Bible Truth or Church Tradition

Finding a Church Built Squarely on the Word of God

Melvin Maxwell

TEACH Services, Inc.
PUBLISHING
www.TEACHServices.com • (800) 367-1844

World rights reserved. This book or any portion thereof may not be copied or reproduced in any form or manner whatever, except as provided by law, without the written permission of the publisher, except by a reviewer who may quote brief passages in a review.

The author assumes full responsibility for the accuracy of all facts and quotations as cited in this book. The opinions expressed in this book are the author's personal views and interpretations, and do not necessarily reflect those of the publisher.

This book is provided with the understanding that the publisher is not engaged in giving spiritual, legal, medical, or other professional advice. If authoritative advice is needed, the reader should seek the counsel of a competent professional.

Copyright © 2015 Melvin Maxwell
Copyright © 2015 TEACH Services, Inc.
ISBN-13: 978-1-4796-0313-8 (Paperback)
ISBN-13: 978-1-4796-0314-5 (ePub)
ISBN-13: 978-1-4796-0315-2 (Mobi)
Library of Congress Control Number: 2014940619

All scripture quotations, unless otherwise indicated, are taken from the King James Version. Public domain.

Scripture quotations marked CEV are from the Contemporary English Version Copyright © 1991, 1992, 1995 American Bible Society, Used by Permission.

Scripture quotations marked NIV are taken from the Holy Bible, New International Version®, NIV®. Copyright © 1973, 1978, 1984, 2011 by Biblica, Inc.™ Used by permission of Zondervan. All rights reserved worldwide.

Scripture quotations marked NKJV™ are taken from the New King James Version®. Copyright © 1982 by Thomas Nelson, Inc. Used by permission. All rights reserved.

Published by

www.TEACHServices.com • (800) 367-1844

Dedication

I dedicate this book to everyone everywhere who desires a genuine relationship with "the only wise God" our heavenly Father, Jesus Christ our Saviour, and the Holy Spirit our guide. Unto Them "be glory and majesty, dominion and power, both now and forever more. Amen." May each receive a spiritual blessing from reading it.

I have read the complete document and believe it would be a valuable tool in the hands of new believers because of all the detailed facts concerning prophecies of both the Old and New Testaments. In my estimation, Mel's research goes beyond that of many authors, thus providing information not found in books of similar content. I hope and pray that he will realize the fruition of his labor and that many souls will be blessed as a result.

—V. L. Bretsch
Retired Minister

Table of Contents

Introduction vii

Chapter 1   First Things First 9

Chapter 2   Receiving the Gift of God 14

Chapter 3   Righteousness Through Christ 17

Chapter 4   Sanctification 21

Chapter 5   The "Doing" of Salvation 25

Chapter 6   Growing in Faith and the Symbol of Baptism 29

Chapter 7   True Conversion 32

Chapter 8   The Devil's Deceptions 35

Chapter 9   The Bible Sabbath 41

Chapter 10   Origins of Sunday Worship 47

Chapter 11   Earth's History Foretold in Dreams 56

Chapter 12   The Roman Empire Predicted 63

Chapter 13   A New Phase for Rome 69

Chapter 14	The Protestant Reformation	79
Chapter 15	Who Made the Claim?	86
Chapter 16	Protestants Come to America	96
Chapter 17	Filtering a Long, Long List	107
Chapter 18	A True Church	125
Chapter 19	Receiving God's Guidance	130
Chapter 20	The End	135
Chapter 21	The Saints and the Wicked	149
Chapter 22	The Final Reward	158
Bibliography		166

Introduction

In the world we live in there are many different forms of theology. With an estimated 34,000 Christian organizations around the world, all claiming to derive their beliefs from Scripture, it is impossible that all of their teachings should be in line with the Scriptures (unless they are all teaching the same message). Untold thousands of people have been deceived into thinking that what they have been taught is found in the Word of God, when it really is not. Research in the Bible and history reveals that there are many mistaken notions taught from the pulpits of churches today. A great number of preachers are unaware that some of what they are teaching as truth is actually church doctrine without a proper basis in Scripture.

Since a person's salvation is based upon biblical truth and not just church doctrine, this study should be of primary interest and concern. It should make every person, desiring to spend eternity with Jesus Christ as Lord and master, to study to know what is truth and what is error. The only way we can be sure we are receiving truth alone is to know what the Bible teaches and compare that knowledge to what is being taught. The Bible alone can be trusted; it is the sure Word of God.

Many wonder if they are doing the right things in their life to be able to enjoy the future life. Many others, of course, simply go about life as if this life is all they have to be concerned with. It surprises me to find so many seemingly intelligent people who do not care about eternity. It is not as if there are not enough books, literature, and help available for anyone who is interested to decide intelligently between eternal life and eternal death.

True surrender to our Creator is a marvelous wealth and joy to everyone who has it while here on this earth, and it comes with the knowledge that we will be able to spend eternity with the God we love and appreciate. Jesus said, "For what shall it profit a man, if he shall gain the whole world, and lose his own soul?" (Mark 8:36).

Many people do not want to know about the truths in the Bible. They think that it really does not matter. As long as they go to church a few times a year, they think they will be all right. Some prefer ignorance, believing that everyone automatically goes to heaven without even knowing the nature of heaven or who it has been prepared for.

I wanted to know about life here on earth as well as life after death. I received many answers to my questions, and they were all different. Finally, one person told me, if you really want to know the truth, then study the Bible and the doctrines of the different churches until you find one whose beliefs are all based on the Bible. Then decide what is correct.

After studying the Bible, history and church traditions, and then comparing the facts of each, I was able to see the difference between what is taught in the churches and what the Bible and history say about theology. I have written this book with the hope that it will awaken people to take an interest in their future lives as well as in the blessings that are here afforded by a true Christian relationship with Jesus as our personal Savior—a gift from God to everyone who accepts what God has done and will do for them. This book is the result of my study of several years, and I hope it will be as helpful to all who read it as it was for me to write.

Only the truth gives us total freedom; without truth, we flounder. What is truth, you say? David said: "Thy word is truth" and Jesus said: "Ye shall know the truth and the truth will make you free."

Chapter 1
First Things First

Many churchgoers take for granted that the things taught week after week and year after year from their pulpits are Bible-based teachings. Whether they actually are or not is a question of the greatest importance, for our future destiny will be determined by what we choose in this life. Depending on our choice, we will either receive eternal life with Jesus or we will receive eternal death. Would you not want to do that which is required to receive eternal life, comparing every aspect of your life to the Bible standard? That is why we need to compare everything we are told to the Scriptures. This book is the author's comparison of the Bible with mainstream Christian teachings.

The Most Important Question

What must a person do to be saved? The apostle Paul says, "For by grace are ye saved through faith; and that not of yourselves: it is the gift of God" (Ephesians 2:8). In the King James Bible, the word "faith" is used two hundred and thirty-one times and the word "saved" is used three hundred and thirty-six times. Yet, what is faith? Let us turn to the Bible for its definition: "Now faith is the substance of things hoped for, the evidence of things not seen" (Hebrews 11:1). Can we see or tangibly feel faith? No, we cannot, but we can see the effects and results of faith. Can we experience faith? Yes, the apostle Paul used the term "substance" to describe faith because "substance" is something that is real or that produces a result. The Contemporary English Version puts it this way: "Faith makes us sure of what we hope for and gives us proof of what we cannot see." The Free Dictionary defines *faith* as ". . . a belief that does not rest on logical proof or material evidence" or as "the theological virtue defined as secure belief in God and a trusting acceptance of God's will" ("Faith," The Free Dictionary by Farlex, http://1ref.us/44). Thus, the words "faith," "belief," and "trust" can be used virtually interchangeably. John 3:16 tells us, "For God so loved the world that he gave his only begotten Son, that whosoever believeth in him should not perish, but have everlasting life." We can use either "faith" or "trust" in this verse and read it as "whosoever has faith in Him" or as "whosoever puts their trust in Him." Of course, the "Him" in the passage refers to Jesus.

In both the King James Version and the Contemporary English Version of the Bible "hope" is used in connection with "faith." So, what is "hope"? It is: "To wish for something with expectation of its fulfillment; to look forward to an event with confidence or expectation that it will happen just as we believed it will; a desire for something and confidence in the probability of its fulfillment" (http://1ref.us/45).

God has promised salvation to those who believe. Yet, the promise of a gift is conditional upon its reception. If someone says that he has a gift for you, but you will not take it, then it will never be yours. The gift of salvation has the same requirement. John 3:16 says that God gave His Son. Thus, God is the giver. Yet, in order for people to take possession of the gift, they must accept it. Since God gave the gift of His Son out of love, the natural response is to reciprocate by giving love back to the Giver.

We cannot see love, yet we can see love's results. In the same way, faith is the means by which hope comes to fruition. We *hope* that we will receive God's gift and then we receive that gift by *faith*. When it comes to salvation, God gave us His Son out of love to redeem us from our sins. Our part is the last part of the verse: "… whosoever believeth in him should not perish, but have everlasting life." Faith receives the gift that God has given. We are to respond in love to the loving gift of God's Son Jesus and what He has done for us.

> **The most important answer to the question, "What must I do to be saved?" is "Believe on the Lord Jesus Christ, and thou shalt be saved" (Acts 16:31)**

Describing Jesus' baptism, John wrote: "The next day John seeth Jesus coming unto him, and saith, Behold the Lamb of God, which taketh away the sin of the world" (John 1:29). Remember his words, "which taketh away the sin of the world." In his first epistle, John wrote: "Whosoever committeth sin transgresseth also the law: for sin is the transgression of the law. And ye know that he was manifested to take away our sins; and in him is no sin. Whosoever abideth in him sinneth not: whosoever sinneth hath not seen him, neither known him" (1 John 3:4–6).

Returning to Hebrews 11:1, we read: "Now faith is the substance of things hoped for, the evidence of things not seen." What is the substance of our faith? It is accepting and holding onto the gift of salvation. The gift is conditional upon its being accepted. God gives graciously, and we receive it by faith. Yet, real faith is made manifest by works. Notice how James described the "Father of faith" in the following verses: "Abraham believed God, and it was imputed unto him for righteousness: and he was called the Friend of God. Ye see then how that by works a man is justified, and not by faith only" (James 2:23, 24). The description of Abraham's friendship with God reads this way in the Contemporary English Version:

> Well, our ancestor Abraham pleased God by putting his son Isaac on the altar to sacrifice him. Now you see how Abraham's faith and deeds worked together. He proved that his faith was real by what he did. This is what the Scriptures mean by saying, "Abraham had faith in God, and God was pleased with him." That's how Abraham became God's friend. You can now see that we please God by what we do and not only by what we believe. (James 2:21–24, CEV)

Thus, pleasing God requires *doing* and not just *believing*. John wrote: "In this the children of God are manifest, and the children of the devil: whosoever doeth not righteousness is not of God, neither he that loveth not his brother" (1 John 3:10). What did Abraham do that pleased God? "… the angel said, 'Now I know that you truly obey God, because you were willing to offer him your only son'" (Genesis 22:12, CEV)

Real faith—living faith—results in corresponding works. James wrote: "What doth it profit, my brethren, though a man say he hath faith, and have not works? Can faith save him? … Yea, a man may say, Thou hast faith, and I have works: shew me thy faith without thy works, and I will shew thee my faith by my works.… For as the body without the spirit is dead, so faith without works is dead also" (James 2:14, 18, 26). Thus, we see that saving faith does not exist by itself; it has corresponding works.

What is the role of faith in salvation and what is the role of works? The answer to this question comes in Paul's epistle to the Romans, where the apostle Paul described salvation by faith. Many people use Paul's writings to assert that works are not necessary for salvation. However, Paul wrote: "For I am not ashamed of the gospel of Christ: for it is the power of God unto salvation to everyone that believeth; to the Jew first, and also to the Greek. For therein is the righteousness of God revealed from faith to faith: as it is written. The just shall live by faith" (Romans 1:16, 17). Consider these verses carefully. Paul is describing "the gospel of Christ." Webster's Dictionary defines "gospel" as the message or teachings of a religious teacher. In this case, it would mean the teachings and message of Jesus. Paul declares, "the gospel of Christ … is the power of God unto salvation." Does the power of God produce works? Yes, it does. The Contemporary English Version puts the passage this way:

> I am proud of the good news! It is God's powerful way of saving all people who have faith, whether they are Jews or Gentiles. The good news tells how God accepts everyone who has faith, but only those who have faith. It is just as the Scriptures say, "The people God accepts because of their faith will live." (Romans 1:16, 17)

Here the Contemporary English Version's equivalent of "gospel" is "good news" and of "believeth" is "have faith." The fundamental phrase, "But only those who have faith," declares an unbreakable truth: no one will make it into heaven without faith.

Continuing on to verse 17, we read: "For therein is the righteousness of God revealed from faith to faith: as it is written, The just shall live by faith" (Romans 1:17). The Contemporary English Version says: "The people God accepts because of their faith will live." Why do people need acceptance with God? It is because sin has separated them from Him. Yet, we have been justified by Jesus' death on the cross; we have been made acceptable to God by Jesus' payment of the penalty for our sin by His death. The law demanded the shedding of blood to remove sin. Jesus said: "For this is my blood of the new testament, which is shed for many for the remission of sins" (Matthew 26:28).

What is the gospel? It is the good news that, through His death, Jesus took the sins of the whole world upon Himself. Paul wrote to the Corinthians: "Moreover, brethren, I declare unto you the *gospel* which I preached unto you, which also ye have received, and wherein ye stand; By which also ye are saved, if ye keep in memory what I preached unto you, unless ye have believed in vain. For I delivered unto you first of all that which I also received, how that *Christ died for our sins* according to the scriptures; And that he was buried, and that he rose again the third day according to the scriptures" (1 Corinthians 15:1–4, emphasis supplied).

Because Jesus' death paid the penalty for our sins, our own blood does not need to be shed. Jesus paid the price; we are justified before God. Thus, "The just shall live by faith" or, as the Contemporary English Version puts it, "The people God accepts because of their faith will live." We continue to be acceptable to God by our faith in what Jesus has done and continues to do for us.

Paul wrote: "Therefore we conclude that a man is justified by faith without the deeds of the law" (Romans 3:28). The law, the Ten Commandments, cannot give us salvation. There is a passage, however, that shows how people can be justified, in one sense, by something they do. Jesus said: "For by thy words thou shalt be justified, and by thy words thou shalt be condemned" (Matthew 12:37). Are our words what save us? No, they are not. We are saved by faith. Thus, in this passage, being justified is not the same as being saved. It is justification by faith that makes us acceptable to God, and salvation comes through Jesus, as Peter declared: "Neither is there salvation in any other: for there is none other name under heaven given among men, whereby we must be saved" (Acts 4:12). Peter made it clear that he meant the name of *Jesus*, for he had said just before this: "Be it known unto you all, and to all the people of Israel, that by the name of Jesus Christ of Nazareth, whom ye crucified, whom God raised from the dead, even by him doth this man stand here before you whole" (Acts 4:10).

Paul later declared the same truth: "And by him [that is, by Jesus] all that believe are justified from all things, from which ye could not be justified by the law of Moses" (Acts 13:39), which means the same as "all that believe in Jesus are justified by faith and not by the law of Moses."

As we have seen before, the keeping of the law will not save us—even if we could keep the Ten Commandment law perfectly. However, all those who will be saved will indeed keep the Ten Commandment law. Those who will be saved at Jesus' second coming are those who "keep the commandments of God, and have the testimony of Jesus Christ" (Revelation 12:17).

Paul wrote: "Therefore by the deeds of the law there shall no flesh be justified in his sight: for by the law is the knowledge of sin" (Romans 3:20). In this statement, he pointed out that the commandments are the means by which we know what sin is, for the commands that God gave require that works be done. When the commandment says, "Thou shalt not" or "Remember," the believer must follow through. Paul wrote: "Therefore being justified by faith, we have peace with God through our Lord Jesus Christ" (Romans 5:1). That "we have peace with God" means that, through faith, we are made acceptable to God—we are justified through Jesus' death for us. Sin separated the human race from God. Through the death of Jesus, we are made acceptable once again. Justification is the first step in salvation, and we accept it by faith.

Paul said that we are reconciled to God through Jesus Christ: "For if, when we were enemies, we were reconciled to God by the death of his Son, much more, being reconciled, we shall be saved by his life" (Romans 5:10). Justification and reconciliation are two aspects of the same thing. Justification comes to us by the death of Jesus as God accepts us through the righteousness of Christ. Reconciliation, in the original Greek, means complete restoration of relationship with God. To bring this about does not require a change in God's attitude; we are the ones who need to change. Sin corrupted the human race; we became enemies of God and could only be reconciled and transformed through the death of Jesus. Having received justification through the death of Jesus, we are now reconciled to God. We are no longer enemies. Like Abraham, we have become God's friends. Abraham's faith was counted to him for righteousness, and we, being reconciled, "shall be saved by his life"—the perfect life of Christ. His life begins in us through faith and good works befitting salvation.

Yet, Christians cannot produce the works of Christ without learning how to use faith correctly. Salvation is a learning process that begins when we accept God's gift of Jesus as our Redeemer and then desire to have a closer relationship with God, the Bible guiding us on how to live.

Chapter 2
Receiving the Gift of God

The apostle Paul pointed to the elements required for salvation: "For by grace are ye saved through faith; and that not of yourselves: it is the gift of God: Not of works, lest any man should boast. For we are his workmanship, created in Christ Jesus unto good works, which God hath before ordained that we should walk in them." (Ephesians 2:8–10).

"Grace" (Ephesians 2:8) and "love" (John 3:16) are both the gift of God. The difference is that John expressed the Father's gift as *love*, while Paul expressed it as *grace*. Paul expanded further on the Father's love because he was addressing Gentiles who did not have the background of the Jews, who were John's audience. The idea of a substitution, that anyone would give up his or her life for another, was something for which the Jews had been prepared for by the sacrificial system, while it was completely unthinkable to Gentiles. On the other hand, faith was something that even the Gentiles knew something about.

Being saved is the same as receiving salvation. In this passage, Paul declares what the Bible requires for salvation: "We are saved by grace." What is grace? Webster answers: "Unmerited divine assistance given humans for their regeneration or sanctification." Like God's love, which is freely poured upon man, salvation, Paul affirms, is not from works, that is, from anything we do to deserve it.

Eternal life is a gift that must be willingly received. Paul called it "the gift of God. The message of John 3:16 is common knowledge to most Christians—"For God so loved the world that He gave His only begotten Son, that whosoever believeth in Him should not perish but have everlasting life" (John 3:16). Yet, before telling people without a Christian background about things we Christians take as common knowledge, try telling them about God up in heaven. They may respond by asking who is God and where is heaven located. The Gentiles of Bible times believed in gods. However, the gods that they worshipped gave them the wrong idea about what the true God is like. After struggling to tell people without a Christian background about the God of heaven, next try telling them about God's begotten Son, Jesus—the One who came from heaven and died so that human beings can have eternal life. Such an announcement would probably trigger new questions, such as: What kind of person would do that? What is eternal life? Is it something I would want? And what do I have to do to get it? They might also imagine that, if God has a Son, He must also have a wife. Imagine what Paul had to teach the Gentiles before they could understand John 3:16!

When Jesus came to this earth, He came in the form of a human being in every respect, exactly like us except that He did not have a sinful nature (Heb. 2:16, 17). There are many different views of Jesus' nature while He was on earth, but what did He say of Himself? He said that He was both the Son of God and the Son of man. Jesus was God in the flesh. Matthew wrote: "Behold, a virgin shall be with child, and shall bring forth a son, and they shall call his name Emmanuel, which being interpreted is, God with us" (Matthew 1:23). "Now the birth of Jesus Christ was on this wise: When as his mother Mary was espoused to Joseph, before they came together, she was found with child of the Holy Ghost" (Matthew 1:18). Joseph married Jesus' mother but did not sleep with her until after Jesus was born; Jesus' "birth father" was the Holy Spirit. His mother was a woman named Mary, who submitted herself fully to the providence of the Holy Spirit (Luke 1:38). The story of Jesus' birth is very simple:

> This is how Jesus Christ was born. A young woman named Mary was engaged to Joseph from King David's family. But before they were married, she learned that she was going to have a baby by God's Holy Spirit.
>
> Joseph was a good man and did not want to embarrass Mary in front of everyone. So he decided to quietly call off the wedding.
>
> While Joseph was thinking about this, an angel from the Lord came to him in a dream. The angel said, "Joseph, the baby that Mary will have is from the Holy Spirit. Go ahead and marry her. Then after her baby is born, name him Jesus, because he will save his people from their sins." So the Lord's promise came true, just as the prophet Isaiah had said, "A virgin will have a baby boy, and he will be called Immanuel," which means "God with us."
>
> After Joseph woke up, he and Mary were soon married, just as the Lord's angel had told him to do. But they did not sleep together before her baby was born. Then Joseph named him Jesus. (Matthew 1:18–25, CEV)

Paul makes it very plain in Romans that eternal life comes through Jesus Christ our Lord and that such life is a gift from God—"For the wages of sin is death; but the gift of God is eternal life through Jesus Christ our Lord" (Romans 6:23).

When the apostle Paul was on trial before King Agrippa because of the accusations of the Jews, he was given permission to speak on his own behalf, and Paul told King Agrippa about how he was given a vision on the road to Damascus. Paul declared that Jesus came "to open their eyes and to turn them from darkness to light, and from the power of Satan unto God, that they may receive forgiveness of sins, and inheritance among them which are sanctified by faith" in Jesus (Acts 26:18).

> **Paul declared that Jesus came "to open their eyes and to turn them from darkness to light, and from the power of Satan unto God, that they may receive forgiveness of sins."**

Here Paul was explaining to King Agrippa the reason that Jesus came to this world, knowledge Paul received from Jesus on the road to Damascus (see Acts 22:6–8).

Salvation is a gift from God, a gift of grace. We did nothing to earn it, and we receive it by believing that Jesus' death on the cross paid the demands of the law ("the wages of sin is death"). When we receive that gift by faith, we are justified through Jesus' death and made eligible for eternal life. Since Jesus paid our penalty, we do not need to offer our own blood to pay the law's demands. Nonetheless, faith in Jesus requires that we do more. Look again at what Paul says: "Therefore, King Agrippa, I was not disobedient to the heavenly vision, but declared first to those in Damascus and in Jerusalem, and throughout all the region of Judea, and then to the Gentiles, that they should repent, turn to God, and do works befitting repentance" (Acts 26:19, 20, NKJV).

What did Paul declare? He declared what Jesus had told him in the heavenly vision. When Paul asked, "Who are You, Lord?" the heavenly Messenger identified Himself, giving Paul his assignment: "I am Jesus, whom you are persecuting. But rise and stand on your feet; for I have appeared to you for this purpose, to make you a minister and a witness both of the things which you have seen and of the things which I will yet reveal to you" (Acts 26:15, 16, NKJV).

Receiving salvation by accepting God's gift of grace through faith, provided by Jesus' death on the cross, we continue in the way of faith, by doing what Jesus wants us to do, which is to "repent, turn to God, and do works befitting repentance" (Acts 26:20, NKJV).

Jesus is God's gift of love. God gave Him to mankind through human birth. His life and death express the great love that the Godhead has for the human family. In John 3:16, "the world" refers to the people in the world and not to the physical planet.

The life of Jesus is an exact portrait of what the Godhead wants Christians to be, which includes gaining victory over sin by the help God gives us through faith. We receive nothing without faith. In faith, we are to ask for whatever we want, believing that we shall receive it. "Now faith is the substance of things hoped for, the evidence of things not seen" (Hebrews 11:1). The apostle Paul used the term "substance" to indicate that faith is something that is real or that produces a result.

The tangible things that we do to receive God's help in overcoming sin is to exercise the belief that God gives us what we ask. It is not enough to *say* that we want victory over sin; we must truly *desire* victory over sin and demonstrate that desire by our actions. Yet, our victory is still a gift received from God. Because of human pride, we need to remind ourselves that Jesus is the source of the power that we receive. We must always remember that, if we rely on ourselves, we can fall away and sin again. To continue receiving God's promises requires that we stay acceptable to God and free from sin.

This is what faith does: it enables us to believe that the death of Jesus was for our forgiveness and for our justification before God. It is Jesus' death that makes us acceptable before God. When Jesus shed His blood on Calvary, He paid our penalty for sin. When God looks at the repentant sinner, He sees the perfect righteousness of His Son Jesus. Yet, this step of faith is only the first step in our relationship with God. At every succeeding step, we must exercise faith in God that we may receive strength from Him to accomplish the further work He has for us to do. Remember, our final goal is getting the victory over sin with the help God gives us.

Chapter 3
Righteousness Through Christ

It is to accomplish this further work that Jesus' righteousness was given to us. Paul wrote: "But for us also, to whom it shall be imputed, if we believe on him that raised up Jesus our Lord from the dead: who was delivered for our offences, and was raised again for our justification" (Romans 4:24, 25). "Imputed" means that it was *given* for our benefit. The same word (imputed) was given to Abraham as a gift from God: "And the scripture was fulfilled which saith, Abraham believed God, and it was imputed unto him for righteousness: and he was called the Friend of God" (James 2:23).

If we trust Jesus for all that He has done for us, we will also trust the Father for all the things that He has done for us. Paul related these two verses in Ephesians: "For by grace are ye saved through faith; and that not of yourselves: it is the gift of God: Not of works, lest any man should boast. For we are his workmanship, created in Christ Jesus unto good works, which God hath before ordained that we should walk in them" (Ephesians 2:8–10).

James put it this way: "Seest thou how faith wrought with his works, and by works was faith made perfect? Ye see then how that by works a man is justified, and not by faith only" (James 2:22, 24). In other words, faith is "made perfect," or complete, through corresponding works.

Abraham provides an example of this kind of belief. Abraham's belief in God resulted in his willingness to sacrifice his only son. Abraham believed that God could bring his son back to life to fulfill the promise of his descendants' becoming a great nation. Faith is more than just believing that God exists. James wrote: "Thou believest that there is one God; thou doest well: the devils also believe, and tremble. But wilt thou know, O vain man, that faith without works is dead? … Ye see then how that by works a man is justified, and not by faith only" (James 2:19, 20, 24).

To be justified to the Godhead we have to have both faith and works. What was the reason God gave Jesus to us as our Savior? It was so that, when we accept His gift of love by faith, we would return love to the Godhead.

When a lawyer asked Jesus, "What is the greatest commandment?" Jesus answered: "Thou shalt love the Lord thy God with all thy heart, and with all thy soul, and with all thy mind. This is the first and great commandment" (Matthew 22:37, 38; cf. Mark 12:30).

In following Jesus' admonition, we will be keeping the first four of the Ten Commandments (Exodus 20:3–11). The "works" of keeping God's commandments demonstrate our love for God. Jesus said, "If ye love me, keep my commandments.... He that hath my commandments, and keepeth them, he it is that loveth me: and he that loveth me shall be loved of my Father, and I will love him, and will manifest myself to him" (John 14:15, 21). Having accepted Jesus' sacrifice in our behalf for the removal of sin in our lives, we show that we truly love God by keeping all of His commandments—which include His Ten Commandments.

> **Having accepted Jesus' sacrifice in our behalf for the removal of sin in our lives, we show that we truly love God by keeping all of His commandments—which include His Ten Commandments.**

John the Baptist said that Jesus, "the Lamb of God," came to take "away the sin of the world" (John 1:29). The apostle James tells us where sin comes from: "But every man is tempted, when he is drawn away of his own lust, and enticed. Then when lust hath conceived, it bringeth forth sin: and sin, when it is finished, bringeth forth death" (James 1:14, 15). This text is rendered by the Contemporary English Version as: "We are tempted by our own desires that drag us off and trap us. Our desires make us sin, and when sin is finished with us, it leaves us dead."

The ultimate goal of salvation is to do away with sin, which would keep us separated from God. We cannot have immortality as long as there is a trace of sin, "for the wages of sin is death" (Romans 6:23). As Paul had said, "... as sin hath reigned unto death, even so might grace reign through righteousness unto eternal life by Jesus Christ our Lord" (Romans 5:21).

The opposite of death is life. When there is no more death, there will only be life—eternal life—"the gift of God" made possible "through Jesus Christ our Lord" (Romans 6:23).

Scripture tells us that grace is what gave us the gift of eternal life: "For by grace are ye saved through faith; and that not of yourselves: it is the gift of God" (Ephesians 2:8). God's grace was given to us to reunite us with God, who loves us beyond measure. The ultimate goal of salvation is to place humankind where we were at the Creation, restoring the relationship we had with the Godhead in the beginning before sin.

Faith Is the Key

Consider another blessing we get from believing God. Paul wrote: "For what saith the scripture? Abraham believed God, and it was counted unto him for righteousness" (Romans 4:3). It is Christ's righteousness that is "counted," credited, or "imputed" to Christians by God. It is given to us for our benefit. Imputed righteousness is received by faith when "a sinner is declared righteous by God purely by God's grace through faith in Christ," and this is by Christ's merit and worthiness alone ("Imputed Righteousness," Wikipedia, http://1ref.us/46).

"Therefore it is of faith, that it might be by grace; to the end the promise might be sure to all the seed; not to that only which is of the law, but to that also which is of the faith of Abraham; who is the father of us all" (Romans 4:16). Paul is declaring to whom God gives His grace. It was to the Jew first and then to the Gentiles who are spiritual Jews.

Justification and righteousness are related terms. Justification means to be made right or acceptable to God; righteousness is given to us by Jesus as a covering of our sins. As the Bible tells us, we did not do anything to earn it—it is a gift that God gave us through Jesus Christ our Lord.

"And being fully persuaded that, what he had promised, he was able also to perform" (Romans 4:21). In other words, Abraham believed that the things God had promised him would come true. About Abraham's faith, Paul declared: "And therefore it was imputed to him for righteousness. Now it was not written for his sake alone, that it was imputed to him; but for us also, to whom it shall be imputed, if we believe on him that raised up Jesus our Lord from the dead: Who was delivered for our offences, and was raised again for our justification" (Romans 4:22–25).

Faith is essential to both salvation and the reception of righteousness for both are gifts from God. Works alone cannot give us salvation. It takes both faith and works—faith comes first, and, through love for God, we return works, doing His will by the strength He provides us.

This should make it clear that the Godhead acts in our behalf for our redemption. "Therefore being justified by faith, we have peace with God through our Lord Jesus Christ: By whom also we have access by faith into this grace wherein we stand, and rejoice in hope of the glory of God" (Romans 5:1, 2). The entire passage in the Contemporary English Version is quite helpful. (Notice that, rather than "grace," the Contemporary English Version uses the word "kindness.") We read:

> By faith we have been made acceptable to God. And now, because of our Lord Jesus Christ, we live at peace with God. Christ has also introduced us to God's undeserved kindness on which we take our stand. So we are happy, as we look forward to sharing in the glory of God. But that's not all! We gladly suffer, because we know that suffering helps us to endure. And endurance builds character, which gives us a hope that will never disappoint us. All of this happens because God has given us the Holy Spirit, who fills our hearts with his love. Christ died for us at a time when we were helpless and sinful. No one is really willing to die for an honest person, though someone might be willing to die for a truly good person. But God showed how much he loved us by having Christ die for us, even though we were sinful.
>
> But there is more! Now that God has accepted us because Christ sacrificed his life's blood, we will also be kept safe from God's anger. Even when we were God's enemies, he made peace with us, because his Son died for us. Yet something even greater than friendship is ours. Now that we are at peace with God, we will be saved by his Son's life. And in addition to everything else, we are happy because God sent our Lord Jesus Christ to make peace with us....

Sin ruled by means of death. But God's kindness now rules, and God has accepted us because of Jesus Christ our Lord. This means that we will have eternal life. (Romans 5:1–10, 21, CEV)

The wages of sin is death, and death is what we had before accepting what Jesus did and is still doing for us. However, if we have any sin left in our lives, our ultimate reward will still be eternal death.

Chapter 4
Sanctification

We have covered most of the major issues regarding biblical faith and have discussed some of the issues regarding biblical works as they pertain to our lives. Yet, there is still more in the life of a Christian—full devotion, which is known as *sanctification*.

If we are justified by the death of Jesus, how are we sanctified? As we have noted, we are justified by the death of Jesus through faith alone. If we do not believe we are made acceptable to God, then we will not be. Paul wrote: "For by grace are ye saved through faith" (Ephesians 2:8). Since justification comes by faith, so also does salvation. They are both given to us by God's grace.

Paul explained to the people in Thessalonica that God knew from the very beginning of time who would accept His gift of His Son for their salvation: "… God hath from the beginning chosen you to salvation through sanctification of the Spirit and belief of the truth" (2 Thessalonians 2:13). Sanctification is the transforming of our mind and patterning it after Jesus. It is an ongoing lifetime process. Through our minds (called the "spirit" in 1 Corinthians 2:11), the Holy Spirit influences our thoughts. The thoughts are linked to a person's conscience. Paul recognized this when he said: "… their conscience also bearing witness, and their thoughts the mean while accusing or else excusing one another" (Romans 2:15).

Peter also used the words "sanctification of the Spirit" in describing that which God uses to bring us into full devotion to Him: "Elect according to the foreknowledge of God the Father, through sanctification of the Spirit, unto obedience and sprinkling of the blood of Jesus Christ: Grace unto you, and peace, be multiplied" (1 Peter 1:2). The progression is "belief of the truth," then "obedience," and lastly the "sprinkling of the blood of Jesus Christ."

> **Sanctification is the transforming of our mind and patterning it after Jesus. It is an ongoing lifetime process.**

Somewhere among the steps we took in becoming followers of Jesus, someone told us about what God the Father and His Son have done for the people of this world to bring about our growth in His love and grace. Jesus told the parable of the sower to help us understand what is required:

And when he sowed, some seeds fell by the way side, and the fowls came and devoured them up: Some fell upon stony places, where they had not much earth: and forthwith they sprung up, because they had no deepness of earth: And when the sun was up, they were scorched; and because they had no root, they withered away. And some fell among thorns; and the thorns sprung up, and choked them: But other fell into good ground, and brought forth fruit, some an hundredfold, some sixtyfold, some thirtyfold. Who hath ears to hear, let him hear. (Matthew 13:4–9)

The understanding of Jesus' parable is vital to everyone who wants to become His disciple. What He meant by the parable is so important that He explained it to His disciples.

When any one heareth the word of the kingdom, and understandeth it not, then cometh the wicked one, and catcheth away that which was sown in his heart. This is he which received seed by the way side. But he that received the seed into stony places, the same is he that heareth the word, and anon with joy receiveth it. Yet hath he not root in himself, but dureth for a while: for when tribulation or persecution ariseth because of the word, by and by he is offended.

He also that received seed among the thorns is he that heareth the word; and the care of this world, and the deceitfulness of riches, choke the word, and he becometh unfruitful.

But he that received seed into the good ground is he that heareth the word, and understandeth it; which also beareth fruit, and bringeth forth, some an hundredfold, some sixty, some thirty. (Matthew 13:19–23)

To believe something to be true requires knowing what it is that we believe in. So, what is truth? Jesus said: "Sanctify them through thy truth: thy word is truth" (John 17:17). The work of sanctification is knowing God's Word and how it is to be applied in our lives. Sanctification is hearing, understanding, and walking. Paul wrote: "As ye have therefore received Christ Jesus the Lord, so walk ye in him: rooted and built up in him, and stablished in the faith, as ye have been taught, abounding therein with thanksgiving" (Colossian 2:6, 7). In His prayer to His Father, Jesus referred to all the people who would accept Him as their Savior: "As thou hast sent me into the world, even so have I also sent them into the world. And for their sakes I sanctify myself, that they also might be sanctified through the truth. Neither pray I for these alone, but for them also which shall believe on me through their word" (John 17:18–20). As we learn the truth of God's Word, we should desire to obey all of it. Obedience is the response of love to God for all the blessings He has given us. Jesus said: "If ye love me, keep my commandments" (John 14:15). Keeping God's commandments shows our love for God. John made the same point when he wrote: "For this is the love of God, that we keep his commandments: and his commandments are not grievous" (1 John 5:3).

Sprinkled by Jesus' Cleansing Blood

The "sprinkling of the blood of Jesus Christ" is a covering that we get when we obey God out of love:

> God the Father decided to choose you as his people, and his Spirit has made you holy. You have obeyed Jesus Christ and are sprinkled with his blood. I pray that God will be kind to you and will keep on giving you peace! Praise God, the Father of our Lord Jesus Christ. God is so good, and by raising Jesus from death, he has given us new life and a hope that lives on. (1 Peter 1:2, 3, CEV)

Notice what Peter said: "You have obeyed Jesus Christ and are sprinkled with his blood." According to Exodus 24:3–8, the people of Israel were sprinkled with sacrificial blood to show they would keep their agreement with God. Hebrews 9 describes the same event: "For when Moses had spoken every precept to all the people according to the law, he took the blood of calves and of goats, with water, and scarlet wool, and hyssop, and sprinkled both the book, and all the people, saying, This is the blood of the testament which God hath enjoined unto you" (Hebrews 9:19, 20). Moses used blood—the blood of bulls and goats mixed with water—to seal the first covenant. It was the blood of Jesus that sealed the New Covenant (see Hebrews 9:18–21). Relating Hebrews 9 to 1 Peter 1:2, we see that sanctification has to do with Jesus' blood: "And almost all things are by the law purged with blood; and without shedding of blood is no remission" (Hebrews 9:22). Remission means "the cancellation of a debt, charge, or penalty." Remission also means the total forgiveness of sin. Because of His love, Jesus shed His blood to pay the penalty for our sins. If we love Him, we have the obligation and burning desire to obey Him.

That is how it was with Jesus, as we find in the epistle to the Hebrews: "Jesus is God's own Son, but still he had to suffer before he could learn what it really means to obey God. Suffering made Jesus perfect, and now he can save forever all who obey him" (Hebrews 5:8, 9, CEV). Our obedience is required before God gives us salvation—willingness to obey what the Bible tells us to do.

Paul tells us that, if we want to share in the glory of eternal life with Jesus, we must also be willing to suffer for His cause: "And if children, then heirs; heirs of God, and joint-heirs with Christ; if so be that we suffer with him, that we may be also glorified together" (Romans 8:17). We can suffer for Jesus by obeying all that the Bible tells us that we should do even when it conflicts with church tradition or when people make fun of us for doing what is right. Romans 5 tells what it means to be acceptable to God:

> By faith we have been made acceptable to God. And now, because of our Lord Jesus Christ, we live at peace with God. Christ has also introduced us to God's undeserved kindness [grace] on which we take our stand. So we are happy, as we look forward to

sharing in the glory of God. But that's not all! We gladly suffer, because we know that suffering helps us to endure. And endurance builds character, which gives us a hope that will never disappoint us. All of this happens because God has given us the Holy Spirit, who fills our hearts with his love. (Romans 5:1–5, CEV)

Because we believe that Jesus' death on the cross justifies us with God, making us acceptable to Him, we live at peace with God because our relationship with Him is no longer one of fear. Paul continues: "Now that God has accepted us because Christ sacrificed his life's blood, we will also be kept safe from God's anger" (Romans 5:9, CEV). We share in the undeserved kindness of God's grace, on which we stand. Firmly believing, we look forward to sharing eternally in the glory of God. "But that is not all!" Paul says, "We gladly suffer"—we put up with the temptations of the devil without succumbing to them by the help we receive from God through prayer. "Suffering helps us to endure," he says. It enables us to become more like Christ. "Endurance builds character," he adds, and character is the only thing we will take to heaven since our mortal bodies must be transformed into immortal ones.

> In a moment, in the twinkling of an eye, at the last trump: for the trumpet shall sound, and the dead shall be raised incorruptible, and we shall be changed. For this corruptible must put on incorruption, and this mortal must put on immortality. So when this corruptible shall have put on incorruption, and this mortal shall have put on immortality, then shall be brought to pass the saying that is written, Death is swallowed up in victory. (1 Corinthians 15:53, 54)

"All of this happens," Paul says, "because God has given us the Holy Spirit, who fills our hearts with his love." It is the Holy Spirit who influences our thoughts to return love to God in response to the love that God gave us. Remember that the Godhead is made up of the Father, the Son, and the Holy Spirit—all working together for the benefit of mankind.

In strictly following the truths of Scripture, we will be at odds with most church traditions. If we truly follow Jesus, then we will be eager to learn all the truths found in the Bible and take our stand for that which is right and not simply for church tradition.

Remember, there is truth preached in most churches. The devil is smart in his approach. He knows that, though he cannot deceive all of the people all of the time, he can deceive some of the people all of the time, and he believes he can deceive all of the people some of the time. This is why it is very important that we compare what the Bible teaches with what the preachers are preaching. John wrote: "Beloved, believe not every spirit, but try the spirits whether they are of God: because many false prophets are gone out into the world" (1 John 4:1). How do we try the spirits? First, we must identify what a spirit is. John calls those who preach the gospel "spirits," and he cautions the people to compare what is being taught to what the Bible teaches. We need to do the same thing by comparing what the preachers teach with what the Bible declares.

Chapter 5
The "Doing" of Salvation

The heart of the gospel is found in Paul's statement in 1 Corinthians:

> Moreover, brethren, I declare unto you the gospel which I preached unto you, which also ye have received, and wherein ye stand; By which also ye are saved, if ye keep in memory what I preached unto you, unless ye have believed in vain. For I delivered unto you first of all that which I also received, how that Christ died for our sins according to the scriptures; and that he was buried, and that he rose again the third day according to the scriptures. (1 Corinthians 15:1–4)

Nonetheless, the gospel includes more than belief in the reality of Jesus' death and resurrection. "Though he were a Son, yet learned he obedience by the things which he suffered; and being made perfect, he became the author of eternal salvation unto all them that obey him" (Hebrews 5:8, 9). According to these verses, Jesus can save, or give eternal life, to all who obey Him because He, as a human, was perfect. Does this make salvation conditional? Yes, it does. And what is the condition? It is obedience, the final result of faith and good works. When we accept Jesus' sacrifice, our lives will be changed as a result.

> **Moreover, brethren, I declare unto you the gospel which I preached unto you, which also ye have received, and wherein ye stand; By which also ye are saved ...**

As Soon as There Was Sin, There Was a Savior

Genesis 2:17 quotes God's words to Adam: "But of the tree of the knowledge of good and evil, thou shalt not eat of it: for in the day that thou eatest thereof thou shalt surely die." Genesis 3 introduces what took place at the tree of knowledge of good and evil:

> Now the serpent was more subtil than any beast of the field which the Lord God had made. And he said unto the woman, Yea, hath God said, Ye shall not eat of every tree

of the garden? And the woman said unto the serpent, We may eat of the fruit of the trees of the garden: but of the fruit of the tree which is in the midst of the garden, God hath said, Ye shall not eat of it, neither shall ye touch it, lest ye die. And the serpent said unto the woman, Ye shall not surely die. (Genesis 3:1–4)

Then God asked Adam and Eve, "Hast thou eaten of the tree, whereof I commanded thee that thou shouldest not eat?" Undoubtedly you know the answer: the man pointed his finger at the woman and the woman pointed hers at the serpent. But they were responsible for their choices. Sin entered this world because Adam and Eve disobeyed a direct command from God. The opposite is to obey God's commands. Had Adam and Eve obeyed, obedience would still be the norm and obedience would have been absolute. Obedience means not disobeying any commands God has given humankind, and we find His commands in the Bible. We cannot afford to neglect any of them.

When a man asked Jesus, "What is the greatest commandment?" Jesus answered: "Thou shalt love the Lord thy God with all thy heart, and with all thy soul, and with all thy mind. This is the first and great commandment. And the second is like unto it, Thou shalt love thy neighbour as thyself. On these two commandments hang all the law and the prophets" (Matthew 22:37–40). Here Jesus summed up the Ten Commandment law of Exodus 20. Complete love for God is the theme of the first four commandments, which are the greatest of all the commandments. The first of these four is: Have no other God. Jehovah is the only true God, the great "I AM." The second is: Do not try to duplicate what only the Creator God can accomplish; make no type of image to worship; only the Creator God is worthy of our worship. The third is: Do not take God's name in vain—do not use His name disrespectfully, and do not claim to be something that you are not, such as a Christian when you are not living like one. The fourth is: "Remember the Sabbath Day to keep it Holy." "Holy" means to set aside for the purpose of giving the day to God alone, a day to place all of our thoughts on Him as thanksgiving for all He has done for us. After creating the world, God set aside the seventh day as a day of rest, and He blessed and sanctified it as a memorial to all that He had done. The word "remember" is the same as "don't forget"—don't forget all the blessings that God has given to us and the things He has done for us.

Jesus continued: "And the second is like unto it, Thou shalt love thy neighbour as thyself" (Matthew 22:39). The last six commandments are instructions on how to treat other human beings. They tell us how to treat all people with respect and love—the same way we would like to be treated.

The fifth is: Obey your parents in the Lord. The sixth is: Do not take the life of another person. The seventh is: Do not have sexual relations with one who is not your spouse. The eighth is: Do not take that which belongs to another. The ninth is: Do not give a false account about someone else, period. The tenth is: Do not let your mind dwell upon that which belongs to another to desire it.

If obedience is the result of our acceptance of God's grace, then love would be equal to it. Love is the reason for obedience. Jesus said, "If ye love me, keep my commandments" (John 14:15). Because of what Jesus has done for us, and is still doing for us, and because of the righteousness He gave to us, we can become obedient to God's will. And we are never to stop growing. Sanctification is the work of a lifetime, and obedience is part of sanctification.

There are people who argue that, because Adam and Eve did not die that very day, God did not really mean what He said, "in the day that thou eatest thereof thou shalt surely die," Why did Adam and Eve not die that very day? According to John, it was because God already had a plan to save mankind—Jesus was "the lamb slain from the foundation of the world" (Revelation 13:8). Jesus pointed to this plan when He said: "Father, I will that they also, whom thou hast given me, be with me where I am; that they may behold my glory, which thou hast given me: for thou lovedst me before the foundation of the world" (John 17:24). The future sacrifice of Jesus already existed in the plan of salvation, and the Father and Son initialized that plan when Adam and Eve fell.

Since everyone in this world has sinned, what must a person *do* to be saved? Jesus wants us to "repent, turn to God, and do works befitting repentance" (Acts 26:20, NKJV). Jesus declared, "If ye love me, keep my commandments" (John 14:15).

When we repent, we will be sorry enough for our sins that we will not want to keep on doing them. Then, using all the strength of body, mind, and soul that Jesus can give, we will overcome our sinful nature. Simply put, sin is disobeying the laws of God. Turning to God is complete surrender to the will of God through the Holy Spirit. Jesus declared: "But ye shall receive power, after that the Holy Ghost is come upon you: and ye shall be witnesses unto me both in Jerusalem, and in all Judaea, and in Samaria, and unto the uttermost part of the earth" (Acts 1:8). Through the Holy Spirit, Jesus gives us strength to completely repent of our sins. With His strength, we will "do works befitting repentance"; we will be His witnesses. A key work of repentance is obeying the great commission given by Jesus in Matthew 28:19, 20: "Go ye therefore, and teach all nations, baptizing them in the name of the Father, and of the Son, and of the Holy Ghost: Teaching them to observe all things whatsoever I have commanded you: and, lo, I am with you alway, even unto the end of the world. Amen" (Matthew 28:19, 20). Starting in Jerusalem, then going on to Judea and to the uttermost part of the earth (Acts 1:8), Jesus sent out His twelve disciples to teach others the good news of His life, death, and resurrection. The testimony of Scripture regarding the early disciples, following His ascension, is: "And the word of God increased; and the number of the disciples multiplied in Jerusalem greatly; and a great company of the priests were obedient to the faith" (Acts 6:7).

> **Since everyone in this world has sinned, what must a person do to be saved? Jesus wants us to "repent, turn to God, and do works befitting repentance" (Acts 26:20, NKJV)**

The types of works that followers of Jesus do are all different, as Paul described: "For as we have many members in one body, and all members have not the same office: So we, being many, are one body in Christ, and every one members one of another" (Romans 12:4, 5).

When the apostles were put in jail in Philippi, God's angel let them out, and the jail keeper said, "Sirs, what must I do to be saved? And they said, Believe on the Lord Jesus Christ, and thou shalt be saved" (Acts 16:30, 31). To receive eternal life we must believe as the Bible tells us—believe *on the Lord Jesus Christ*. Saving faith is believing in God. The Contemporary English Version uses "have faith" for "believe" in Acts 16:30, 31: "Have faith in the Lord Jesus and you will be saved." Saving faith requires believing everything that Jesus has said and has done in our behalf.

Jesus said; "Search the scriptures; for in them ye think ye have eternal life: and they are they which testify of me." (John 5:39) When Jesus made this statement, the Old Testament was all the Scriptures they had, the New Testament was not written yet. The Jews spent a lot of time searching the Scriptures. They thought that, by following the laws of Moses, which were the rules of ordinance, it would give them eternal life. However, in the New Testament Jesus spent a great deal of time explaining that, along with keeping God's commandments it is necessary to have faith in Him as the only Son of God and in His life, death and resurrection. Paul and Silas told the jailer in Philippi: "Believe on the Lord Jesus Christ, and thou shalt be saved" (Acts 16:31). True belief encompasses many different things. We must believe that Jesus was truly the only Son of God, was truly human, and was without sin. We must believe that Jesus died on the cross and was raised to life, that His death took away our sins and justified our relation with God the Father, that Jesus represents us before the Father by His shed blood, and that Jesus will give us eternal life if we obey the Bible and all His commandments. We must have complete trust in Jesus as our Savior: "For God sent not his Son into the world to condemn the world; but that the world through him might be saved" (John 3:17).

Chapter 6

Growing in Faith and the Symbol of Baptism

Where does faith come from? As Paul wrote, "God hath dealt to every man the measure of faith" (Romans 12:3). This means that everyone has been given sufficient faith to believe, yet "faith cometh by hearing, and hearing by the word of God" (Romans 10:17). In order to increase our faith, we need to spend regular time studying God's Word.

Justification is an essential part of salvation, for without it we are not acceptable to God and cannot have eternal life. It was through the death of Jesus that we became justified. It is through Jesus' life that we see how to "live in order to please God" (1 Thessalonians 4, NIV). This follows repentance. Peter's message on the day of Pentecost was: "Repent, and be baptized every one of you in the name of Jesus Christ for the remission of sins" (Acts 2:38). What is the purpose of repentance? "Repent ye therefore, and be converted, that your sins may be blotted out" (Acts 3:19). The result of repenting is conversion. When we repent, Jesus covers our sins by His blood, as Hebrews says: "without shedding of blood is no remission" (Hebrews 9:22).

The New King James Version of the great commission reads: "Go therefore and make disciples of all the nations, baptizing them in the name of the Father and of the Son and of the Holy Spirit" (Matthew 28:19, NKJV). Bible.org defines the term "disciples" as "devoted followers of a great religious leader or teacher." If we want to become Christians, then we must become disciples of Jesus Christ and give Him our devotion, making every effort to be Christ-like followers of His. Devotion requires following in the footsteps of Jesus and repenting of our sins first. It is the devil who wants us to think that we need to be baptized first and then we can work on repentance. This is backwards. Baptism is the outward sign that we have repented of our sins and put them away.

Baptism *by immersion* symbolizes two parts of our relationship with God: death to sin and

> **Justification is an essential part of salvation, for without it we are not acceptable to God and cannot have eternal life.**

resurrection to new life. Paul wrote: "Know ye not, that so many of us as were baptized into Jesus Christ were baptized into his death?" (Romans 6:3). Paul explained what John's baptism pointed to: "John verily baptized with the baptism of repentance, saying unto the people, that they should believe on him which should come after him, that is, on Christ Jesus" (Acts 19:4). Mark described the focus of John's baptism: "And there went out unto him all the land of Judaea, and they of Jerusalem, and were all baptized of him in the river of Jordan, confessing their sins" (Mark 1:5). The baptism that the believers in Acts 19 needed went further than John's did. They needed the baptism of the Holy Ghost: "Then remembered I the word of the Lord, how that he said, John indeed baptized with water; but ye shall be baptized with the Holy Ghost" (Acts 11:16). They needed the baptism that connects the believer with Christ: "For as many of you as have been baptized into Christ have put on Christ [or accepted Christ]" (Galatians 3:27). They needed the baptism that buries the old life and brings the believer forth in newness of life: "For if we have been planted [baptized] together in the likeness of his death, we shall be also in the likeness of his resurrection" (Romans 6:5).

Our brain, which is where we do our thinking, is referred to as our heart many times in the Bible. We need to change the way we think. Remember, we can receive what we ask for from God through faith. Yet, we need to be converted for God to be able to change our thinking from worldly things to spiritual things and to study the Bible to find His will for our life. Following conversion, we need to take the next step of faith—we need to be baptized in the name of Jesus Christ. Sadly, all too often people are baptized without putting away sin. Everyone has been given a measure of faith, and Jesus has made us acceptable to God. These first two parts we receive by grace, and, if we appreciate what has been done for us through love, then we will want to study the Word of God and ask Him what He wants for us to do, and then we are to do it. We are not to stand still—"For we walk by faith, not by sight" (2 Corinthians 5:7).

What does the Bible say about baptism? Consider the following verses: "One Lord, one faith, one baptism" (Ephesians 4:5). Here Paul says that there is one Lord, the only Creator God—the heavenly Father, Son, and Holy Spirit. These are the personages that make up the Trinity. Paul also states there is only one faith—in the unity of heaven, there will not be any different beliefs.

John the Baptist declared what type of baptism is required of the believer: "I indeed baptize you with water unto repentance: but he that cometh after me is mightier than I, whose shoes I am not worthy to bear: he shall baptize you with the Holy Ghost and with fire" (Matthew 3:11). In the footnotes of the Contemporary English Version, it is pointed out that baptism "unto repentance" means being baptized "because you have given up your sins." Mark notes where John baptized Jesus: "And it came to pass in those days, that Jesus came from Nazareth of Galilee, and was baptized of John in Jordan" (Mark 1:9). The Jordan River runs from north to south in Israel. Mark also tells the type of baptism John used: "John did baptize in the wilderness, and preach the baptism of repentance for the remission of sins" (Mark 1:4). Thus, John the Baptist baptized in the Jordan River and preached repentance (turning from our worldly ways of sin) into following the teachings of Jesus. Peter wrote: "Baptism is more than just washing your body. It means turning to God with a clear conscience, because Jesus Christ was raised from death" (1 Peter 3:21, CEV).

The apostle Paul often uses the term "clear conscience" referring to our relationship to God as a perfected relationship (Acts 23:1; 24:16; 2 Corinthians 1:12; 1 Timothy 1:19; 3:9; 2 Timothy 1:3). Many people have the mistaken idea that baptism by itself gives us eternal life. Others think that believing that Jesus was the Son of God is the only requirement for salvation. The Bible says that we must believe that Jesus was a human like us and that He was also the Son of God:

> Forasmuch then as the children are partakers of flesh and blood, he also himself likewise took part of the same; that through death he might destroy him that had the power of death, that is, the devil.... Wherefore in all things it behoved him to be made like unto his brethren, that he might be a merciful and faithful high priest in things pertaining to God, to make reconciliation for the sins of the people. (Hebrews 2:14, 17)

How should we prepare ourselves for baptism? The "baptism" of repentance is needed to change our heart and mind. Together with the measure of faith that God gives us, we need to believe that Jesus takes away our sins and that He was truly human and that He was also the Son of God, and then we must "repent [turn from sin in our lives] and be baptized" (Acts 2:38). Some churches are more interested in the number of those who are baptized than that the candidates have true repentance, yet Jesus said: "But seek ye first the kingdom of God, and his righteousness: and all these things shall be added unto you" (Matthew 6:33). Baptism is an outward sign that we have repented within and that we have received conversion of heart. Though many preachers advocate getting baptized first and then letting the Spirit change the heart, such a notion is not in the Bible. According to Acts 2:38, the proper order is to repent first and then to be baptized "in the name of Jesus Christ for the remission of sins." Being baptized "in the name of Jesus Christ" means believing that Christ is your Savior and that you need to obey everything He commanded His followers to do. Obedience is the gift of love returned through love—and the response to a convicted conscience: "And they which heard it, being convicted by their own conscience" (John 8:9). Paul testified about the conscience: "Which shew the work of the law written in their hearts, their conscience also bearing witness" (Romans 2:15). "I say the truth in Christ, I lie not, my conscience also bearing me witness in the Holy Ghost" (Romans 9:1). The Contemporary English Version puts this nicely: "I am a follower of Christ, and the Holy Spirit is a witness to my conscience. So I tell the truth and I am not lying..." (Romans 9:1, CEV).

The conscience needs the Holy Spirit's guidance. If we abuse the conscience, it is no longer a good guide. To receive the Holy Spirit's guidance we must be a follower of Jesus Christ. All things are accomplished through Jesus, as He has promised: "All power is given unto me in heaven and in earth" (Matthew 28:18).

Chapter 7
True Conversion

To the same resurrected Lord, there were two reactions: "And when they saw him [Jesus], they worshipped him: but some doubted" (Matthew 28:17). We choose to worship God because we love Him for who He is and we appreciate the marvelous things that He has done for us. If we ever forget these things, we will begin to doubt the necessity of worshiping Him.

Drawing from the qualities of little children, Jesus mentioned two qualities people need in order to enter heaven. First, they need to be converted. Second, they need to become as a little child in simplicity of faith. "Verily I say unto you, Except ye be converted, and become as little children, ye shall not enter into the kingdom of heaven" (Matthew 18:3). A converted mind that believes God without doubting is willing to follow Jesus in everything He asks us to do in fulfillment of the Christian life. About little children Jesus said: "But whoso shall offend one of these little ones which believe in me, it were better for him that a millstone were hanged about his neck, and that he were drowned in the depth of the sea" (Matthew 18:6). By this He meant that a person who offended even one of these little ones would be better off dead.

This principle can also be applied in not causing people who are new in the faith to stumble. As Paul wrote to the Galatians: "If you think you are better than others, when you really aren't, you are wrong" (Galatians 6:3, CEV). If we have been Christians a long time, it is good to remember that not everyone has the same amount of knowledge. Look at the following texts and see how they can apply: "I have shewed you all things, how that so labouring ye ought to support the weak, and to remember the words of the Lord Jesus, how he said, It is more blessed to give than to receive" (Acts 20:35). "We then that are strong ought to bear the infirmities of the weak, and not to please ourselves" (Romans 15:1). "But take heed lest by any means this liberty of yours become a stumblingblock to them that are weak" (1 Corinthians 8:9). Paul is saying that we who have been long in the faith need to be mindful of those who are new in the faith. "But when ye sin so against the brethren, and wound their weak

> **Jesus mentioned two qualities people need in order to enter heaven. First, they need to be converted. Second, they need to become as a little child in simplicity of faith.**

conscience, ye sin against Christ" (1 Corinthians 8:12). Remembering to uplift the weak (new believers) with words of encouragement and love and reminding them of what Christ has done for them, Paul uses the word "infirmities" to describe one who is "discouraged." He encouraged believers: "Now the God of patience and consolation grant you to be likeminded one toward another according to Christ Jesus: That ye may with one mind and one mouth glorify God, even the Father of our Lord Jesus Christ" (Romans 15:5, 6).

How is treating others the way we want to be treated a sign of "true conversion"? It is a change in the way we think and act, signifying to others that we know Jesus. Our salvation was given to us as a gift of grace through faith—through believing what God has promised. It is a thought process.

Remember what Jesus said about the greatest commandment? The first commandment is supreme love for God; the second is similar to the first: "Thou shalt love thy neighbour as thyself" (Matthew 22:39). All mankind are our neighbors. Paul wrote: "There is neither Jew nor Greek, there is neither bond nor free, there is neither male nor female: for ye are all one in Christ Jesus" (Galatians 3:28).

In this world, there are many people who do not want to be followers of Jesus. True conversion involves people who have chosen to be Christ's followers and have accepted the Bible as the only rule for governing their lives. The sacrifice of Jesus will not help anyone who does not accept His life, death, and resurrection for their salvation. People who have not accepted salvation through Christ may have faith that certain biblical events took place. However, such faith will not help any of them to obtain salvation or eternal life.

Some denominations teach that belief is all that is required to enter heaven. Yet, conversion means a change of mind. Sadly, there are many people who claim to have been converted and to believe the teachings of the Bible, yet they are deceived in believing only the parts of Scripture that suit them. Scripture plainly declares: "For there shall arise false christs, and false prophets, and shall shew great signs and wonders; insomuch that, if it were possible, they shall deceive the very elect" (Matthew 24:24). "But there were false prophets also among the people, even as there shall be false teachers among you, who privily shall bring in damnable heresies, even denying the Lord that bought them, and bring upon themselves swift destruction" (2 Peter 2:1). "And many false prophets shall rise, and shall deceive many" (Matthew 24:11). Jesus predicted a time when imposters would portray themselves as bearers of the gospel, even claiming to be Christ Himself. Look at what Paul wrote in his second letter to Timothy:

> This know also, that in the last days perilous times shall come. For men shall be lovers of their own selves, covetous, boasters, proud, blasphemers, disobedient to parents, unthankful, unholy, without natural affection, trucebreakers, false accusers, incontinent, fierce, despisers of those that are good, traitors, heady, highminded, lovers of pleasures more than lovers of God; having a form of godliness, but denying the power thereof: from such turn away. (2 Timothy 3:1–5)

Consider also the cautions of Jesus, John, and Paul: "But in vain they do worship me, teaching for doctrines the commandments of men" (Matthew 15:9). "Beloved, believe not every spirit, but try the spirits whether they are of God: because many false prophets are gone out into the world" (1 John 4:1). "If any man will do his will, he shall know of the doctrine, whether it be of God, or whether I speak of myself" (John 7:17). "Now the Spirit speaketh expressly, that in the latter times some shall depart from the faith, giving heed to seducing spirits, and doctrines of devils" (1 Timothy 4:1).

There are many people who have been deceived by believing human doctrines instead of the teachings of the Bible. But, of course, that is what Paul predicted: "For the time will come when they will not endure sound doctrine; but after their own lusts shall they heap to themselves teachers, having itching ears" (2 Timothy 4:3). Some people who claim to be Christians rationalize in this way: I will believe it if it is what I want to hear. Such a view sees doctrines more in terms of entertainment than of biblical soundness. Paul's admonition to Titus was: "Holding fast the faithful word as he hath been taught, that he may be able by sound doctrine both to exhort and to convince the gainsayers" (Titus 1:9).

The devil has a counterfeit for everything that God has given to mankind. In 1 Timothy 4:1, Paul spoke of the role of the Holy Spirit, referring to Him as "the Spirit." Peter referred to the Holy Spirit as "the Holy Ghost": "For the prophecy came not in old time by the will of man: but holy men of God spake as they were moved by the Holy Ghost" (2 Peter 1:21).

Paul also refers to false spirits as seducing spirits and to the doctrines of devils, which shows that they originate with Satan.

Satan and his fallen angels have one purpose—to deceive as many people as they can. They even use people who preach the gospel while mixing in error.

> Even him, whose coming is after the working of Satan with all power and signs and lying wonders, and with all deceivableness of unrighteousness in them that perish; because they received not the love of the truth, that they might be saved. And for this cause God shall send them strong delusion, that they should believe a lie: That they all might be damned who believed not the truth, but had pleasure in unrighteousness. (2 Thessalonians 2:9–12)

Deception began when sin came into this world. Eve repeated to the serpent: "God hath said, Ye shall not eat of it ... lest ye die. And the serpent said unto the woman, Ye shall not surely die" (Genesis 3:3, 4). The devil does not want anyone to believe all that the Bible teaches, but he does not mind if people believe some truth as long as they also believe some of his deceptions.

> **Satan and his fallen angels have one purpose—to deceive as many people as they can. They even use people who preach the gospel while mixing in error.**

Chapter 8
The Devil's Deceptions

The devil works under many guises. Revelation mentions several of these: "And the great dragon was cast out, that old serpent, called the Devil, and Satan, which deceiveth the whole world: he was cast out into the earth, and his angels were cast out with him" (Revelation 12:9).

It may come as a great surprise to many, but the favorite tool of the devil is actually the Bible. That is right—the Bible. "How is that possible?" you say. Look again at Genesis 3, where the serpent provocatively said to the woman:

> Yea, hath God said, Ye shall not eat of every tree of the garden? And the woman said unto the serpent, We may eat of the fruit of the trees of the garden: But of the fruit of the tree which is in the midst of the garden, God hath said, Ye shall not eat of it, *neither shall ye touch it*, lest ye die. And the serpent said unto the woman, Ye shall not surely die. (Genesis 3:1–4; italicized words were not in God's original statement in Genesis 2:17)

In that first temptation, the devil, working through the guise of the serpent, used Eve's misquoting of what God said to trick Eve. The same deception can come to us when we question what the Bible says. God speaks through the Bible just as surely today as He spoke to Adam and Eve in person before sin entered the world. One of the devil's most insidious deceptions is to influence people to change the exact meaning of Bible texts by taking a statement out of context, using just part of the statement, or adding human words to the words of God. This is what the devil did in the Garden of Eden. God had said not to eat of the fruit, or they would die. "… the serpent said unto the woman, Ye shall not surely die. For God doth know that in the day ye eat thereof, then your eyes shall be opened, and ye shall be as gods, knowing good and evil" (Genesis 3:4, 5).

> **It may come as a great surprise to many, but the favorite tool of the devil is actually the Bible.**

The devil first tried to trick Eve regarding the exact words God used. Then he contradicted God and quickly added words that sounded very appealing, "And ye shall be as gods, knowing good and evil." Here is the devil's clincher: they were to partake of divinity, knowing good and evil! The promise of knowledge Eve did not posses as she was talking with the devil sounded especially good.

Notice that in Eve's reply she added words that God had not told her. "Neither shall ye touch it," she said. God's actual words are recorded in the previous chapter: "And the LORD God commanded the man, saying, Of every tree of the garden thou mayest freely eat: but of the tree of the knowledge of good and evil, thou shalt not eat of it: for in the day that thou eatest thereof thou shalt surely die" (Genesis 2:16, 17).

Picture the scene. In the middle of the garden is a beautiful tree with attractive fruit growing on it. Resting in its branches is a beautiful golden serpent with wings to fly, holding and eating a piece of luscious fruit.

Would such a scene not only attract your attention but also arouse your curiosity? It certainly worked well on Eve. There was the serpent, not only touching the tree but also eating of the very fruit of which God had said, "Do not eat it lest you die." Picture Eve looking very intensely, waiting for the serpent to fall out of the tree dead. Instead, the serpent spoke to her, insinuating that it was the eating of the fruit that gave him the power of speech and, better yet, that allowed him to read her thoughts. How powerful the serpent must have appeared to her! Is it any wonder why Eve started believing what the serpent said? This was deception at its very finest.

Death: The Consequence of Sin

People still have a problem knowing what God has instructed them to do or not to do, and they sometimes argue that, because Adam and Eve did not die the very day they ate the forbidden fruit, that God must have meant a different kind of death. So, just what is death? Death is separation from life, God is the giver of life and the very day that Adam and Eve ate the forbidden fruit, they were separated from God. What in the Bible confirms this? Consider the description in Genesis 3: "And the eyes of them both were opened, and they knew that they were naked; and they sewed fig leaves together, and made themselves aprons" (Genesis 3:7). Adam told God, "'I was afraid, because I was naked; and I hid myself.' And God said, 'Who told thee that thou wast naked? Hast thou eaten of the tree, whereof I commanded thee that thou shouldest not eat?'" (Genesis 3:7, 10, 11). The fallen pair hid from God. They had separated themselves from God with eternal separation, and they were in need of a Savior.

Most Christians do not realize that today the same false doctrine—that humans are not really dead when they die—is taught in the majority of Christian churches. If people go to heaven or hell when they die, whether in body or spirit as many teach, then they are not really dead. Yet, this is not what God teaches in Scripture. God declared through Solomon: "For the living know that they shall die: but the dead know not any thing, neither have they any more a reward; for the memory of them is forgotten" (Ecclesiastes 9:5).

The part of the verse "neither have they any more a reward" makes it plain that, when we die, we do not *go* anywhere except to the grave. The idea that a person goes to heaven through his spirit is directly contradicted by what Jesus told Mary on the morning of the resurrection. Jesus said that He had not ascended to His Father: "Jesus saith unto her, Touch me not; for I am not yet ascended to my Father: but go to my brethren, and say unto them, I ascend unto my Father, and your Father; and to my God, and your God" (John 20:17; see also Luke 23:46).

Those who believe that they either go to heaven or hell at death are simply taking someone else's word without verifying it from Scripture. As a result, they are perpetuating the devil's lie, for such a teaching is not found in God's Word.

Look at how easy it is for the devil to deceive people today. He has practically the whole world believing that first lie. God said plainly that, if they ate of the fruit, they would die. He has also told us in Ecclesiastes 9:5 what it is like to be dead: it is just like being sound asleep—we do not know anything that is going on. There is no conscious spirit floating around anywhere; the person is just dead.

When speaking about Lazarus, Jesus referred to death as being a sleep:

> These things said he: and after that he saith unto them, Our friend Lazarus sleepeth; but I go, that I may awake him out of sleep. Then said his disciples, Lord, if he sleep, he shall do well. Howbeit Jesus spake of his death: but they thought that he had spoken of taking of rest in sleep. Then said Jesus unto them plainly, Lazarus is dead. (John 11:11–14)

Several Bible texts tell us what happens to humans at death. "For that which befalleth the sons of men befalleth beasts; even one thing befalleth them: as the one dieth, so dieth the other; yea, they have all one breath; so that a man hath no preeminence above a beast: for all is vanity. All go unto one place; all are of the dust, and all turn to dust again" (Ecclesiastes 3:19, 20). Notice that they return to dust. Genesis tells us that that is what God made human beings out of: "And the LORD God formed man of the dust of the ground, and breathed into his nostrils the breath of life; and man became a living soul" (Genesis 2:7). What makes the difference between a living person and a dead one is that a living person is still breathing while a dead one is not.

Solomon clearly tells us where we go when we die: "and all turn to dust again" (Ecclesiastes 3:20). King David wrote: "His breath goeth forth, he returneth to his earth; in that very day his thoughts perish" (Psalms 146:4). Isaiah wrote: "Thy dead men shall live; together with my dead body shall they arise. Awake and sing, ye that dwell in dust: for thy dew is as the dew of herbs, and the earth shall cast out the dead" (Isaiah 26:19). Isaiah is describing what will happen when Jesus returns. In his Thessalonian letter, Paul described Jesus' return: "For the Lord himself shall descend from heaven with a shout, with the voice of the archangel, and with the trump of God: and the dead in Christ shall rise first" (1 Thessalonians 4:16). In this same passage, Paul described those who die believing in Jesus as those who "sleep in Jesus." Other Bible passages describe the lack of consciousness in death. David wrote: "For in death there is no remembrance of thee: in the grave who shall give thee thanks"

(Psalms 6:5). "The dead praise not the Lord, neither any that go down into silence" (Psalm 115:17). "What profit is there in my blood, when I go down to the pit [the grave]? Shall the dust praise thee? Shall it declare thy truth?" (Psalms 30:9). Isaiah declared: "For the grave cannot praise thee, death can not celebrate thee: they that go down into the pit cannot hope for thy truth" (Isaiah 38:18). Here Isaiah refers to the grave as "the pit." Job said: "All flesh shall perish together, and man shall turn again unto dust" (Job 34:15). The great Creator formed humans out of the dust of the earth. "In the sweat of thy face shalt thou eat bread, till thou return unto the ground; for out of it wast thou taken: for dust thou art, and unto dust shalt thou return" (Genesis 3:19).

Some people claim that the words of Paul in Philippians 1:20-25 support believers' going to heaven when they die. Let us take a closer look:

> According to my earnest expectation and my hope, that in nothing I shall be ashamed, but that with all boldness, as always, so now also Christ shall be magnified in my body, whether it be by life, or by death. For to me to live is Christ, and to die is gain. But if I live in the flesh, this is the fruit of my labour: yet what I shall choose I wot not. For I am in a strait betwixt two, having a desire to depart, and to be with Christ; which is far better: Nevertheless to abide in the flesh is more needful for you. And having this confidence, I know that I shall abide and continue with you all for your furtherance and joy of faith.

Because of his confidence in the return of Christ, Paul said, "Christ shall be magnified in my body, whether it be by life, or by death." He was confident that those who die in Christ will be raised to life, as he told the Thessalonians: "For the Lord himself shall descend from heaven with a shout, with the voice of the archangel, and with the trump of God: and the dead in Christ shall rise first" (1 Thessalonians 4:16). Paul knew that as long as he was alive, he could use his physical brain and his physical lips and vocal chords to proclaim the gospel of salvation to Jew and Gentile. By preaching this message, he magnified the life, death, and resurrection of Christ. Yet, how could Paul magnify Christ if he were dead?

Look at the words of Jesus in Matthew: "And this gospel of the kingdom shall be preached in all the world for a witness unto all nations; and then shall the end come" (Matthew 24:14). "Teaching them to observe all things whatsoever I have commanded you: and, lo, I am with you alway, even unto the end of the world" (Matthew 28:20).

Jesus commanded His followers to preach until the end of time, teaching the things that Jesus did as an example. Time has extended nearly two thousand years since the time of the early believers. How would Jesus expect the apostles to live from then until the end of time? He would not, and Paul had confidence that the message he preached would still be preached by others after his death and that his death for Jesus would be a faithful witness to His Lord. That is what Paul rejoiced in—that the gospel would be preached whether he was alive or dead.

What was it that magnified Christ? Was it Paul's life or death or was it the gospel that he preached? Of course it was—and still is—the gospel, which was not only preached by Paul, but also by many others. Paul knew that the gospel would magnify Christ whether he was alive or dead.

"For to me to live is Christ, and to die is gain." As long as Paul was alive, he would preach the everlasting gospel, and, if he were to die, he knew that, by his faithful example, he would inspire others to preach the same everlasting gospel. Instead of there being only one person preaching, there would be many more. More is "gain"—Paul knew that more people would be learning about the gift of salvation through Jesus Christ our Lord and what He has done for us. "But if I live in the flesh, this is the fruit of my labour: yet what I shall choose I wot not. For I am in a strait betwixt two, having a desire to depart, and to be with Christ; which is far better" (Philippians 1:22, 23). The reward of being alive is seeing people accept Jesus' gift of salvation and choosing to always follow Him.

How will those who die in the Lord be *with* Christ? Paul himself said: "For the Lord himself shall descend from heaven with a shout, with the voice of the archangel, and with the trump of God: and the dead in Christ shall rise first: then we which are alive and remain shall be caught up together *with them in the clouds*, to meet the Lord in the air: and so shall we ever be *with the Lord*" (1 Thessalonians 4:16, 17, emphasis supplied). Because Paul knew that he would be with Christ at Jesus' second coming, to die and have all the pain and suffering gone would be wonderful—that would be far better than the life he had to live on earth. If he had accomplished all that God had for him to do, what better thing than to go to sleep and wait until Jesus' return? Paul completed his thought: "Nevertheless to abide in the flesh is more needful for you. And having this confidence, I know that I shall abide and continue with you all for your furtherance and joy of faith" (Philippians 1:24, 25). Paul knew that his ministry was not yet finished and that God had work for him to do in ministering to others and fulfilling God's command, "And the second is like unto the first, that ye love one another as I have loved you."

There is nothing in Philippians 1:20–25 to indicate that people go to heaven at death, but the devil has used the passage to lead people to believe that to be the case. Such deception is what Jesus predicted: "For there shall arise false Christs, and false prophets, and shall shew great signs and wonders; insomuch that, if it were possible, *they shall deceive the very elect*" (Matthew 24:24, emphasis supplied).

There are many more examples in the Bible that show the deceiving power of the devil. Yet, to list them all would make this book too large. This particular lie of the devil started at the very beginning of time, and it will continue until the very end, causing the ruin of many of God's created beings. How sad it is that people will believe a lie!

The apostle Paul was only one of many to proclaim the gospel of Jesus, but he was the apostle who Jesus commissioned to go to the Gentiles. If we look around the world today, we find far more believing Gentiles than believing Jews, a thought that makes this author very happy since that is what gave him the chance to know the Word of God and receive salvation.

Adam and Eve did not die the very day they ate the forbidden fruit, a symbol of disobeying God. Yet, on that day, they did die spiritually and their spiritual death would have brought eternal separation from God had a Savior not come to their rescue. Thankfully, the Savior did not come for Adam and Eve alone but for all people who have ever lived on this planet. Salvation has been extended to all mankind through Jesus Christ our Lord.

In our next chapter, we will consider a deception that is as equally misleading as believing that humans live on in heaven when they die.

Chapter 9
The Bible Sabbath

In chapter 3 we discussed "righteousness through Christ" and noted that, in receiving Christ's righteousness, we will keep God's Ten Commandments in faith. The Bible gives us all the information we need to discover how God wants us to live. As humans, we start out in life as a baby, and then, because someone cares for us, we grow stronger and more mature because they feed us the kind of food that is good for our bodies. We also begin to learn and develop our minds with the help of mothers, fathers, grandparents, and even our siblings. Growth of both body and mind are made possible because someone cared for us. That care is called love, and, as we grow bigger, we begin to use our mind to make choices about what we want to become.

In our spiritual life, that someone who cares for us is God, and the food we need to eat so we can grow is the Bible. What would happen to us after birth if no one cared enough to feed us? We would die physically. Likewise, if we do not receive spiritual food, we will die spiritually.

Knowing the difference between good and evil helps us to properly choose to maintain our spiritual well being. We choose to follow either good or evil, God or the devil. There are only two choices. There is no such thing as neutral, and Jesus made it very plain: "He that is not with me is against me; and he that gathereth not with me scattereth abroad" (Matthew 12:30).

Yet, in order to choose between different things, we need to know the options available. In the Bible, God shows us both sides. He shows us good and evil, and that is why it is so important for us to learn what is in the Word of God, for the devil distorts the truths of the Bible, using the Bible very effectively against humans.

Genesis begins by telling us that God created the heavens and the earth. The apostle Paul wrote: "For the invisible things of him from the creation of the world are clearly seen, being understood by the things that are made, even his eternal power and Godhead; so that they are without excuse" (Romans 1:20). Paul is saying that every human being knows of God by the things we see—nature speaks of the power and wisdom of God as the Creator. No one who has the use of his or her mind can use the excuse that he or she did not know, for God's designing capability is clearly seen in His created works.

Regarding the Jesus' role as creator, Paul wrote: "For by him were all things created, that are in heaven, and that are in earth, visible and invisible, whether they be thrones, or dominions, or principalities, or powers: all things were created by him, and for him" (Colossians 1:16). This verse says, "For by him were all things created." Who is the word "him" referring to? Ephesians 3:9 gives the answer: "And to make all men see what is the fellowship of the mystery, which from the beginning of the world hath been hid in *God, who created all things by Jesus Christ*" (emphasis supplied). What did he mean by "the fellowship of the mystery"? Consider the verse in context from the Contemporary English Version:

> In fact, this letter tells you a little about how God has shown me his mysterious ways. As you read the letter, you will also find out how well I really do understand the mystery about Christ. No one knew about this mystery until God's Spirit told it to his holy apostles and prophets. And the mystery is this: Because of Christ Jesus, the good news has given the Gentiles a share in the promises that God gave to the Jews. God has also let the Gentiles be part of the same body.… God was kind and chose me to tell the Gentiles that because of Christ there are blessings that cannot be measured. (Ephesians 3:3–8, CEV)

The mystery Paul was describing is the "good news" of the gospel given to us by Jesus Christ, which gives us "blessings that cannot be measured." One of these blessings is salvation, and who is it that does not want anyone to be saved? It is the devil, and the best way he has to insure his wishes is to confuse people's minds about the truths of God's Word.

The devil has used biblical counterfeits and deceptions to deceive people. One of these is regarding what happens to people when they die. Another is which day God calls upon humans to worship Him as Creator.

So, which day is it? The answer becomes apparent in the first book of the Bible, which recounts the beginning of this world's history. We begin in Genesis 1.

Creation day one. "And God said, Let there be light: and there was light" (Genesis 1:3).

Creation day two. "And God said, Let there be a firmament in the midst of the waters, and let it divide the waters from the waters.… And God called the firmament Heaven. And the evening and the morning were the second day" (Genesis 1:6, 8).

Creation day three. "And God said, Let the waters under the heaven be gathered together unto one place, and let the dry land appear: and it was so. And God called the dry land Earth; and the gathering together of the waters called he Seas: and God saw that it was good. And God said, Let the earth bring forth grass, the herb yielding seed, and the fruit tree yielding fruit after his kind, whose seed is in itself, upon the earth: and it was so. And the earth brought forth grass, and herb yielding seed after his kind, and the tree yielding fruit, whose seed was in itself, after his kind: and God saw that it was good" (Genesis 1:9–12).

Creation day four. "And God said, Let there be lights in the firmament of the heaven to divide the day from the night; and let them be for signs, and for seasons, and for days, and years: And let them be for lights in the firmament of the heaven to give light upon the earth: and it was so. And God made two great lights; the greater light to rule the day, and the lesser light to rule the night: he made the stars also. And God set them in the firmament of the heaven to give light upon the earth, and to rule over the day and over the night, and to divide the light from the darkness: and God saw that it was good" (Genesis 1:14–18).

Creation day five. "And God said, Let the waters bring forth abundantly the moving creature that hath life, and fowl that may fly above the earth in the open firmament of heaven. And God created great whales, and every living creature that moveth, which the waters brought forth abundantly, after their kind, and every winged fowl after his kind: and God saw that it was good. And God blessed them, saying, Be fruitful, and multiply, and fill the waters in the seas, and let fowl multiply in the earth" (Genesis 1:20–22).

Creation day six. "And God said, Let the earth bring forth the living creature after his kind, cattle, and creeping thing, and beast of the earth after his kind: and it was so. And God made the beast of the earth after his kind, and cattle after their kind, and every thing that creepeth upon the earth after his kind: and God saw that it was good.

"And God said, Let us make man in our image, after our likeness: and let them have dominion over the fish of the sea, and over the fowl of the air, and over the cattle, and over all the earth, and over every creeping thing that creepeth upon the earth. So God created man in his own image, in the image of God created he him; male and female created he them. And God blessed them, and God said unto them, Be fruitful, and multiply, and replenish the earth, and subdue it: and have dominion over the fish of the sea, and over the fowl of the air, and over every living thing that moveth upon the earth" (Genesis 1:24–28).

The chapter describes days one through six of the Creation. There is nothing about worship in any of these six days, nothing that memorializes the work of God. Following this account, Genesis summarizes God's activity in creation: "Thus the heavens and the earth were finished, and all the host of them" (Genesis 2:1). Everything necessary for the function of this earth and the universe had been created. Yet, Genesis mentions one day more:

Creation day seven. "And on the seventh day God ended his work which he had made; and he rested on the seventh day from all his work which he had made. And God blessed the seventh day, and sanctified it: because that in it he had rested from all his work which God created and made. These are the generations of the heavens and of the earth when they were created, in the day that the Lord God made the earth and the heavens" (Genesis 2:2–4).

The Bible says that God rested on the seventh day of creation; it also says that He gave the seventh day His blessing and sanctified it, that is, He set it aside as special because in it He had rested from all His work of creating. Does God get tired? Did He need physical rest? No. Remember who it was that did the creating. "God … created all things by Jesus Christ" (Ephesians 3:9). So it was Jesus who *made* the Sabbath, and He made it, as He said in Mark, *for man:* "The sabbath was made for man, and not man for the sabbath" (Mark 2:27).

The same Jesus who created all things declares that the Sabbath was made for man. In the Creation, what came first, man or the Sabbath? Man was created on the sixth day and Jesus set aside the Sabbath for man on the seventh day. It is His having made the Sabbath that gives Him lordship over it. "Therefore the Son of man is Lord also of the sabbath" (Mark 2:28). Then, both in Luke and in Matthew, He makes the same declaration: "And he said unto them, That the Son of man is Lord also of the sabbath" (Luke 6:5). "For the Son of man is Lord even of the sabbath day" (Matthew 12:8).

In Bible times, the priests were the teachers of the people to instruct them in the ways of the Lord. They also sat as judges. The high priest was like a Supreme Court judge in that he had the final judgment over the people, as Ezekiel described: "And in controversy they [the priests] shall stand in judgment; and they shall judge it according to my judgments: and they shall keep my laws and my statutes in all mine assemblies; and they shall hallow [set aside] my sabbaths" (Ezekiel 44:24).

> "Moreover also I gave them my sabbaths, to be a sign between me and them, that they might know that I am the LORD that sanctifies them" (Ezekiel 20:12).

According to the Bible, if there is a controversy over church doctrine, it should be decided according to God's judgments. In all God's assemblies, wherever they may take place, the people were to keep the Ten Commandment law and God's counsels recorded in Scripture.

"And hallow my sabbaths; and they shall be a sign between me and you, that ye may know that I am the LORD your God" (Ezekiel 20:20). "Moreover also I gave them my sabbaths, to be a sign between me and them, that they might know that I am the LORD that sanctifies them" (Ezekiel 20:12).

These statements are direct commands from God. They tell us the reason for hallowing the Sabbath: it is a sign between God and His people, pointing to His identity as the LORD God, the Creator of the heavens and earth. "Hallow" is also translated "make holy" or "set specially apart for worshiping God."

Some people have been deceived into thinking that the days of creation were different in the beginning from the twenty-four hour day that we have today. However, according to the fourth day of creation, God placed the same sun, moon, and stars to mark time just as they do today. "And God said, Let there be lights in the firmament of the heaven to divide the day from the night; and let them be for signs, and for seasons, and for days, and years" (Genesis 1:14).

The question about which day of the week is the Sabbath frequently surfaces among seekers after truth. If we are willing to accept it, the fourth commandment plainly tells us which day of the week is the Sabbath:

> But the seventh day is the sabbath of the LORD thy God: in it thou shalt not do any work, thou, nor thy son, nor thy daughter, thy manservant, nor thy maidservant, nor thy cattle, nor thy stranger that is within thy gates: For in six days the LORD made heaven and earth, the sea, and all that in them is, and rested the seventh day: wherefore the LORD blessed the sabbath day, and hallowed it. (Exodus 20:8, 10, 11)

Prior to God's giving the commandment, Moses had told the people: "This is that which the Lord hath said, to morrow is the rest of the holy sabbath unto the Lord" (Exodus 16:23). After giving the commandments, God told Moses: "Speak thou also unto the children of Israel, saying, Verily my sabbaths ye shall keep: for it is a sign between me and you throughout your generations; that ye may know that I am the Lord that doth sanctify you" (Exodus 31:13).

The Seventh-Day Sabbath Is the Seal of the Creator God

The statement about the sign of the Sabbath was given by the Lord to Moses during Israel's encampment at Mount Sinai in Exodus 31, and some nine hundred years later the Lord told Ezekiel the same thing in Ezekiel 20. The Bible assures us that God does not change: "For I am the Lord, I change not; therefore ye sons of Jacob are not consumed" (Malachi 3:6). Some people assume that God is not so particular under the new covenant and that He changed the day of worship. Yet, nothing in Scripture says that He did. The New Testament declares Jesus the Creator to be "the same yesterday, to day, and for ever" (Hebrews 13:8).

The devil still distorts the Bible just enough in quoting it that some people accept his distortion as truth. How jealous is God for His written word? Consider the following passage:

> Ye shall keep the sabbath therefore; for it is holy unto you: every one that defileth it shall surely be put to death: for whosoever doeth any work therein, that soul shall be cut off from among his people. Six days may work be done; but in the seventh is the sabbath of rest, holy to the Lord: whosoever doeth any work in the sabbath day, he shall surely be put to death. Wherefore the children of Israel shall keep the sabbath, to observe the sabbath throughout their generations, for a perpetual covenant. (Exodus 31:14–16)

The ending of this passage is very beautiful. It describes the seventh-day Sabbath as a "perpetual covenant," showing the relationship that God wants with everyone who accepts Christ's sacrifice and gift, giving them eternal life in strict obedience to His Word.

What does this have to do with Bible truth or church traditions? None of the above is possible without both faith and works. We must first believe that the Bible is the Word of God and a guide for our life and that we can only obtain eternal life in "the obedience of faith" and good works, "that they should repent and turn to God, and do works meet for repentance" (Acts 26:20)—faithfully obeying what the Bible tells us to do.

> If a brother or sister be naked, and destitute of daily food, And one of you say unto them, Depart in peace, be ye warmed and filled; notwithstanding ye give them not those things which are needful to the body; what doth it profit? Even so faith, if it hath not works, is dead, being alone.… Ye see then how that by works a man is justified, and

not by faith only.... For as the body without the spirit is dead, so faith without works is dead also. (James 2:15–17, 24, 26)

If we have genuine faith, we will not only believe what the Bible tells us regarding God's plan for us, we will also produce the good works of doing what God has told us to do.

As we continue through the next chapters, we will be confronted with many things that the devil does not want us to read or understand. This is where faith and works are put to the test for any of us who really want to be true followers of God.

The chapter shows what the truth about the seventh-day Sabbath is and how the devil has tried to eliminate the seventh-day Sabbath and replace it with his counterfeit day of Sunday.

> **If we have genuine faith, we will not only believe what the Bible tells us regarding God's plan for us, we will also produce the good works of doing what God has told us to do.**

Chapter 10
Origins of Sunday Worship

In our last chapter, we looked at some of the Bible references pertaining to the seventh-day Sabbath and that which God expects true followers of Jesus to do. In this chapter, we will answer the question of how Sunday came to be the day of worship for so many Christians. There are many possible answers to this question. The most popular of these is that Christians worship on Sunday to commemorate Jesus' resurrection. Yet, is there any evidence in the New Testament that the first Christians rested or worshipped on Sunday? No, but there is evidence about what Jesus and His disciples did on the seventh-day Sabbath. Here is one example:

> At that time Jesus went on the sabbath day through the corn; and his disciples were an hungered, and began to pluck the ears of corn, and to eat. But when the Pharisees saw it, they said unto him, Behold, thy disciples do that which is not lawful to do upon the sabbath day.... And when he [Jesus] was departed thence, he went into their synagogue. (Matthew 12:1, 2, 9)

The Jews, who bore the name "Jew" because they were descendants of the tribe of Judah and what was left of the other tribes, followed the Jewish traditions of the law. One area of addition had to do with the many rules they had of things that were unlawful to do on the Sabbath day. One of these was about how far a person could walk on the Sabbath. Another was about how much one could carry as a "burden" on the Sabbath—a handkerchief being such a "burden." Still another rule was what they considered to be work on the Sabbath. They considered picking even a few heads of grain to be thrashing or harvesting, activities which should be saved for the other days of the week. In Matthew 12, we see how Jesus answered the Pharisees' charge that what His disciples were doing was unlawful:

> But he said unto them, Have ye not read what David did, when he was an hungered, and they that were with him; how he entered into the house of God, and did eat the shewbread, which was not lawful for him to eat, neither for them which were with him, but only for the priests? Or have ye not read in the law, how that on the sabbath days the priests in the temple profane the sabbath, and are blameless. (Matthew 12:3–5)

Remember that, in the days of Jesus, the Old Testament was all the Bible that they had. So, from their Bible, Jesus referred to David's actions in running from King Saul and the priests' work on the Sabbath, for which they were "blameless," as examples which proved that Jesus' disciples were guiltless in pulling off a few heads of grain while walking through the field (Matthew 12:7). The Pharisees never brought up the charge again in the Gospel of Matthew.

What else did Jesus do on the Sabbath? "And they went into Capernaum; and straightway on the sabbath day he entered into the synagogue, and taught" (Mark 1:21). "And when the sabbath day was come, he began to teach in the synagogue: and many hearing him were astonished, saying, From whence hath this man these things? And what wisdom is this which is given unto him, that even such mighty works are wrought by his hands?" (Mark 6:2). "And he came to Nazareth, where he had been brought up: and, as his custom was, he went into the synagogue on the sabbath day, and stood up for to read." (Luke 4:16). These three texts tell us that Jesus attended the synagogue in observance of the Sabbath. Mark 1:21 uses the word "they," which indicates that it was talking about more than Jesus. It was Jesus *and* His disciples. There are more references to Jesus' Sabbath activities: "And he came down to Capernaum, a city of Galilee, and taught them on the sabbath days" (Luke 4:31). "And it came to pass also on another sabbath that he entered into the synagogue and taught" (Luke 6:6). "And he was teaching in one of the synagogues on the sabbath" (Luke 13:10). These samplings from the Gospels are good indicators of Jesus' teaching, preaching, and healing on the Sabbath day.

After Christ's ascension, what did Jesus' followers do on the Sabbath, and what did they teach about Sabbath observance? Luke describes a significant visit of Paul's: "But when they departed from Perga, they came to Antioch in Pisidia, and went into the synagogue on the sabbath day, and sat down" (Acts 13:14). In Acts 12 and 13, Luke identifies who "they" were. "They" includes Barnabas and Saul (who later became known as Paul), and John (who was called Mark). Acts says that John Mark went back to Jerusalem. Who was Paul's audience on this occasion? From Luke's account, we determine that Paul was talking to a group of people who were mostly Jews but also some Gentiles. Paul also mentions the Sabbath in declaring: "For they that dwell at Jerusalem, and their rulers, because they knew him not, nor yet the voices of the prophets which are read every sabbath day, they have fulfilled them in condemning him" (Acts 13:27).

> "And on the sabbath we went out of the city by a river side, where prayer was wont to be made; and we sat down, and spake unto the women which resorted thither" (Acts 16:13).

Paul was referring to the Jewish leaders at Jerusalem, who wanted to kill Jesus because they would not accept Him as the Messiah. Ironically, in condemning Jesus, they were fulfilling what they had read from Sabbath to Sabbath in the Old Testament prophecies, leaving them without excuse. Next, something surprising occurred. Luke's account of events continues: "And when the Jews were gone out of the synagogue, the Gentiles besought that these words might be preached to them the next sabbath" (Acts 13:42). Amazingly, "the next sabbath day came almost the whole city together to hear the word of God" (Acts 13:44).

This is a wonderful chapter! In it we find Paul preaching the gospel—the good news about Jesus the Savior of the world—the same Jesus who came to this earth as a baby while being both the Son of God and the Son of Man, the same Jesus who died and rose from the dead on the third day, and who returned to heaven to intercede for all who accept His sacrifice for the forgiveness of sin and who choose to follow Him through obedience to God's law.

There are other instances of Paul's meeting with people on the Sabbath. "And on the sabbath we went out of the city by a river side, where prayer was wont to be made; and we sat down, and spake unto the women which resorted thither" (Acts 16:13). This incident illustrates Paul's desire to find other believers worshipping the true God on the Sabbath. In this case, it was a group of ladies led by a non-Jewish businesswoman named Lydia. Chapter 17 of Acts establishes Paul's "manner" or weekly pattern: "And Paul, as his manner was, went in unto them, and three sabbath days reasoned with them out of the scriptures" (Acts 17:2). This pattern is repeated in chapter 18: "And he [Paul] reasoned in the synagogue every sabbath, and persuaded the Jews and the Greeks" (Acts 18:4).

Thus, the story of Jesus' life on earth, as told by Matthew, Mark, Luke, and John, and the story of the apostle Paul as he traveled the regions of Asia and the Mediterranean, as recorded in the book of Acts, illustrate what Jesus and His early followers did on the Sabbath. If you would like to locate where these Sabbath meetings occurred, most Bibles have a map in the back pages, showing the different journeys of Paul. Paul's writings also tell where he preached as he took the gospel to the Gentiles. All the worship meetings recorded in Acts were held on Sabbath.

So where did Sunday worship come from, and when did it begin? Since there is no record of Sunday worship in the Bible, we will have to go to history to find it. Yet, first, let us go back in biblical history.

Israel's Flirtation With False Gods

What was the false worship that Israel fell into anciently? It was idol worship. The first instance of this in Scripture has to do with Aaron and the golden calf, described in Exodus: "And he received them at their hand, and fashioned it with a graving tool, after he had made it a molten calf: and they said, "These be thy gods, O Israel, which brought thee up out of the land of Egypt" (Exodus 32:4). The people whom God had just saved from Egypt turned away from Him when Moses went up into the mount, and they worshiped an idol resembling the Egyptian god Apis.

The second instance of idol worship among the Israelites is in the story of Balaam and Balak. Balak was the king of the Moabites. He was afraid of the Israelites because they had followed the instructions of the Lord and defeated Og the king of Bashan and Sihon the king of all the Amorites. Balak secured the services of the prophet Balaam to curse Israel.

The account of Balaam's attempt to curse them begins: "And it came to pass on the morrow, that Balak took Balaam, and brought him up into the high places of Baal, that thence he might see the utmost part of the people [of Israel]" (Numbers 22:41). This would indicate that the nations living in the land of Canaan at that time worshiped Baal. That the account mentions "the high places of Baal" indicates that there was more than one high place. After Balaam could not curse Israel and subsequently counseled Balak to bring in women to entice Israel's men to follow their religion, "And Israel joined himself unto Baalpeor: and the anger of the LORD was kindled against Israel" (Numbers 25:3). Baal Peor, which is a name of Jordanian-Moabite origin, describes both the sun god and the moon goddess. Reading all of Numbers 25, we discover what the Lord told Moses to do to all the men who had joined themselves unto Baalpeor. Notice the connection to the sun in their punishment, which indicates the focus of Baal worship:

> And the LORD said unto Moses, Take all the heads of the people, and hang them up before the LORD *against the sun*, that the fierce anger of the LORD may be turned away from Israel. And Moses said unto the judges of Israel, Slay ye every one his men that were joined unto Baalpeor. (Numbers 25:3–5, emphasis supplied)

All the worship of gods and goddesses was a form of sexual immorality just like that practiced by the Israelites when they worshiped at Baalpeor with the sacred poles and sacrificed to idols. The results were horrible: "And those that died in the plague were twenty and four thousand" (Numbers 25:9). Israel, the chosen people of the Lord, after promising to follow "all that the Lord has said we will do," began to worship the gods that were worshiped by the nations in the land of Canaan. In violation of the first commandment, this placed another god before the God of creation.

How repulsive it is to God when His children break the commandments that He has given them? Referring to the twenty-four thousand who were killed in Numbers 25, Moses said: "Your eyes have seen what the LORD did because of Baalpeor: for all the men that followed Baalpeor, the LORD thy God hath destroyed them from among you" (Deuteronomy 4:3). During the period of the judges, Israel's apostasy was rampant: "And the children of Israel did evil in the sight of the LORD, and served Baalim: … And they forsook the LORD, and served Baal and Ashtaroth" (Judges 2:11, 13).

> **"Take all the heads of the people, and hang them up before the LORD against the sun, that the fierce anger of the LORD may be turned away from Israel."**

In this passage, we find another god that Israel began to worship—Ashtaroth, who was an equivalent of the Babylonian goddess Ishtar, the earlier Sumerian goddess Inanna, and the Phoenician goddess Astarte. Wikipedia describes the god/goddess this way: "Astaroth (also Ashtaroth, Astarot, and Asteroth), in demonology, is a Crowned Prince of Hell. He is a male figure named after the Canaanite Ashtoreth.… The name "Astaroth" as a male demon is first known from *The Book of Abramelin*, purportedly written in Hebrew ca. 1458 [BC].… In art … Astaroth is depicted as a nude man with feathered wings, wearing a crown, holding a serpent in one hand, and riding a beast with dragon-like wings and a serpent-like tail" ("Astaroth," Wikipedia, http://1ref.us/47).

This description could easily fit the depiction of Satan found in the book of Revelation: "And the great dragon was cast out, that old serpent, called the Devil, and Satan, which deceiveth the whole world: he was cast out into the earth, and his angels were cast out with him" (Revelation 12:9).

Other foreign gods that the Israelites worshiped can be found in the record of the Kings: "Because that they have forsaken me, and have worshipped Ashtoreth the goddess of the Zidonians, Chemosh the god of the Moabites, and Milcom the god of the children of Ammon, and have not walked in my ways, to do that which is right in mine eyes, and to keep my statutes and my judgments" (1 Kings 11:33).

Chemosh was the national God of the Moabites, as Baal was of the Zidonians, and Milcom (also spelled Moloch or Malcam) was the god of the Ammonites. Moloch was the god to whom Israel sacrificed their children. The name Moloch means "king." Moloch was "the sun god of the Canaanites (Ammonites?) in old Palestine and sometimes associated with the Sumerian Baal, although Moloch (or Molekh) was entirely malevolent. In the 8th–6th century BCE, firstborn children were sacrificed to him by the Israelites in the Valleye of Hinnom, south-east of Jerusalem … These sacrifices to the sun god were made to renew the strength of the sun fire. This ritual was probably borrowed from surrounding nations, and was also popular in ancient Carthage" ("Moloch," *Encyclopedia Mythica*, http://1ref.us/48).

In Deuteronomy 17, God warned Israel what the consequences would be if they left Him "and served other gods, and worshipped them, either the sun, or moon, or any of the host of heaven" (Deuteronomy 17:3). They would be stoned (Deuteronomy 17:5). He also identified who worshippers of false gods were really serving: "They sacrificed *unto devils*, not to God; to gods whom they knew not, to new gods that came newly up, whom your fathers feared not" (Deuteronomy 32:17, emphasis supplied). Sadly, Israel did just what He commanded them not to do. "And the children of Israel did evil again in the sight of the Lord, and served Baalim, and Ashtaroth, and the gods of Syria, and the gods of Zidon, and the gods of Moab, and the gods of the children of Ammon, and the gods of the Philistines, and forsook the Lord, and served not him" (Judges 10:6).

Even though the people worshipped these seven foreign gods rather than the true God, they still wanted God to protect them. Are we any different than they? God still expects believers to keep His commandments (1 Corinthians 7:19; 1 John 5:2), yet many professed Christians make excuses for not doing so. God's indictment of Israel was: "Yet ye have forsaken me, and served other gods: wherefore I will deliver you no more. Go and cry unto the gods which ye have chosen; let them deliver you in the time of your tribulation" (Judges 10:13, 14).

Later in their history, when the king of Assyria took the people of Israel out of the region of Samaria and put other people in their land from Babylon, Cuthah, Ava, Hamath, and Sepharvaim, the new inhabitants did not respect the God of Israel: "Howbeit every nation made gods of their own, and put them in the houses of the high places which the Samaritans had made, every nation in their cities wherein they dwelt" (2 Kings 17:29).

Dagon was the most important god to the Philistines and was represented as a fish. The Babylonians also had a fish god, which was half man and half fish. The symbol of the fish god has consistently been found in the sculptures of Nineveh. The book of Judges describes the Philistine's worship of Dagon after their victory over Samson:

> Then the lords of the Philistines gathered them together for to offer a great sacrifice unto Dagon their god, and to rejoice: for they said, Our god hath delivered Samson our enemy into our hand. And when the people saw him, they praised their god: for they said, Our god hath delivered into our hands our enemy, and the destroyer of our country, which slew many of us. (Judges 16:23, 24)

Samson became weak when he let the Philistines cut off his hair. Since the Israelites were worshiping idols and not the Creator of heaven and earth, God let the surrounding nations overrun their land and take them captive.

Dagon was represented with outstretched arms and a hollow interior. The people would kindle a fire inside the Dagon idol and place a newborn baby on its arms. Then when Dagon got hot enough to change colors, the priests of Dagon would move the arms toward the mouth as if to eat the baby, causing the baby to fall into the fire and be consumed. Israel worshiped this same false deity when they burned their babies on the altars.

In one of the later battles that Israel had with the Philistines, the Philistines captured the ark of the covenant and took it to the temple of Dagon. This was seen as a sign of Dagon's superiority to the Lord God. However, the Lord God—the Creator of heaven and earth—had a way to show who the important deity was, as the account in 1 Samuel reveals:

> When the Philistines took the ark of God, they brought it into the house of Dagon, and set it by Dagon. And when they of Ashdod arose early on the morrow, behold, Dagon was fallen upon his face to the earth before the ark of the Lord.
>
> And they took Dagon, and set him in his place again. And when they arose early on the morrow morning, behold, Dagon was fallen upon his face to the ground before the ark of the Lord; and the head of Dagon and both the palms of his hands were cut off upon the threshold; only the stump of Dagon was left to him. (1 Samuel 5:2–4)

There are many ways that people have blasphemed the Lord through the worship of false gods, and the apostasy is not over yet. People even now worship false gods. However, most have been deceived and led astray by the teachings of men and by the devil himself. Devil worship has been around since the time of the flood. Jesus declared, "He that is not with me is against me" (Matthew 12:30).

Worship of the sun

Sun worship has been described as far back as the Tower of Babel. It was associated with the rituals of the pagan sun god. We find it in Genesis 10, immediately following Noah's genealogy: "Now these are the generations of the sons of Noah, Shem, Ham, and Japheth … And the sons of Ham;

Cush, and Mizraim, and Phut, and Canaan.... And Cush begat Nimrod: he began to be a mighty one in the earth.... And the beginning of his kingdom was Babel ... in the land of Shinar. Out of that land went forth Asshur, and builded Nineveh ..." (Genesis 10:1, 6, 8, 10, 11). Thus, Nimrod was the great-grandson of Noah (Genesis 10:6–8). The account of the flood states: "And the ark rested in the seventh month, on the seventeenth day of the month, upon the mountains of Ararat" (Genesis 8:4). Just after the flood, the knowledge of evil was still on the minds of Noah's sons, grandsons, and great-grandsons.

About the post-flood inhabitants of the earth, Genesis says: "And as they journeyed from the east, that they found a plain in the land of Shinar; and they dwelt there.... Therefore is the name of it called Babel" (Genesis 11:2, 9). This links Nimrod with the place where the people built the tower of Babel. In Jewish tradition, the kingdom of Nimrod is associated with Babylon in the plains of Shinar. Nimrod, who created this state system to serve him as god, is credited with a primary role in the construction of the Tower of Babel. Nimrod was killed and his body was smeared all over the streets of the place. But that did not stop the people from worshipping him as a god, for his widow declared that he did not die, but that "he rose into heaven," and had now become the sun god.

Various ancient sources on mythology list Semiramis as the first wife of Nimrod, sometimes calling her "Sumerimus" or "Tamuramus." She was apparently the high priestess of the religion of Babel and the founder of all mystery religions. She was worshiped as a goddess and known by many other names in different countries. In Syria she was called Ishtar; in Phoenicia, Astarte; in Egypt, Isis; in Greece, Aphrodite; in Rome, Venus. Yet, she was always known as the deity of sexual love and fertility. Semiramis, as the accounts go, had become pregnant by someone other than her husband, Nimrod. She claimed that "the rays of the sun had impregnated" her and that the baby that was born was a reincarnation of her husband—a virgin birth counterfeited by the devil to take away from the real virgin birth of Jesus Christ (Matthew 1:23). The baby, whom she named Tammuz (sometimes spelled "Tamu" or "Tamus" in some ancient stories), was born during the winter solstice on December 25.

The sun god cult often included human sacrifice. On December 25, adherents of the Tammuz cult held a child mass, killing infants, burning them as offerings to Tammuz. Tamuramus was said to die, 'ascend into heaven,' and be reborn on the fertile equinox in the spring, the longest day of equal sunlight and darkness, returning to earth in a giant egg, which landed in the Euphrates River, broke open, and turned a bird into an egg-laying rabbit, declaring Tamuramus's divinity. This occurred yearly on the first Sunday after the equinox in spring. Sun god worship is known all over the eastern world under different names.

A freak hunting accident cost the supposedly reincarnated Tammuz his life as he was gored to death by a wild boar on his fortieth birthday. In memory of Tammuz, every year after that, his followers would weep for forty days and nights for each year of his mortal life, and this action was supposed to give Tammuz a better afterlife. These forty days preceded Easter Sunday when the mother was supposedly reincarnated as the goddess of fertility. This celebration was transformed into Lent, a period of forty days during which people are supposed to deny themselves of pleasures. Lent is a Catholic observance. On Easter Sunday, after forty days of mourning for Tamu the sun god, his followers would kill a wild boar and eat it at the early Sunday service, just as the sun rose and filled the eastern-facing caves where they worshipped with light. The priests of the Tamu sun god worshipers would impregnate virgins in the cave and then, nine months later, would sacrifice their babies in the same cave, dipping eggs in the blood of the sacrificed babies. The sons of Canan moved from Shinar and squatted in the Promised Land.

Tammuz was considered the consort of Ishtar and the god of the underworld and came to be known under other names: in Phoenicia, he was called Baal; in Egypt, he was Osiris; in Greece, he was Eros; and in Rome, he was Cupid (adapted from a posting by "rahbbayrahb420," accompanying a video entitled "Awaken Part I," and other sources). Some Romans referred to Tamu as Mithras—"The Light of the World." In Persia, Mithras was a spirit or archangel of the sun and of fire, and he was worshiped as the sun god. Mithras was also adopted as the sun god in early Roman civilizations. The ancient sun god identified as Sol Invictus ("the Invincible Sun") was associated with Mithras under Mithraism. Sol Invictus. "In 270 AD, the popularity in the Roman Empire of the Mithraic Mysteries and Mithraism led to Emperor Aurelian's establishment of Sol Invictus ("the unconquered sun") as the Empire's official religion. Mithra, or Mithras, was the Persian sun god, and his worship was very popular throughout the Roman Empire for hundreds of years. In 274 AD, Emperor Aurelian established December 25th, the winter solstice (the shortest solar day of the year under the Julian calendar), as the day the goddess Cybele, the Queen of Heaven, gave birth to the sun, Mithras" ("Mithras & Sol Invictus ("the unconquered sun"), Tek Gnostics, http://1ref.us/49). Thus, the birthday of the Invincible Sun supposedly took place on December 25. Mithras resembled Jesus in symbolism. The Roman sun god's sacrifice was a person nailed to a cross made from a tree. This means of punishment was adopted from the Persians under the Babylonian Empire. Actually, to be nailed to a tree meant to be cursed by God and man, as Paul wrote in Galatians, "Cursed is every one that hangeth on a tree" (Galatians 3:13; cf. Deuteronomy 21:23).

While Tamu was the ancient Persian/Babylonian sun god, the Egyptians adopted the practice of sun worship from them and named their sun god Ra, who was also said to be born on December 25, as was the Roman god Zeus. When the invading Roman general invaded Judea, he went up to the altar of burnt offerings in the Jewish temple at Jerusalem and set up Zeus in God's holy temple, on Zeus's birthday—December 25. The Romans adopted the sun god Zeus from the Greeks. Zeus was the first Greek god and was the chief God as God of the sky. Since Zeus was the Greek god above all other gods, the Romans attributed the greatest power to Zeus and made him the father of the sun god.

When Semele, the mortal bride of Zeus, was found with child, Zeus, being immortal and the father of the unborn child, proclaimed that the child would be his son and would be a god. Semele, being Zeus's favored daughter, would produce the offspring as the sun god and be worshiped above all other gods.

We have noted that many Christians today believe that worship on Sunday was established in commemoration of Jesus' resurrection. We should also note that sun worship had been attached to Sunday at least before the time of the destruction of Pompeii in AD 79, for a calendar with a day devoted to the sun has been found in Pompeii's ruins. Moreover, sun worship goes back to the time of Nimrod and the building of the Tower of Babel—long before Jesus' resurrection. Sunday worship was pagan worship; worshipping the sun was really worshiping the devil and his power in the belief that the sun gives light and reproduction to all things on the earth. This belief was in almost all the nations throughout the whole earth.

Sacrificing to Devils

The devil does not care how much truth people teach so long as they include some error. God's admonition against false worship was clear: "And they shall no more offer their sacrifices unto devils, after whom they have gone a whoring. This shall be a statute for ever unto them throughout their generations" (Leviticus 17:7). If Israel had not been offering sacrifices to devils, God would not have warned Israel against it.

People, who were not from the tribes of Israel were Gentiles, which literally means "the nations." They were descendants of the people who would, under Rome, be called "pagans." The Gentiles were descendants of the people from Canaan, Babylon, Egypt, Greece, and every other place on earth. The apostle Paul was very familiar with the secular knowledge of that time and of the writings of the prophets in the Old Testament. He recognized that the devil was behind all of these sacrifices and that the people of Corinth, who had not accepted Christ, still worshiped in this way. This knowledge is reflected in his letter to the Corinthians: "But I say, that the things which the Gentiles sacrifice, they sacrifice to devils, and not to God: and I would not that ye should have fellowship with devils. Ye cannot drink the cup of the Lord, and the cup of devils: ye cannot be partakers of the Lord's table, and of the table of devils" (1 Corinthians 10:19, 20).

Until the time of Jesus' death and resurrection and the signaling of the Jewish nation's rejection of Jesus at the stoning of Stephen, Israel remained God's chosen people. David tells us how the Israelites adopted the ways of earth's descendants and the evils that were associated with the practices of those whom God had not yet called—the idol-worshipping Gentiles:

> But were mingled among the heathen, and learned their works. And they served their idols: which were a snare unto them. Yea, they sacrificed their sons and their daughters unto devils, and shed innocent blood, even the blood of their sons and of their daughters, whom they sacrificed unto the idols of Canaan: and the land was polluted with blood. (Psalms 106:35–38)

God spent centuries trying to get the children of Israel to love Him and abide by the laws that He gave through Moses. Yet, Israel wanted to follow the nations around them, and they turned to the worship of idols.

In our next chapter, we will see how God revealed to Israel His prophetic timeline of probationary time for turning from false gods to the One who had redeemed them.

Chapter 11

Earth's History Foretold in Dreams

History—the stories of human activities through time—can be very interesting if one can follow who is involved and what is going on. To make the outline of history simple enough that a child can understand it, we turn to the Bible as our guide. Did you know that the prophecies of Daniel outline earth's history in a very simple way? Since we are looking for time elements, we will skip the parts of Daniel that do not relate to specific times. For background, we will begin with chapter 1. The first verses describe how God allowed the king of Babylon, Nebuchadnezzar, to capture Jerusalem and take captives back to Babylon. By verse seventeen, Daniel and his three companions had excelled in their studies: "As for these four children, God gave them knowledge and skill in all learning and wisdom: and Daniel had understanding in all visions and dreams" (Daniel 1:17).

After the king gave them their "final exam," he found that God had blessed them with their simple diet, giving them understanding beyond their peers: "And in all matters of wisdom and understanding, that the king enquired of them, he found them ten times better than all the magicians and astrologers that were in all his realm" (Daniel 1:20). Exalted to positions of responsibility, a crisis would soon arise:

> **Did you know that the prophecies of Daniel outline earth's history in a very simple way?**

> And in the second year of the reign of Nebuchadnezzar Nebuchadnezzar dreamed dreams, wherewith his spirit was troubled, and his sleep brake from him. Then the king commanded to call the magicians, and the astrologers, and the sorcerers, and the Chaldeans, for to shew the king his dreams. So they came and stood before the king. And the king said unto them, I have dreamed a dream, and my spirit was troubled to know the dream. (Daniel 2:1–3)

The wise men that came in could not tell the king what he had dreamed, so he ordered all of them to be killed. When Daniel caught wind of the king's decree, he told Arioch, the king's captain, "Why is the decree so hasty from the king?" (Daniel 2:15). Arioch explained what had happened. "Then Daniel went in, and desired of the king that he would give him time …" (Daniel 2:16). It was granted, and Daniel went back to pray with his three companions, and God answered Daniel's prayers. "Then was the secret revealed unto Daniel in a night vision" (Daniel 2:19). Giving glory to the God in heaven for the dream and the interpretation, Daniel boldly went in before Nebuchadnezzar and told him that "there is a God in heaven that revealeth secrets, and maketh known to the king Nebuchadnezzar what shall be in the latter days. Thy dream, and the visions of thy head upon thy bed, are these. As for thee, O king, thy thoughts came into thy mind upon thy bed, what should come to pass hereafter: and he that revealeth secrets maketh known to thee what shall come to pass" (Daniel 2:28, 29).

Thus, he began to reveal the history of the earth's kingdoms as revealed through the king's dream. Three times Daniel mentioned that the dream was about the future.

> Thou, O king, sawest, and behold a great image. This great image, whose brightness was excellent, stood before thee; and the form thereof was terrible. This image's head was of fine gold, his breast and his arms of silver, his belly and his thighs of brass, His legs of iron, his feet part of iron and part of clay. Thou sawest till that a stone was cut out without hands, which smote the image upon his feet that were of iron and clay, and break them to pieces. Then was the iron, the clay, the brass, the silver, and the gold, broken to pieces together, and became like the chaff of the summer threshingfloors; and the wind carried them away, that no place was found for them: and the stone that smote the image became a great mountain, and filled the whole earth. (Daniel 2:31–35)

As Daniel was revealing what the dream was, Nebuchadnezzar listened with great intent as the dream was coming back to him. Daniel described a great image standing before him, (images were familiar to Nebuchadnezzar), "and the form thereof was terrible." Notice that Daniel went right into naming the parts. It had a head of gold, breast and arms of silver, belly and his thighs of brass, legs of iron, and feet part of iron and part of clay (Daniel 2:32, 33).

At this point, Daniel takes his first breath since beginning with the head of gold. "Thou sawest till that a stone was cut out without hands." Daniel knows that stonework was not anything new to the king; stonework was used for building throughout the city of Babylon but all of the building stones had to be cut out by hand.

Daniel continued: "… which smote the image upon his feet that were of iron and clay, and break them to pieces. Then was the iron, the clay, the brass, the silver, and the gold, broken to pieces together" (Daniel 2:34, 35).

What would a person think today if they had a dream like this one? Call it a nightmare, but if you could not remember it, it would haunt you forever. Think of the frame of mind King Nebuchadnezzar must have been in.

Daniel continued: "… and became like the chaff of the summer threshingfloors; and the wind carried them away, that no place was found for them" (Daniel 2:35). Daniel used figures of speech that were everyday occurrences to the people; a threshing floor was used every time the people threshed grain.

"… and the stone that smote the image became a great mountain, and filled the whole earth" (Daniel 2:35). King Nebuchadnezzar must have been sitting on the edge of his seat in anticipation of the interpretation. Daniel pronounced it thoughtfully:

> Thou, O king, art a king of kings: for the God of heaven hath given thee a kingdom, power, and strength, and glory. And wheresoever the children of men dwell, the beasts of the field and the fowls of the heaven hath he given into thine hand, and hath made thee ruler over them all. Thou art this head of gold. And after thee shall arise another kingdom inferior to thee, and another third kingdom of brass, which shall bear rule over all the earth. (Daniel 2:37–39)

It is interesting to note here that Daniel did not call attention to the material of the kingdom following Babylon, though he had identified it in verse 32 as silver. He simply pointed to its being inferior to Nebuchadnezzar's kingdom. Now, Daniel arrived at the fourth kingdom:

> And the fourth kingdom shall be strong as iron: forasmuch as iron breaketh in pieces and subdueth all things: and as iron that breaketh all these, shall it break in pieces and bruise. And whereas thou sawest the feet and toes, part of potters' clay, and part of iron, the kingdom shall be divided; but there shall be in it of the strength of the iron, forasmuch as thou sawest the iron mixed with miry clay. And as the toes of the feet were part of iron, and part of clay, so the kingdom shall be partly strong, and partly broken. And whereas thou sawest iron mixed with miry clay, they shall mingle themselves with the seed of men: but they shall not cleave one to another, even as iron is not mixed with clay. (Daniel 2:40–43)

Daniel explained that the fourth kingdom was going to be like iron and then went on to give the last of the interpretation:

> And in the days of these kings shall the God of heaven set up a kingdom, which shall never be destroyed: and the kingdom shall not be left to other people, but it shall break in pieces and consume all these kingdoms, and it shall stand for ever. Forasmuch as thou sawest that the stone was cut out of the mountain without hands, and that it brake in pieces the iron, the brass, the clay, the silver, and the gold: the great God hath made known to the king what shall come to pass hereafter: and the dream is certain, and the interpretation thereof sure. (Daniel 2:44, 45)

Four times Daniel gave the God of heaven all praise for revealing the dream and its interpretation to him; never did he take it for himself. We should do likewise. Give all honor, glory and praise to the God of heaven, our Creator God and to His Son and to the Holy Spirit, now and forever more, Amen.

Chapters 3 through 6 of Daniel do not deal with revelations about the future, so we will skip to Daniel 7. God gave this revelation to Daniel without also giving it to anyone else.

> Daniel spake and said, I saw in my vision by night, and, behold, the four winds of the heaven strove upon the great sea. And four great beasts came up from the sea, diverse one from another.... The first was like a lion, and had eagle's wings: I beheld till the wings thereof were plucked, and it was lifted up from the earth, and made to stand upon the feet as a man, and a man's heart was given to it. And behold another beast, a second, like to a bear, and it raised up itself on one side, and it had three ribs in the mouth of it between the teeth of it: and they said thus unto it, Arise, devour much flesh. After this I beheld, and lo another, like a leopard, which had upon the back of it four wings of a fowl; the beast had also four heads; and dominion was given to it. After this I saw in the night visions, and behold a fourth beast, dreadful and terrible, and strong exceedingly; and it had great iron teeth: it devoured and brake in pieces, and stamped the residue with the feet of it: and it was diverse from all the beasts that were before it; and it had ten horns. I considered the horns, and, behold, there came up among them another little horn, before whom there were three of the first horns plucked up by the roots: and, behold, in this horn were eyes like the eyes of man, and a mouth speaking great things. (Daniel 7:2, 4–8)

To identify the symbols used here we are going to need some help from various books in the Bible: "... the four winds of the heaven strove upon the great sea" (Daniel 7:2). What does the wind represent? Jesus said: "And he shall send his angels with a great sound of a trumpet, and they shall gather together his elect from the four winds, from one end of heaven to the other" (Matthew 24:31). "And then shall he send his angels, and shall gather together his elect from the four *winds*, from the uttermost part of the earth to the uttermost part of heaven" (Mark 13:27). John the Revelator wrote: "And after these things I saw four angels standing on the four corners of the earth, holding the four winds of the earth, that the wind should not blow on the earth, nor on the sea, nor on any tree" (Revelation 7:1). Jeremiah wrote: "And upon Elam will I bring the four winds from the four quarters of heaven, and will scatter them toward all those winds; and there shall be no nation whither the outcasts of Elam shall not come" (Jeremiah 49:36). These four verses and the wording in

> **Give all honor, glory and praise to the God of heaven, our Creator God and to His Son and to the Holy Spirit, now and forever more, Amen.**

Daniel all indicate that wind in prophecy represents war, strife or conflict.

In verse 2, the winds are coupled with waters. What do waters represent? Isaiah wrote: "Woe to the multitude of many people, which make a noise like the noise of the seas; and to the rushing of nations, that make a rushing like the rushing of mighty waters" (Isaiah 17:12). Luke wrote: "The sea and the waves roaring" (Luke 21:25). John wrote: "And he saith unto me, The waters which thou sawest, where the whore sitteth, are peoples, and multitudes, and nations, and tongues" (Revelation 17:15). Water represents people in large numbers. Daniel also indicates the four winds where the people are to come from is the north, south, east, and west. In simple language, Daniel presents a picture of strife and conflict upon people over the whole earth at different times in history.

Verse 3 says: "And four great beasts came up from the sea, diverse one from another." What do the beasts represent? "These great beasts, which are four, are four kings, which shall arise out of the earth" (Daniel 7:17). We now know that a beast in prophecy represents a king or a kingdom. It can also represent the head ruler of a group of people or a government who makes rules for people to obey.

We move on next to the individual beasts and their descriptions: "The first was like a lion, and had eagle's wings: I beheld till the wings thereof were plucked, and it was lifted up from the earth, and made to stand upon the feet as a man, and a man's heart was given to it" (Daniel 7:4).

Since a kingdom is represented by a beast, certainly a lion, "the king of beasts," would represent a superior kingdom with strength and power. The addition of eagle's wings would represent a kingdom that conquered with great speed.

As Daniel watched, "the wings were plucked off," which means that, after a time, this kingdom lost its ability to accomplish things with speed.

"And it was lifted up from the earth" (Daniel 7:4). If something is lifted up above the earth, it would be exalted to the heavens, signaling great majesty like a divine being of some kind.

It was "made to stand upon the feet as a man." Beasts move about on all four feet but this beast was made to stand up. God gave humans dominion over the beasts indicating a greater intelligence.

"A man's heart was given to it." In the Bible, the heart is where a man thinks (Proverbs 23:7). This beast could reason like a human, indicating what this beast was. It was a king or kingdom with great power with movements that were very fast until it lost its wings. It was above all other earthly powers, it ruled over the nations, and it could make choices like a human being. Who was this beast? It was Babylon as illustrated in the image of Daniel 2 as the head of gold.

"And behold another beast, a second, like to a bear, and it raised up itself on one side, and it had three ribs in the mouth of it between the teeth of it: and they said thus unto it, Arise, devour much flesh" (Daniel 7:5). This second beast or kingdom is described as being "like to a bear." People have pitted lion against bear and the lion won. Therefore, the bear is inferior to the lion. It is still a beast, representing a kingdom, but it is not as strong as the first beast or kingdom was. Nonetheless, it would overthrow the first kingdom.

"It raised up itself on one side." This would denote that one part of the kingdom was stronger than the other side and was perhaps the uniting of two separate kingdoms, one stronger than the other.

"It had three ribs in the mouth of it between the teeth of it." Have you ever tried to take a bone away from a dog that held it in its teeth? This kingdom has ultimate control over the three ribs, whatever they stand for.

"They said thus unto it, Arise, devour much flesh." Who could this beast represent? First of all, it was not as strong as the first beast. A lion is a fitting symbol for Babylon, and the symbol of the lion corresponded to the head of gold in the king's dream, which Daniel identified in the statement, "Thou art this head of gold" (Daniel 2:38). Daniel had told the king that the second kingdom was to be inferior to the first (Daniel 2:39), and we know that the kingdom that overthrew Babylon was Medo-Persia.

Daniel 5 tells of the downfall of Babylon. The king at this time was Belshazzar, who was actually the grandson of King Nebuchadnezzar. As the chapter opens, he was giving a great party for all the royal princes of Babylon. In celebration of Babylon's superiority, he called for the gold and silver vessels that were taken from the temple in Jerusalem so they could drink wine from them. As they raised these vessels in blasphemous revelry, a man's hand was seen writing on the plaster wall across from the king. It scared him so badly that his knees smote together. At once, he called for all the wise men of Babylon to come and interpret the writing for him. Yet, none of them could read what was written. The queen mother remembered Daniel's previous life.

> Then was Daniel brought in before the king. And the king spake and said unto Daniel, Art thou that Daniel, which art of the children of the captivity of Judah, whom the king my father brought out of Jewry? I have even heard of thee, that the spirit of the gods is in thee, and that light and understanding and excellent wisdom is found in thee. (Daniel 5:13, 14)

Daniel was prince over all of the wise men in Babylon, having received his position from King Nebuchadnezzar, the grandfather of Belshazzar. In Daniel 5:16 it says, "And I have heard of thee, that thou canst make interpretations, and dissolve doubts: now if thou canst read the writing, and make known to me the interpretation thereof, thou shalt be clothed with scarlet, and have a chain of gold about thy neck, and shalt be the third ruler in the kingdom." Daniel refused Belshazzar's offer. "Then Daniel answered and said before the king, Let thy gifts be to thyself, and give thy rewards to another; yet I will read the writing unto the king, and make known to him the interpretation" (Daniel 5:17).

Daniel 4 tells how King Nebuchadnezzar honored himself for all the power and glory that the God of heaven had given him and, as a result, had to go out and eat grass with the beasts of the field until he gave all the glory to the God of heaven. Daniel addressed the proud and foolish Belshazzar: "And thou his son, O Belshazzar, hast not humbled thine heart, though thou knewest all this; but hast lifted up thyself against the Lord of heaven: … and thou hast praised the gods of silver, and gold, of brass, iron, wood, and stone, which see not, nor hear, nor know, and the God in whose hand thy breath is, hast thou not glorified" (Daniel 5:22, 23). Daniel's first rebuke was to tell the king how he had given all the credit for the good life he enjoyed to false gods. He acted just like his grandfather had done at first—he was proud and arrogant—and now the God of heaven would tell him what his future would be by the message inscribed on the wall of his palace.

> And this is the writing that was written, MENE, MENE, TEKEL, UPHARSIN. This is the interpretation of the thing: MENE; God hath numbered thy kingdom, and finished it. TEKEL; Thou art weighed in the balances, and art found wanting. PERES; Thy kingdom is divided, and given to the Medes and Persians.… In that night was Belshazzar the king of the Chaldeans slain. And Darius the Median took the kingdom, being about threescore and two years old. (Daniel 5:25–28, 30, 31)

The Medo-Persian soldiers fought without regard for soldiers or civilians and with the ferocity of a bear, a fitting symbol of the Medes and Persians. The three ribs in the bear's mouth fitly represent three nations: Ethiopia, Lydia, and Egypt. These three nations were all conquered about the same time, and Darius ruled over them all from Babylon.

Moving on, Daniel said: "After this I beheld, and lo another, like a leopard, which had upon the back of it four wings of a fowl; the beast had also four heads; and dominion was given to it" (Daniel 7:6). In the vision, Daniel beheld a third beast like a leopard; it had four wings and four heads. We have seen how the first two beasts were the same as the gold and silver sections of the image and represented the same kingdoms—Babylon and Medo-Persia.

Is it not likely that the third beast represented Greece, corresponding to the brass in the third part of the image, which is inferior to silver? (In Daniel 8, a parallel symbol is specifically identified as "Grecia.") This third beast was like a leopard. The lion, as the "king of beasts" was a fitting symbol of Nebuchadnezzar, who was a king above kings (Daniel 2:37). The bear, which is a ferocious beast, was a very fitting symbol for the armies of Medo-Persia. A leopard is a very fleet-footed animal, representing a world power that conquered quickly. Having four wings would make it even faster. History tells us that Alexander the Great, leader of the Greek army, conquered the kingdoms of the earth with great speed. Another reason that the third beast would represent Grecia is that its four heads aptly symbolize Grecia's four divisions after Alexander's death. Generals have to have a good head to win battles and conquer quickly. When Alexander the Great died, his four generals divided the kingdom into four parts. All the details of the symbol fit the kingdom of Grecia.

Chapter 12

The Roman Empire Predicted

Describing the fourth beast, Daniel said: "After this I saw in the night visions, and behold a fourth beast, dreadful and terrible, and strong exceedingly; and it had great iron teeth: it devoured and brake in pieces, and stamped the residue with the feet of it: and it was diverse from all the beasts that were before it; and it had ten horns" (Daniel 7:7).

The description of the fourth beast includes greater detail than the descriptions of the previous beasts. This indicates the importance of the beast and the different nature of its kingdom, since it crushed out all opposition.

A beast that was "dreadful and terrible" would seem to be one that was too disgusting to look at or whose actions were painful to watch. The kingdom represented by the beast would commit terrible and inhuman atrocities. "Strong exceedingly" means that it was so strong that no one could stand against it. Following this beast, no other unified earthly kingdom comes, but rather a conglomerate of kingdoms represented by feet and toes of iron mixed with clay.

The fourth beast in Daniel 7 had great iron teeth, which it used to devour its prey and tear what remained into pieces. It used its powerful feet to crush whatever remained. It was "diverse" from the other beasts, meaning that it had a different character or a different way of thinking.

What kingdom followed the Grecian empire? It was Rome, under its pagan rulers—a kingdom that ruled with an iron hand.

> "... Behold a fourth beast, dreadful and terrible, and strong exceedingly; and it had great iron teeth: it devoured and brake in pieces..."

The fourth beast also had ten horns. In Daniel 2, the iron legs represented the pagan Roman Empire. Connected to these were the feet and toes of iron and clay. Presumably the image had ten toes, though Daniel does not mention this detail.

In Daniel 7, the fourth beast has ten horns. The number ten depicts the ten divisions of Rome. Rome was not overthrown by a fifth world power; it was overrun by barbarian Germanic tribes from the north. Daniel described what he saw next: "I considered the horns, and, behold, there came up among them another little horn, before whom there were three of the first horns plucked up by the roots: and, behold, in this horn were eyes like the eyes of man, and a mouth speaking great things" (Daniel 7:8).

Modern commentators are not in agreement regarding the specific identity of each of the ten horns, but they do agree that the toes of Daniel 2 and the horns of Daniel 7 represent the same thing, namely, ten separate kingdoms that overthrew the Roman Empire with help from certain Roman emperors.

A point of contention between expositors is whether all ten kingdoms needed to exist for the same length of time until the "stone cut out without hands" at the second coming of Jesus, crushing all ten at once. Yet, we must recognize that the power of the ten kingdoms of Daniel 2 and Daniel 7 is not equal. Daniel says that the toes were to be "partly strong and partly broken" (Daniel 2:42). Also, the vision of Daniel 7 portrays the "little horn" plucking up three of the horns before the second coming of Jesus. This is evidence that they do not have to all exist until the end; rather only what remained of the ten kingdoms need to exist until Jesus returns.

There is general agreement among interpreters of this prophecy that the ten barbaric tribes were the Ostrogoths, Visigoths, Franks, Vandals, Suevi, Burgundians, Heruli, Anglo-Saxons, Lombards, and the Alamanni. These ten nations were the most instrumental in breaking up the Roman Empire. Some interpreters name the Huns instead of the Alamanni.

History clearly establishes that the three horns plucked up were the Heruli (in AD 493), the Vandals (in AD 534), and the Ostrogoths (in AD 553). The seven other nations remained. The ten kingdoms are also indicated by symbols in Revelation 13: "And I stood upon the sand of the sea, and saw a beast rise up out of the sea, having seven heads and ten horns, and upon his horns ten crowns, and upon his heads the name of blasphemy" (Revelation 13:1).

The book of Daniel says that the "little horn" blasphemed the God of heaven, and Revelation says that the heads of the beast carried "the name of blasphemy." This may indicate that the kingdoms represented by the seven remaining horns would follow the "little horn," doing what they are told to do by that power.

> "And there appeared another wonder in heaven; and behold a great red dragon, having seven heads and ten horns, and seven crowns upon his heads."

The beasts of Daniel 7 are a lion, a bear, and a leopard; the beast that was in power in Revelation had the resemblance or characteristics of these three beasts. "And the beast which I saw was like unto a leopard, and his feet were as the feet of a bear, and his mouth as the mouth of a lion: and the dragon gave him his power, and his seat, and great authority" (Revelation 13:2). John, in Revelation, tells us who the power is behind the beasts: "the dragon gave him his power, and his seat, and great authority" (Revelation 13:2). John also revealed the identity of the dragon (Revelation 12:9) and what it would do:

And there appeared another wonder in heaven; and behold a great red dragon, having seven heads and ten horns, and seven crowns upon his heads. And his tail drew the third part of the stars of heaven, and did cast them to the earth … And there was war in heaven: Michael and his angels fought against the dragon; and the dragon fought and his angels, and prevailed not; neither was their place found any more in heaven. (Revelation 12:3–8)

What was the result of this heavenly battle? "And the great dragon was cast out, that old serpent, called the Devil, and Satan, which deceiveth the whole world: he was cast out into the earth, and his angels were cast out with him" (Revelation 12:7–9). From these verses, there should be no doubt who it was that gave the "beast" its power—it was Satan.

"And I saw one of his heads as it were wounded to death; and his deadly wound was healed: and all the world wondered after the beast" (Revelation 13:3). This verse contains a tell-tale identifying mark for the fourth beast. It had to be a kingdom or power that had its earthly dominion taken away and later restored. When we identify who it was that removed the three nations by AD 553, we will know who is represented by the little horn. So, what power came up among the ten Germanic tribes? As pagan Rome was fading, a religious power was rising.

It was the Catholic emperors of the Roman Empire who formed papal Rome. Church historian Mervyn Maxwell wrote: "The Catholic Emperor Zeno in AD 474–491 arranged a treaty with the Ostrogoths in AD 487 which resulted in the eradication of the kingdom of the Arian Heruls in AD 493. The Catholic Emperor Justinian (AD 527–565) exterminated the Arian Vandals in AD 534 and significantly broke the power of the Arian Ostrogoths by AD 538" (*God Cares*, vol. 1, p. 129). Christianity had not always held such a privileged place. "The Pagan Roman Empire began fierce persecution of the Christians in AD 250. The Emperor Decius enforced edicts which commanded all citizens to sacrifice to the traditional Roman gods, , those who did not obey were executed" ("Nero Caesar," LUSENET, The Greenspun Family Server, http://1ref.us/4a).

A reminder here of the traditional Roman gods takes us back to what we studied about sun worship through the centuries and in different nations, beginning with Tamu the sun god in the time of Nimrod and the Tower of Babel. This is where Sunday worship had its beginning.

There was a turnaround in the persecution of Christians with Emperor Constantine. "Yet it was only shortly before his death that Constantine received baptism. The story of his baptism at Rome by Pope Sylvester in 326" (Kreis, "Constantine the Great, c. 274–337," The History Guide, http://1ref.us/4d). Emperor Theodosius made Christianity the sole religion of the remaining Roman Empire.

"For many centuries the Emperors were not only the highest military leader, supreme judge, but also the protector of the church and orthodoxy. Justinian reached the height of imperial influence in religious matters" ("Nero Caesar," LUSENET, The Greenspun Family Server, http://1ref.us/4a). In all matters of belief and rituals his was the final decision. "Nothing now stood in the way of the pope exercising the power conferred upon him by Justinian five years previous" (Emahiser, "Daniel Prophesied the Roman Catholic Church," Israelite Watchmen, http://1ref.us/4b).

The Roman Catholic Church claims that the apostle Peter was the first bishop or pope of Rome and supports this claim by Matthew 16:18. Yet, a broader study of Scripture and Catholic history does not support this contention. Consider the following from www.gotquestions.org:

Question: "What is the origin of the Catholic Church?"

Answer: The Roman Catholic Church contends that its origin is the death, resurrection, and ascension of Jesus Christ in approximately A.D. 30. The Catholic Church proclaims itself to be the church that Jesus Christ died for, the church that was established and built by the apostles. Is that the true origin of the Catholic Church? [No.] On the contrary. Even a cursory reading of the New Testament will reveal that the Catholic Church does not have its origin in the teachings of Jesus or His apostles. In the New Testament, there is no mention of the papacy, worship/adoration of Mary (or the immaculate conception of Mary, the perpetual virginity of Mary, the assumption of Mary, or Mary as co-redemptrix and mediatrix), petitioning saints in heaven for their prayers, apostolic succession, the ordinances of the church functioning as sacraments, infant baptism, confession of sin to a priest, purgatory, indulgences, or the equal authority of church tradition and Scripture. So, if the origin of the Catholic Church is not in the teachings of Jesus and His apostles, as recorded in the New Testament, what is the true origin of the Catholic Church?

For the first 280 years of Christian history, Christianity was banned by the Roman Empire, and Christians were terribly persecuted. This changed after the so called "conversion" of the Roman Emperor Constantine. Constantine "legalized" Christianity with the Edict of Milan in A.D. 313. Later, in A.D. 325, Constantine called the Council of Nicea in an attempt to unify Christianity. Constantine envisioned Christianity as a religion that could unite the Roman Empire, which at that time was beginning to fragment and divide. While this may have seemed to be a positive development for the Christian church, the results were anything but positive. Just as Constantine refused to fully embrace the Christian faith, but continued many of his pagan beliefs and practices, so the Christian church that Constantine promoted was a mixture of true Christianity and Roman paganism.

Constantine found that with the Roman Empire being so vast, expansive, and diverse, not everyone would agree to forsake his or her religious beliefs to embrace Christianity. So, Constantine allowed, and even promoted, the "Christianization" of pagan beliefs. Completely pagan and utterly unbiblical beliefs were given new "Christian" identities. Some clear examples of this are as follows:

(1) The Cult of Isis, an Egyptian mother-goddess religion, was absorbed into Christianity by replacing Isis with Jesus' mother Mary. Many of the titles that were used for Isis, such as "Queen of Heaven," "Mother of God," and *theotokos* ("God-bearer") were attached to Mary. Mary was given an exalted role in the Christian faith, far beyond what the Bible ascribes to her, in order to attract Isis worshippers to a faith they would not otherwise embrace. Many temples to Isis were, in fact, converted into temples dedicated to Mary. The first clear hints of Catholic Mariology occur in the writings of Origen, who lived in Alexandria, Egypt, which happened to be the focal point of Isis worship.

(2) Mithraism was a religion in the Roman Empire in the 1st through 5th centuries A.D. It was very popular among the Romans, especially among Roman soldiers, and was possibly the religion of several Roman emperors. While Mithraism was never given "official" status in the Roman Empire, it was the de facto official religion until Constantine and succeeding Roman emperors replaced Mithraism with Christianity. One of the key features of Mithraism was a sacrificial meal, which involved eating the flesh and drinking the blood of a bull. Mithras, the god of Mithraism, was "present" in the flesh and blood of the bull, and when consumed, granted salvation to those who partook of the sacrificial meal (this is known as theophagy, the eating of one's god). Mithraism also had seven "sacraments," making the similarities between Mithraism and Roman Catholicism too many to ignore. Constantine and his successors found an easy substitute for the sacrificial meal of Mithraism in the concept of the Lord's Supper/Christian communion. Sadly, some early Christians had already begun to attach mysticism to the Lord's Supper, rejecting the biblical concept of a simple and worshipful remembrance of Christ's death and shed blood. The Romanization of the Lord's Supper made the transition to a sacrificial consumption of Jesus Christ, now known as the Catholic Mass/Eucharist, complete.

(3) Most Roman emperors (and citizens) were henotheists. A henotheist is one who believes in the existence of many gods, but focuses primarily on one particular god or considers one particular god supreme over the other gods. For example, the Roman god Jupiter was supreme over the Roman pantheon of gods. Roman sailors were often worshippers of Neptune, the god of the oceans. When the Catholic Church absorbed Roman paganism, it simply replaced the pantheon of gods with the saints. Just as the Roman pantheon of gods had a god of love, a god of peace, a god of war, a god of strength, a god of wisdom, etc., so the Catholic Church has a saint who is "in charge" over each of these, and many other categories. Just as many Roman cities had a god specific to the city, so the Catholic Church provided "patron saints" for the cities.

(4) The supremacy of the Roman bishop (the papacy) was created with the support of the Roman emperors. With the city of Rome being the center of government for the Roman Empire, and with the Roman emperors living in Rome, the city of Rome rose to prominence in all facets of life. Constantine and his successors gave their support to the bishop of Rome as the supreme ruler of the church. Of course, it is best for the unity of the Roman Empire that the government and state religion be centered in the same location. While most other bishops (and Christians) resisted the idea of the Roman bishop being supreme, the Roman bishop eventually rose to supremacy, due to the power and influence of the Roman emperors. When the Roman Empire collapsed, the popes took on the title that had previously belonged to the Roman emperors—*Pontifex Maximus*.

Many more examples could be given. These four should suffice in demonstrating the true origin of the Catholic Church. Of course the Roman Catholic Church denies the pagan origin of its beliefs and practices. The Catholic Church disguises its pagan beliefs under layers of complicated theology. The Catholic Church excuses and denies its pagan origin beneath the mask of "church tradition." Recognizing that many of its beliefs and practices are utterly foreign to Scripture, the Catholic Church is forced to deny the authority and sufficiency of Scripture.

The origin of the Catholic Church is the tragic compromise of Christianity with the pagan religions that surrounded it. Instead of proclaiming the gospel and converting the pagans, the Catholic Church "Christianized" the pagan religions, and "paganized" Christianity. By blurring the differences and erasing the distinctions, yes, the Catholic Church made itself attractive to the people of the Roman Empire. One result was the Catholic Church becoming the supreme religion in the "Roman world" for centuries. However, another result was the most dominant form of Christianity apostatizing from the true gospel of Jesus Christ and the true proclamation of God's Word. (Houdmann, "What is the origin of the Catholic Church?" http://1ref.us/4c)

This subject will be fully covered in our next chapter. Please note that the Roman Catholic Church will be designated by the term "the Church" (Christian or Christians) unless otherwise stated.

Chapter 13

A New Phase for Rome

Citing Susan Tyler Hitchcock's *Geography of Religion* and Edward Norman's *The Roman Catholic Church, an Illustrated History*, Wikipedia summarizes the Catholic view of the founding of the Roman Catholic Church (clarifications have been added in brackets):

Origins

Catholic doctrine teaches that the Catholic Church was founded by Jesus Christ. It interprets the Confession of Peter as acknowledging Christ's designation of Apostle Peter and his successors to be the temporal head of his Church. Thus, it asserts that the Bishop of Rome has the sole legitimate claim to Petrine authority and the primacy due to the Roman Pontiff. The Catholic Church claims legitimacy for its bishops and priests via the doctrine of apostolic succession and authority of the Pope via the unbroken line of popes, claimed as successors to Simon Peter.

In [AD] 313, the struggles of the Early Church were lessened by the legalisation of Christianity by the Emperor Constantine I. In [AD] 380, under Emperor Theodosius I, Christianity became the state religion of the Roman Empire by the decree of the Emperor, which would persist until the fall of the Western Empire, and later, with the Eastern Roman Empire, until the Fall of Constantinople. During this time (the period of the Seven Ecumenical Councils) there were considered five primary sees according to Eusebius: Rome, Constantinople, Antioch, Jerusalem and Alexandria, known as the Pentarchy.

After the destruction of the western Roman Empire, the church in the West was a major factor in the preservation of classical civilization, establishing monasteries, and sending missionaries to convert the peoples of northern Europe, as far as Ireland in the north. In the East, the Byzantine Empire preserved Orthodoxy, well after the massive invasions of Islam in the mid–7th century. The invasions of Islam devastated three of the five Patriarchal sees, capturing Jerusalem first, then Alexandria, and then finally in the mid-8th century, Antioch.

The whole period of the next five centuries was dominated by the struggle between Christianity and Islam throughout the Mediterranean Basin. The battles of Poitiers, and Toulouse preserved the Catholic west, even though Rome itself was ravaged in [AD] 850 and Constantinople was besieged. In the 11th century, already strained relations between the primarily Greek church in the East, and the Latin church in the West, developed into the East-West Schism, [mostly] due to conflicts over Papal Authority. The fourth crusade, and the sacking of Constantinople by renegade crusaders proved the final breach.

> "The whole period of the next five centuries was dominated by the struggle between Christianity and Islam throughout the Mediterranean Basin."

In the 16th century, in response to the Protestant Reformation, the Church engaged in a process of substantial reform and renewal known as the Counter-Reformation. In subsequent centuries, Catholicism spread widely across the world despite experiencing a reduction in its hold on European populations due to the growth of Protestantism and also because of religious scepticism during and after the Enlightenment. The Second Vatican Council in the 1960s introduced the most significant changes to Catholic practices since the Council of Trent three centuries before.

Origins

Catholic tradition holds that the Catholic Church was founded by Jesus Christ. The New Testament records Jesus' activities and teaching, his appointment of the twelve Apostles, and his instructions to them to continue his work.... Peter is also thought to be Rome's first bishop and the consecrator of Linus as its next bishop, thus starting the line which includes the most current pontiff, Pope Francis. Conditions in the Roman Empire facilitated the spread of new ideas. The empire's well-defined network of roads and waterways allowed easier travel, while the Pax Romana made it safe to travel from one region to another. The government had encouraged inhabitants, especially those in urban areas, to learn Greek, and the common language allowed ideas to be more easily expressed and understood. Jesus's apostles gained converts in Jewish communities around the Mediterranean Sea, and over 40 [Apostolic] Christian communities had been established by [AD] 100. Although most of these were in the Roman Empire, notable [Apostolic] Christian communities were also established in Armenia, Iran and along the Indian Malabar Coast. The new religion was most successful in urban areas, spreading first among slaves and people of low social standing, and then among aristocratic women [and worshiped on the seventh day of the week,

Sabbath as did the apostles].

At first, [Apostolic] Christians continued to worship alongside Jewish believers, which historians refer to as Jewish Christianity, but within twenty years of Jesus's death, Sunday was being regarded as the primary day of worship [among many people]. As preachers such as Paul of Tarsus began converting Gentiles, [Apostolic] Christianity began growing away from Jewish practices to establish itself as a separate religion, though the issue of Paul of Tarsus and Judaism is still debated today. To resolve doctrinal differences among the competing factions within the [Apostolic] Church, in or around the year [AD] 50, the apostles convened the first Church council, the Council of Jerusalem. This council affirmed that Gentiles could become [Apostolic] Christians without adopting all of the Mosaic Law. Growing tensions soon led to a starker separation that was virtually complete by the time [Apostolic] Christians refused to join in the Bar Khokba Jewish revolt of [AD] 132, however some groups of [Apostolic] Christians retained elements of Jewish practice. [This included Sabbath observance; Sunday observance will be addressed later.]

The early Christian Church was very loosely organized, resulting in diverse interpretations of Christian beliefs. In part to ensure a greater consistency in their teachings, by the end of the 2nd century Christian communities had evolved a more structured hierarchy, with a central bishop having authority over the clergy in his city, leading to the development of the Metropolitan bishop. The organization of the Church began to mimic that of the Empire; bishops in politically important cities exerted greater authority over bishops in nearby cities. The churches in Antioch, Alexandria, and Rome held the highest positions. Beginning in the 2nd century, bishops often congregated in regional synods to resolve doctrinal and policy issues. Duffy claims that by the 3rd century, the bishop of Rome began to act as a court of appeals for problems that other bishops could not resolve.

Doctrine was further refined by a series of influential theologians and teachers, known collectively as the Church Fathers. From the year [AD] 100 onward, proto-orthodox teachers like Ignatius of Antioch and Irenaeus defined Catholic teaching in stark opposition to other things, such as Gnosticism. In the first few centuries of its existence, the Church formed its teachings and traditions into a systematic whole under the influence of theological apologists such as Pope Clement I, Justin Martyr and Augustine of Hippo.

Persecutions

Unlike most religions in the Roman Empire, [Apostolic] Christianity required its adherents to renounce all other gods, a practice adopted from Judaism, see Idolatry.

[Apostolic] Christians' refusal to join pagan celebrations meant they were unable to participate in much of public life, which caused non-Christians-including government authorities-to fear that the [Apostolic] Christians were angering the gods and thereby threatening the peace and prosperity of the Empire. In addition, the peculiar intimacy of [Apostolic] Christian society and its secrecy about its religious practices spawned rumors that [Apostolic] Christians were guilty of incest and cannibalism; the resulting persecutions, although usually local and sporadic, were a defining feature of [Apostolic] Christian self-understanding until [Catholic] Christianity was legalized in the 4th century. A series of more centrally organized persecutions of [Apostolic] Christians emerged in the late 3rd century, when emperors decreed that the Empire's military, political, and economic crises were caused by angry gods. All residents were ordered to give sacrifices or be punished. Jews were exempted as long as they paid the Jewish Tax. Estimates of the number of [Apostolic] Christians who were executed ranges from a few hundred to 50,000. Many fled or renounced their beliefs. Disagreements over what role, if any, these apostates should have in the Church led to the Donatist and Novatianist schisms. Relations between the Church and the Empire were not consistent: "Tiberius wanted to have Christ placed in the Pantheon and refused first of all to persecute the [Apostolic] Christians. Later on his attitude changed. How are we to explain the fact that men like Trajan and above all Marcus Aurelius should have so relentlessly persecuted the [Apostolic] Christians? On the other hand Commodus and other villainous emperors rather favoured them." In spite of these persecutions, evangelization efforts persisted, leading to the Edict of Milan which legalized Christianity in [AD] 313. By [AD] 380, Christianity had become the state religion of the Roman Empire. Religious philosopher Simone Weil wrote: "By the time of Constantine, the state of apocalyptic expectation must have worn rather thin. [The imminent coming of Christ, expectation of the Last Day—constituted 'a very great social danger.'] Besides, the spirit of the old law, so widely separated from all mysticism, was not so very different from the Roman spirit itself. Rome could come to terms with the God of Hosts." [*Gateway to God*, pp. 144, 145; bracketed material from Wikipedia]

Late antiquity

When Constantine became emperor of the Western Roman Empire in [AD] 312, he attributed his victory to the Christian God. Many soldiers in his army were Christians, and his army was his base of power. With Licinius, (Eastern Roman emperor), he issued the Edict of Milan which mandated toleration of all religions in the empire. The edict had little effect on the attitudes of the people. New laws were crafted to codify some Christian beliefs and practices. Constantine's biggest effect on Christianity was his patronage. He gave large gifts of land and money to the Church and offered tax exemptions and other special legal status to Church property and personnel. These gifts and later ones combined to make the Church the largest landowner in the West by the 6th century. Many of these gifts were funded through severe taxation of pagan cults. Some pagan cults were forced to disband for lack of funds; when this happened the Church took over the cult's previous role of caring for the poor. In a reflection of their increased standing in the Empire, clergy began to adopt the dress of the royal household, including the cope [this is still prominent in today's Catholic churches]. Acts 8:9–21

During Constantine's reign, approximately half of those who identified themselves as Christian did not subscribe to the mainstream version of the faith. Constantine feared that disunity would displease God and lead to trouble for the Empire, so he took military and judicial measures to eliminate some sects. To resolve other disputes, Constantine began the practice of calling ecumenical councils to determine binding interpretations of Church doctrine.

Decisions made at the Council of Nicea ([AD] 325) about the divinity of Christ led to a schism; the new religion, Arianism flourished outside the Roman Empire. Partially to distinguish themselves from Arians, Catholic devotion to Mary became more prominent. This led to further schisms.

In [AD] 380, mainstream Catholicism—as opposed to Arianism–became the official religion of the Roman Empire. Christianity became more associated with the Empire, resulting in persecution for [non-Catholic] Christians living outside of the empire, as their rulers feared [these] Christians would revolt in favor of the Emperor. In [AD] 385, this new legal authority of the Church resulted in the first use of capital punishment being pronounced as a sentence upon a [non-Catholic] Christian 'heretic', namely Priscillian.

> **"Prior to these Councils or Synods, the Bible had already reached a form that was nearly identical to the form in which it is now found."**

During this period, the Bible as it has come down to the 21st century was first officially laid out in Church Councils or Synods through the process of official 'canonization'. Prior to these Councils or Synods, the Bible had already reached a form that was nearly identical to the form in which it is now found. According to some accounts, in [AD] 382 the Council of Rome first officially recognized the Biblical canon, listing the accepted books of the *Old* and *New Testament*, and in [AD] 391 the Vulgate Latin translation of the Bible was made…. The Council of Ephesus in [AD] 431 clarified the nature of Jesus' incarnation, declaring that he was both fully man and fully God.

Two decades later, the Council of Chalcedon solidified Roman papal primacy which added to continuing breakdown in relations between Rome and Constantinople, the see of the Eastern Church. Also sparked were the Monophysite disagreements over the precise nature of the incarnation of Jesus which led to the first of the various Oriental Orthodox Churches breaking away from the Catholic Church.

Early Middle Ages

After the fall of the Western Roman Empire in [AD] 476, the Catholic faith competed with Arianism for the conversion of the barbarian tribes. The [AD] 496 conversion of Clovis I, pagan king of the Franks, saw the beginning of a steady rise of the faith in the West.

In [AD] 530, Saint Benedict wrote his *Rule of St Benedict* as a practical guide for monastic community life. Its message spread to monasteries throughout Europe. Monasteries became major conduits of civilization, preserving craft and artistic skills while maintaining intellectual culture within their schools, scriptoria and libraries. They functioned as agricultural, economic and production centers as well as a focus for spiritual life. During this period the Visigoths and Lombards moved away from Arianism for Catholicism. Pope Gregory the Great played a notable role in these conversions and dramatically reformed the ecclesiastical structures and administration which then launched renewed missionary efforts. Missionaries such as Augustine of Canterbury, who was sent from Rome to begin the conversion of the Anglo-Saxons, and, coming the other way in the Hiberno-Scottish mission, Saints Colombanus, Boniface, Willibrord, Ansgar and many others took Christianity into northern Europe and spread Catholicism among the Germanic, and Slavic peoples, and reached the Vikings and other Scandinavians in later centuries. The Synod of Whitby of [AD] 664, though not as decisive as sometimes claimed, was an important moment in the reintegration of the Celtic Church of the British Isles into the Roman hierarchy, after having been effectively cut off from contact with Rome by the pagan invaders.

In the early 8th century, Byzantine iconoclasm became a major source of conflict between the Eastern and Western parts of the Church. Byzantine emperors forbade the creation and veneration of religious images, as violations of the Ten Commandments. Other major religions in the East such as Judaism and Islam had similar prohibitions. Pope Gregory III vehemently disagreed. A new Empress Irene siding with the pope, called for an Ecumenical Council. In AD 787, the fathers of the Second Council of Nicaea "warmly received the papal delegates and his message". At the conclusion, 300 bishops, who were led by the representatives of Pope Hadrian I adopted the "Pope's teaching", in favor of icons.

With the coronation of Charlemagne by Pope Leo III in AD 800, his new title as

Patricius Romanorum, and the handing over of the keys to the Tomb of Saint Peter, the papacy had acquired a new protector in the West. This freed the pontiffs to some degree from the power of the emperor in Constantinople but also led to a schism, because the emperors and patriarchs of Constantinople interpreted themselves as the true descendants of the Roman Empire dating back to the beginnings of the Church. Pope Nicholas I had refused to recognize Patriarch Photios I of Constantinople, who in turn had attacked the pope as a heretic, because he kept the filioque in the creed, which referred to the Holy Spirit emanating from God the Father and the Son. The papacy was strengthened through this new alliance, which in the long term created a new problem for the Popes, when in the Investiture Controversy succeeding emperors sought to appoint bishops and even future popes. After the disintegration of the Charlemagne empire and repeated incursions of Islamic forces into Italy, the papacy, without any protection, entered a phase of major weakness....

Renaissance Church

In Europe, the Renaissance marked a period of renewed interest in ancient and classical learning. It also brought a re-examination of accepted beliefs. Cathedrals and churches had long served as picture books and art galleries for millions of the uneducated. The stained glass windows, frescoes, statues, paintings and panels retold the stories of the saints and of biblical characters. The Church sponsored great Renaissance artists like Michelangelo and Leonardo da Vinci, who created some of the world's most famous artworks. The acceptance of humanism had its effects on the Church, which embraced it as well. In AD 1509, a well known scholar of the age, Erasmus, wrote *The Praise of Folly,* a work which captured a widely held unease about corruption in the Church. The Papacy itself was questioned by conciliarism expressed in the councils of Constance and the Basel. Real reforms during these ecumenical councils and the Fifth Lateran Council were attempted several times but thwarted. They were seen as necessary but did not succeed in large measure because of internal feuds within the Church, ongoing conflicts with the Ottoman Empire and Saracenes and the simony and nepotism practiced in the Renaissance Church of the 15th and early 16th centuries. As a result, rich, powerful and worldly men like Roderigo Borgia (Pope Alexander VI) were able to win election to the papacy.

Reformation Era wars

The Fifth Lateran Council issued some but only minor reforms in March 1517. A few months later, on October 31, 1517, Martin Luther posted his Ninety-Five Theses in public, hoping to spark debate. His theses protested key points of Catholic doctrine as well as the sale of indulgences. Huldrych Zwingli, John Calvin, and others also criticized Catholic teachings. These challenges, supported by powerful political forces in the region, developed into the Protestant Reformation. In Germany, the Reformation led to war between the Protestant Schmalkaldic League and the Catholic Emperor Charles V. The first nine-year war ended in [AD] 1555 but continued tensions produced a far graver conflict, the Thirty Years' War, which broke out in [AD] 1618. In France, a series of conflicts termed the French Wars of Religion was fought from [AD] 1562 to 1598 between the Huguenots and the forces of the French Catholic League. A series of popes sided with and became financial supporters of the Catholic League. This ended under Pope Clement VIII, who hesitantly accepted King Henry IV's 1598 Edict of Nantes, which granted civil and religious toleration to Protestants.

England

The English Reformation was ostensibly based on Henry VIII's desire for annulment of his marriage with Catherine of Aragon, and was initially more of a political, and later a theological dispute. The Acts of Supremacy made the English monarch head of the English church thereby establishing the Church of England. Then, beginning in [AD] 1536, some 825 monasteries throughout England, Wales and Ireland were dissolved and Catholic churches were confiscated. When he died in [AD] 1547, all monasteries, friaries, convents of nuns and shrines were destroyed or dissolved. Mary I of England reunited the Church of England with Rome and, against the advice of the Spanish ambassador, persecuted Protestants during the Marian Persecutions. After some provocation, the following monarch, Elizabeth I enforced the Act of Supremacy. This prevented Catholics from becoming members of professions, holding public office, voting or educating their children. Executions of Catholics under Elizabeth I, who reigned much longer, then surpassed the Marian persecutions and persisted under subsequent English monarchs. Penal laws were also enacted in Ireland but were less effective than in England. In part because the Irish people associated Catholicism with nationhood and national identity, they resisted persistent English efforts to eliminate the Catholic Church.

Council of Trent

... Spiritual renewal and reform were inspired by many new saints like Teresa of Avila, Francis de Sales and Philip Neri whose writings spawned distinct schools of spirituality within the Church (Oratorians, Carmelites, Salesian), etc. Improvement to the education of the laity was another positive effect of the era, with a proliferation of secondary schools reinvigorating higher studies such as history, philosophy and theology. To popularize Counter-Reformation teachings, the Church encouraged the Baroque style in art, music and architecture. Baroque religious expression was stirring and emotional, created to stimulate religious fervor.

Elsewhere, Jesuit missionary Francis Xavier introduced Christianity to Japan, and by the end of the 16th century tens of thousands of Japanese followed Roman Catholicism. Church growth came to a halt in [AD] 1597 under the Shogun Toyotomi Hideyoshi who, in an effort to isolate the country from foreign influences, launched a severe persecution of Christians. Japanese were forbidden to leave the country and Europeans were forbidden to enter. Despite this, a minority Christian population survived into the 19th century. [So far in this chapter, the terms "Christian," Christianity, and "the Church" refer to the Roman Catholic Church.]

Marian Devotions

The Council of Trent generated a revival of religious life and Marian devotions in the Roman Catholic Church. During the Reformation, the Church had defended its Marian beliefs against Protestant views. At the same time, the Catholic world was engaged in ongoing Ottoman Wars in Europe against Turkey which were fought and won under the auspices of the Virgin Mary. The victory at [the] Battle of Lepanto ([AD] 1571) was accredited to her "and signified the beginning of a strong resurgence of Marian devotions, focusing especially on Mary, the Queen of Heaven and Earth and her powerful role as mediatrix of many graces". The Colloquium Marianum, an elite group, and the Sodality of Our Lady based their activities on a virtuous life, free of cardinal sins.

Pope Paul V and Gregory XV ruled in [AD] 1617 and 1622 to be inadmissible to state, that the virgin was conceived non-immaculate.... Alexander VII declared in [AD] 1661, that the soul of Mary was free from original sin. Pope Clement XI ordered the feast of the Immaculata for the whole Church in [AD] 1708. The feast of the Rosary was introduced in [AD] 1716, the feast of the Seven Sorrows in [AD] 1727. The Angelus prayer was strongly supported by Pope Benedict XIII in [AD] 1724 and by Pope Benedict XIV in [AD] 1742. Popular Marian piety was even more colourful and varied than ever before: Numerous Marian pilgrimages, Marian Salve devotions, new Marian litanies, Marian theatre plays, Marian hymns, Marian processions. Marian fraternities, today mostly defunct, had millions of members.

Enlightenment Secularism

The Enlightenment constituted a new challenge of the Church. Unlike the Protestant Reformation, which questioned certain Christian doctrines, the enlightenment questioned Christianity as a whole. Generally, it elevated human reason above divine revelation and down-graded religious authorities such as the papacy based on it. Parallel the Church attempted to fend off Gallicanism and Conciliarism, ideologies which threatened the papacy and structure of the Church.

Toward the latter part of the 17th century, Blessed Pope Innocent XI viewed the increasing Turkish attacks against Europe, which were supported by France, as the major threat for the Church. He built a Polish-Austrian coalition for the Turkish defeat at Vienna in [AD] 1683. Scholars have called him a saintly pope because he reformed abuses by the Church, including simony, nepotism and the lavish papal expenditures that had caused him to inherit a papal debt of 50,000,000 scudi. By eliminating certain honorary posts and introducing new fiscal policies, Innocent XI was able to regain control of the church's finances. In France, the Church battled Jansenism and Gallicanism, which supported Conciliarism, and rejected papal primacy, demanding special concessions for the Church in France. This weakened the Church's ability to respond to gallicanist thinkers such as Denis Diderot, who challenged fundamental doctrines of the Church.

In [AD] 1685 gallicanist King Louis XIV of France issued the Revocation of the Edict of Nantes, ending a century of religious toleration. France forced Catholic theologians to support conciliarism and deny Papal infallibility. The king threatened Pope Innocent XI with a general council and a military take-over of the Papal state. The absolute French State used Gallicanism to gain control of virtually all major Church appointments as well as many of the Church's properties. State authority over the Church became popular in other countries as well. In Belgium and Germany, Gallicanism appeared in the form of Febronianism, which rejected papal prerogatives in an equal fashion. Emperor Joseph II of Austria ([AD] 1780–1790) practiced Josephinism by regulating Church life, appointments, and massive confiscation of Church properties. ("History of the Catholic Church," Wikipedia, http://1ref.us/4e)

The years from AD 1800 forward have seen many changes in the way the Catholic Church has evolved. Many differences between individual beliefs have been eliminated to bring the customs and beliefs of most Catholics into line.

Throughout its history, the Catholic Church has undergone many changes in belief and practice through exposure to outside influences and the influence of the leadership of the Church itself. Yet, differences of opinion still exist among individual Catholics and the different orders and societies that have formed within the church. Differences of opinion are what make up the different ideals of people today. Each one of us form our beliefs and individual practices on what we read, see, and hear and that is what makes each one of us unique.

We will now trace the development of the Protestant Reformation.

Chapter 14

The Protestant Reformation

The following is taken from Wikipedia on the "History of Protestantism":

The Protestant Reformation of the early 16th century was an attempt to reform the Catholic Church. German theologian Martin Luther wrote his Ninety-Five Theses on the sale of indulgences in [AD] 1517. Parallel to events in Germany, a movement began in Switzerland under the leadership of Ulrich Zwingli. The political separation of the Church of England from Rome under Henry VIII, beginning in [AD] 1529 and completed in [AD] 1536, brought England alongside this broad Reformed movement. The Scottish Reformation of [AD] 1560 decisively shaped the Church of Scotland and, through it, all other Presbyterian churches worldwide.

Following the excommunication of Luther and condemnation of the Reformation by the Pope, the work and writings of John Calvin were influential in establishing a loose consensus among various groups in Switzerland, Scotland, Hungary, Germany and elsewhere. In the course of this religious upheaval, the German Peasants' War of [AD] 1524–1525 swept through the Bavarian, Thuringian and Swabian principalities. The confessional division of the states of the Holy Roman Empire eventually erupted in the Thirty Years' War of [AD] 1618–1648. This left Germany weakened and fragmented for more than two centuries, until the unification of Germany under the German Empire of [AD] 1871.

The success of the Counter-Reformation on the Continent and the growth of a Puritan party dedicated to further Protestant reform polarized the Elizabethan Age,

> "The Protestant Reformation of the early 16th century was an attempt to reform the Catholic Church."

although it was not until the Civil War of the [AD] 1640s. that England underwent religious strife comparable to what her neighbors had suffered for many years.

The "Great Awakenings" were periods of rapid and dramatic religious revival in Anglo-American religious history, generally recognized as beginning in the [AD] 1730s. They have also been described as periodic revolutions in colonial religious thought.

In the 20th century, Protestantism, especially in the United States, was characterized by accelerating fragmentation. The century saw the rise of both liberal and conservative splinter groups, as well as a general secularization of Western society. Notable developments in the 20th century of US Protestantism was the rise of Pentecostalism, Christian fundamentalism and Evangelicalism. While these movements have spilled over to Europe to a limited degree, the development of Protestantism in Europe was more dominated by secularization, leading to an increasingly "post-Christian Europe."

History and Origins

Protestants generally trace their beginning to the 16th century with their separation from the Catholic Church. Mainstream Protestantism began with the *Magisterial Reformation*, so called because the movement received support from the magistrates (that is, the civil authorities) as opposed to the *Radical Reformation*, which had no state sponsorship. Older Protestant churches, such as the Unitas Fratrum (Unity of the Brethren), Moravian Brethren or the Bohemian Brethren trace their origin to the time of Jan Hus in the early 15th century. As the Hussite movement was led by a majority of Bohemian nobles and recognized for a time by the Basel Compacts, this is considered by some to be the first Magisterial Reformation in Europe. In Germany, a hundred years later, protests against the Roman Catholic authorities erupted in many places at once, during a time of threatened Islamic Ottoman invasion which distracted German princes in particular. To some degree, the protest can be explained by the events of the previous two centuries in Europe and particularly in Bohemia. Earlier in the south of France, where the old influence of the Cathars led to the growing protests against the pope and his authorities, Guillaume Farel (b. [AD] 1489) preached reformation as early as [AD] 1522 in Dauphiné, where the French Wars of Religion later originated in [AD] 1562, also known as Huguenot wars. These also spread later to other parts of Europe.

Roots and Precursors: 14th Century and 15th Century

Unrest due to the Avignon Papacy and the Papal Schism in the Roman Catholic Church ([AD] 1378–1416) had excited wars between princes, uprisings among the peasants, and widespread concern over corruption in the Church. A new nationalism also challenged the relatively internationalist medieval world. The first of a series of disruptive and new perspectives came from John Wycliffe at Oxford University, then from Jan Hus at the University of Prague (Hus had been previously influenced by Wycliffe during a trip to England). The Catholic Church officially concluded debate over Hus' teachings at the Council of Constance ([AD] 1414–1417). The conclave condemned Jan Hus, who was executed by burning at the stake in spite of a promise of safe-conduct. At the command of Pope Martin V, Wycliffe was posthumously exhumed and burned as a heretic twelve years after his burial.

The Council of Constance confirmed and strengthened the traditional medieval conception of Churches and Empires. It did not address the national tensions, or the theological tensions which had been stirred up during the previous century. The council could not prevent schism and the Hussite Wars in Bohemia....

[Schism in religion is "a split or division between strongly opposed sections or parties, caused by differences in opinion or belief" ("Schism," Oxford Dictionaries, http://1ref.us/4f).]

But as recovery and prosperity progressed, enabling the population to reach its former levels in the late 15th and 16th centuries, the combination of both a newly-abundant labor supply as well as improved productivity, were 'mixed blessings' for many segments of Western European society. Despite tradition, landlords started the move to exclude peasants from "common lands". With trade stimulated, landowners increasingly moved away from the manorial economy. Woollen manufacturing greatly expanded in France, Germany, and the Netherlands and new textile industries began to develop.

> "The conclave condemned Jan Hus, who was executed by burning at the stake in spite of a promise of safe-conduct."

The invention of movable type would lead to the Protestant zeal for translating the Bible and getting it into the hands of the laity. This would advance the culture of Biblical literacy.

The "humanism" of the Renaissance period stimulated unprecedented academic ferment, and a concern for academic freedom. Ongoing, earnest theoretical debates occurred in the universities about the nature of the church, and the source and extent of the authority of the papacy, of councils, and of princes.

16th Century

The protests against Rome began in earnest when Martin Luther, an Augustinian monk and professor at the university of Wittenberg, called in [AD] 1517 for a reopening of the debate on the sale of indulgences. Luther's dissent marked a sudden outbreak of a new and irresistible force of discontent which had been pushed underground but not resolved. The quick spread of discontent occurred to a large degree because of the printing press and the resulting swift movement of both ideas and documents, including the *95 Theses*. Information was also widely disseminated in manuscript form, as well as by cheap prints and woodcuts amongst the poorer sections of society.

Parallel to events in Germany, a movement began in Switzerland under the leadership of Ulrich Zwingli. These two movements quickly agreed on most issues, as the recently introduced printing press spread ideas rapidly from place to place, but some unresolved differences kept them separate. Some followers of Zwingli believed that the Reformation was too conservative, and moved independently toward more radical positions, some of which survive among modern day Anabaptists. Other Protestant movements grew up along lines of mysticism or humanism (cf. Erasmus), sometimes breaking from Rome or from the Protestants, or forming outside of the churches.

After this first stage of the Reformation, following the excommunication of Luther and condemnation of the Reformation by the Pope, the work and writings of John Calvin were influential in establishing a loose consensus among various groups in Switzerland, Scotland, Hungary, Germany and elsewhere.

The Reformation foundations engaged with Augustinianism. Both Luther and Calvin thought along lines linked with the theological teachings of Augustine of Hippo. The Augustinianism of the Reformers struggled against Pelagianism, a heresy that they perceived in the Catholic Church of their day.… In the course of this religious upheaval, the German Peasants' War of [AD] 1524–1525 swept through the Bavarian, Thuringian and Swabian principalities, leaving scores of Catholics slaughtered at the hands of Protestant bands, including the Black Company of Florian Geier, a knight from Giebelstadt who joined the peasants in the general outrage against the Catholic hierarchy.

Even though Luther and Calvin had very similar theological teachings, the relationship between their followers turned quickly to conflict. Frenchman Michel de Montaigne told a story of a Lutheran pastor who once claimed that he would rather celebrate the mass of Rome than participate in a Calvinist service.…

Martin Luther, John Calvin, and Ulrich Zwingli are considered Magisterial Reformers because their reform movements were supported by ruling authorities or "magistrates". Frederick the Wise not only supported Luther, who was a professor at the university he founded, but also protected him by hiding Luther in Wartburg Castle in Eisenach. Zwingli and Calvin were supported by the city councils in Zurich and Geneva. Since the term "magister" also means "teacher", the Magisterial Reformation is also characterized by an emphasis on the authority of a teacher. This is made evident in the prominence of Luther, Calvin, and Zwingli as leaders of the reform movements in their respective areas of ministry. Because of their authority, they were often criticized by Radical Reformers as being too much like the Roman Popes. For example, Radical Reformer Andreas von Bodenstein Karlstadt referred to the Wittenberg theologians as the "new papists".

Humanism to Protestantism

… The polarization of the scholarly community in Germany over the Reuchlin ([AD] 1455–1522) affair, attacked by the elite clergy for his study of Hebrew and Jewish texts, brought Luther fully in line with the humanist educational reforms who favored academic freedom. At the same time, the impact of the Renaissance would soon backfire against traditional Catholicism, ushering in an age of reform and a repudiation of much of medieval Latin tradition. Led by Erasmus, the humanists condemned various forms of corruption within the Church, forms of corruption that might not have been any more prevalent than during the medieval zenith of the church. Erasmus held that true religion was a matter of inward devotion rather than outward symbols of ceremony and ritual. Going back to ancient texts, scriptures, from this viewpoint the greatest culmination of the ancient tradition, are the guides to life. Favoring moral reforms and de-emphasizing didactic ritual, Erasmus laid the groundwork for Luther.…

Luther borrowed from the humanists the sense of individualism, that each man can be his own priest (an attitude likely to find popular support considering the rapid rise of an educated urban middle class in the North), and that the only true authority is the Bible, echoing the reformist zeal of the Conciliar movement and opening up the debate once again on limiting the authority of the Pope. While his ideas called for the sharp redefinition of the dividing lines between the laity and the clergy, his ideas were still, by this point, reformist in nature. Luther's contention that the human will was incapable of following good, however, resulted in his rift with Erasmus finally distinguishing Lutheran reformism from humanism.

Luther affirmed a theology of the Eucharist called Real Presence, a doctrine of the presence of Christ in the Eucharist which affirms the real presence yet upholding that the bread and wine are not "changed" into the body and blood; rather the divine elements adhere "in, with, and under" the earthly elements. He took this understanding of Christ's presence in the Eucharist to be more harmonious with the Church's teaching on the Incarnation. Just as Christ is the union of the fully human and the fully divine (cf. Council of Chalcedon) so to the Eucharist is a union of Bread and Body, Wine and Blood. According to the doctrine of real presence, the substances of the body and the blood of Christ and of the bread and the wine were held to coexist together in the consecrated Host during the communion service. While Luther seemed to maintain the perpetual consecration of the elements, other Lutherans argued that any consecrated bread or wine left over would revert to its former state the moment the service ended. Most Lutherans accept the latter. ("History of Protestantism," Wikipedia, http://1ref.us/4g)

Thus, it would appear that most churches came from the same source. In describing the mission of the apostles after Jesus' ascension, most of Luke's history in Acts relates to Roman dominance of the then-known world. Most if not all of today's Christian churches can be traced to the Roman Catholic Church or branches of that church. It is commonly believed that the Orthodox Churches came from the splitting of power in Rome where the pope remained in Rome and the Eastern Orthodox Churches power was in Constantinople.

Very interesting parts of the early Christian churches come from the idea that two of the different churches came from the same personage. Both the Roman Catholic Church and the Eastern Orthodox Church make the claim that they came from Jesus Christ Himself. The Roman Catholic Church claims to have evolved from Jesus Christ using the text in Matthew 16:18, making the following claim of itself:

> And I say also unto thee, That thou art Peter, and upon this rock I will build my church; and the gates of hell shall not prevail against it.

> The Orthodox Church is the one Church founded by Jesus Christ and his apostles, begun at the day of Pentecost with the descent of the Holy Spirit in the year 33 A.D. It is also known (especially in the contemporary West) as the Eastern Orthodox Church or the Greek Orthodox Church. It may also be called the Orthodox Catholic Church, the Orthodox Christian Church, … the Body of Christ, the Bride of Christ, or simply the Church.
>
> The bishops of the Orthodox Churches trace unbroken succession to the very apostles themselves, therefore ultimately receiving their consecrations from our Lord Jesus Christ. All the bishops of the Eastern Orthodox Churches, no matter their titles, are equal in their sacramental office. The various titles given to bishops are simply administrative or honorific in their essence. At an ecumenical council, each bishop may cast only one vote, whether he is the Ecumenical Patriarch or simply an auxiliary bishop without a diocese. Thus, there is no equivalent to the Roman Catholic papacy within the Eastern Orthodox Churches.
>
> As with its Apostolic succession, the faith held by the Catholic Church is that which was handed by Christ to the apostles.… Throughout history, various heresies have afflicted the Catholic Church, and at those times the Catholic Church makes dogmatic pronouncements (especially at ecumenical councils) delineating in new language what has always been believed by the Church, thus preventing the spread

of heresy and calling to repentance those who rend asunder the Body of Christ. ("Orthodox Church," Orthodox Wiki, http://1ref.us/4h)

What are the differences in the basic beliefs of the Roman Catholic Church and Eastern Orthodox Church? The question of salvation by faith and works is viewed differently by these two churches. The Roman Catholic Church's belief on the sale of indulgences was what led German theologian Martin Luther to write his Ninety-Five Theses denouncing the need of works for salvation and emphasizing "the just shall live by faith." The Eastern Orthodox Church asserts of itself:

> Each church has always had independent administration, but, with the exception of the Church of Rome, which finally separated from the others in the year 1054, are united in faith, doctrine, Apostolic tradition, sacraments, liturgies, and services. Together they constitute what is called the "Orthodox Church", literally meaning "right teaching" or "right worship", derived from two Greek words: *orthos*, "right," and *doxa*, "teaching" or "worship." (Ibid.)

Was the separation of the Orthodox Churches from the Roman Catholic Church because of a great difference in fundamental beliefs or was it mostly because of political disagreement? Based upon its own self definition the Eastern Orthodox Church should have taken all its beliefs from the Bible. However, in separating from the western church, it maintained many beliefs based on tradition. The major factor in the separation of the Eastern and Western Churches in AD 1054 was who would be the head of the Catholic Church since both claimed to be the original Catholic Church with an unbroken succession from Jesus Christ. The top official in the Eastern Church was a patriarch, whereas the Western Church's top official was the pope, and the Eastern Church did not recognize the pope's authority given to him.

In breaking from the Roman Catholic Church, would the Orthodox Church not be considered "protestant"? Looking at the differences between Orthodox Churches and those churches called Protestant today, there seems to be about the same differences as what disunited the early churches one from another. Remember, the devil does not care how much truth a church holds so long as he can get it to embrace some error. There are only two ways to travel through life: the right way or the wrong way, choosing good or evil, doing God's will or the devil's.

Chapter 15
Who Made the Claim?

Who made the claim that the day of worship should be Sunday instead of Saturday? In researching this topic on the Internet, I found more than 300 million articles with pertinent information. In this chapter, we will examine some of the relevant quotations I found. Follow along, for this is interesting history, which most Sunday-going Christians are not aware of. Yet, watch and see that, even after knowing the facts and being shown from their own Bible that God's law is higher than tradition, many Christians will still insist upon tradition, while others will choose to follow their Bible and be given a hard time for it. In the Old Testament there is no doubt but that Saturday was the Sabbath day and that all the Jews who accepted the message of Jesus continued to keep the Sabbath as God commanded. Consider the factors that led to the abandonment of the Sabbath:

> The pagan Romans hated the Jews because of Jewish rebellions throughout the empire. In A.D. 115, Jews revolted in Cyrene, Egypt and Cyprus. More than 220,000 Greeks and Romans perished in Cyrene alone, according to Roman historian Dio Cassius. After ruthlessly suppressing each revolt, the Romans would tighten their yoke around the Jews. (Goldstein, "The Origin of Sunday Worship," From Sabbath to Sunday, http://1ref.us/4i)

> The Roman emperor Hadrian said he would rebuild the temple of the Jews, but it would be dedicated to a Roman Deity. A Jew named Bar Kochba proclaimed himself to be the long awaited messiah and began a revolt in Palestine in 132–135 AD. In the first year of the revolt, the Romans were driven out of more than 50 cities and villages. Bar Kochba proclaimed himself king and even struck his own coinage. Hadrian had his top general Julius Severus to lead the troops into a three year battle to crush the rebellion and finally killed Bar Kochba.
>
> These rebellions inflamed Roman Anti-Judaism. After the Bar Kochba revolt, Jews were forbidden to enter Jerusalem. Hadrian outlawed Judaism, the study of the Torah, and Sabbath-keeping....

Christianity was still in its infancy and it was caught between Roman Imperialism and Jewish Nationalism. Since Christianity originated in the land of the Jews, its Holy Writings were Jewish, Christians were mistaken for Jews. A small number of Christians after 200 AD, eased away from the seventh day Sabbath so as to appear different from the Jews. ("The History of the Change of God's Sabbath from Saturday to Sunday," http://1ref.us/4j)

Up until well into the second century AD, very few Christians observed the first day of the week, which we call Sunday, as a unique day of worship. The majority observed the seventh day, which we call Saturday, as their regular weekly day of worship. Evidences of the divergence of views about Sunday can be seen in a dispute that arose around AD 200 over observing one day annually in honor of Jesus' resurrection. This dispute was known as the Quartodeciman or Easter controversy.

"The Church of Rome suggested Sunday, but all the other churches preferred Nisan 16 regardless of which day it fell on. Rome's insistence on Sunday prevailed and all accepted that day as a yearly celebration" ("The History of the Change of God's Sabbath from Saturday to Sunday," http://1ref.us/4j). Later on, an agitation arose over introducing Lent into the Roman Church, and "it was decided to keep every Sunday during those 40 days" in remembrance of the resurrection. In the fourth century, "a decision was made to keep every Sunday in the year" (Ibid.).

> **This is why many Sunday-keeping churches today believe that Sunday was first observed in honor of Christ's resurrection.**

It was not long until many pagan customs were introduced into the Roman Church—so many, in fact, that church historian James Wharey wrote: "Indeed we shall find, that when Christianity became the established religion of the Roman Empire, and took the place of paganism, it assumed, in a great degree, the forms and rites of paganism, and participated in no small measure of its spirit also. Christianity as it existed in the dark ages, might be termed, without much impropriety of language, baptized paganism" (*Sketches of Church History*, p. 23).

The evidence of history indicates that, up until AD 300 and beyond, both Saturday and Sunday were kept. Christians honored both the Sabbath and the resurrection. Other factors also exalted Sunday after AD 300. "Through the influence of eastern sun cults, sun worship had become dominant in Rome by the early second century" (Ibid.). Obelisks and altars to the sun proliferated throughout the city, and Roman Christians started favoring Sunday, the day of the resurrection, over the Sabbath. As sun worship started to fade in the empire, the resurrection became the primary motive for worship, as it still is today. This is why many Sunday-keeping churches today believe that Sunday was first observed in honor of Christ's resurrection. In the early fourth century, Constantine the Great issued the first known secular Sunday observance, ordering Sunday rest instead of Sabbath rest. In church councils that followed, the Catholic Church enforced Sunday observance through shunning, torture, and even death. When it comes to the claim about who made the change of the Sabbath, Catholic authorities have not been shy. Notice a few authoritative Catholic sources on the subject:

The Roman Church's Claim About Changing the Sabbath

You will tell me that Saturday was the Jewish Sabbath, but that the Christian Sabbath has been changed to Sunday. Changed! but by whom? Who has the authority to change an express commandment of God? When God has spoken and said, Thou shalt keep holy the seventh day, who shall dare to say, Nay, thou mayest work and do all manner of worldly business on the seventh day; but thou shalt keep holy the first day in its stead? This is a most important question, which I know not how you can answer. [Tuberville, *An Abridgment of the Christian Doctrine*, p. 58.]

You are a Protestant, and you profess to go by the Bible and the Bible only; and yet in so important a matter as the observance of one day in seven as a holy day, you go against the plain letter of the Bible, and put another day in the place of that day which the Bible has commanded. The command to keep holy the seventh day is one of the ten commandments; you believe that the other nine are still binding; who gave you authority to tamper with the fourth? If you are consistent with your own principles, if you really follow the Bible and the Bible only, you ought to be able to produce some portion of the New Testament in which this fourth commandment is expressly altered … (Brotherhood of St. Vincent of Paul, "Why Don't You Keep Holy the Sabbath-Day? A Question for All Bible Christians," *The Clifton Tracts*, pp. 5, 6)

Consider the following question sent to Pope Piux XI in 1934:

Thomaston, Georgia
May 22, 1934

Pope Pius XI
Rome, Italy

Dear Sir:

Is the accusation true that Protestants accuse you of? They say you changed the seventh day Sabbath to the so-called Christian Sunday—identical with the first day of the week. If so, when did you make the change, and by what authority?

Yours very truly,

J. L. Day

Here was the pope's deputy's reply:

> THE CATHOLIC EXTENSION MAGAZINE
> *180 Wabash Ave., Chicago, Illinois*
> (Under the Blessing of Pope Pius XI)
>
> Dear Sir:
>
> Regarding the change from the observance of the Jewish Sabbath to the Christian Sunday, I wish to draw your attention to the facts:
>
> (1) That Protestants, who accept the Bible as the only rule of faith and religion, should by all means go back to the observance of the Sabbath. The fact that they do not, but on the contrary observe Sunday, stultifies them in the eyes of every thinking man.
>
> (2) We Catholics do not accept the Bible as the only rule of faith. Besides the Bible we have the living Church, the authority of the Church, as a rule to guide us. We say, this Church instituted by Christ, to teach and guide men through life, has the right to change the ceremonial laws of the Old Testament and hence, we accept her change of the Sabbath to Sunday. We frankly say, "Yes, the Church made this change, made this law, as she made many other laws; for instance, the Friday Abstinence, the unmarried priesthood, the laws concerning mixed marriages, the regulation of Catholic marriages, and a thousand other laws.
>
> (3) We also say that of all Protestants, the Seventh-day Adventists are the only group that reason correctly and are consistent with their teachings. It is always somewhat laughable to see the Protestant Churches, in pulpit and legislature, demand the observance of Sunday, of which there is nothing in the Bible.
>
> With best wishes,
> Peter R. Tramer, Editor

("A Letter to the Pope," SDA Global, http://1ref.us/4k)

Archbishop of Reggio nailed the coffin on any pretense that the Roman Catholic Church based Sunday observance upon Scripture:

> Finally, at the last opening on the eighteenth of January, 1562, their last scruple was set aside: the Archbishop of Reggio made a speech in which he openly declared that tradition stood above Scripture. The authority of the church could therefore not be bound to the authority of the Scriptures, because the church had changed Sabbath into Sunday, not by the command of Christ, but by its own authority. (Holtzmann,

Kanon und Tradition, p. 263, translated in *The Protestant Magazine*, vol. 5, no. 2 (Feb. 1913), p. 71)

I need to remind the reader that this testimony does not come from a critic of Catholicism, but from an authorized representative of the church itself. To repeat his testimony is not to slander anyone, but to examine the basis for the difference between Catholic doctrine and the teachings of Scripture. Such an appraisal favors no particular religious group, but seeks to establish the basis for salvation and biblical truth on the Bible and the Bible alone. If it leads to a particular religious group, it is only because the "last straw in the pile" has been selected by Scripture (see "The Roman Church's Admission of Changing The Sabbath," http://1ref.us/4l).

Why did Christianity lean toward a day not singled out in Scripture? We have already quoted author William Frederick as saying it was to influence the Gentiles by observing their day.

One might be surprised to hear, in his commentary on Exodus 16:4, 22–30, Martin Luther's acknowledgement about the Sabbath and those who continued to observe it, yet here it is: "Hence, you can see that the Sabbath was before the Law of Moses came, and has existed from the beginning of the world. Especially have the devout, who have preserved the true faith, met together and called upon God on this day" (Walch, ed., *Auslegung des Alten Testaments* [Commentary on the Old Testament], in *Dr. Martin Luthers Sämmtliche Schriften* [Collected Writings], vol. 3, Colossians 950).

After presenting a lengthy argument in favor of abandoning the seventh-day Sabbath, Steve Keohane of BibleProbe.com presents what is called "the alternative argument" (note the bracketed explanatory comments that have been added):

> This argument denies that Christians are free from the bondage of the Law (Galatians 4:1–26; Romans 6:14). [The argument actually affirms that we are free from the bondage of trying to obey the law in dependence upon our sinful nature (Romans 8:3, 7) and emphasizes keeping the law of God by the Holy Spirit (Romans 8:4) with God's laws written in heart and mind (Hebrews 8:10; 10:16).] It says that Sabbath (Saturday) keeping is required of the Christian.
>
> In Mark 2:23–28. Jesus allowed His disciples to pluck heads of grain to eat as they walked through grain fields on the Sabbath. He was challenged on this point by the Pharisees, who had added more than 60 legalistic "dos and don'ts" to the Sabbath—of their own human devising. But Jesus said, "The Sabbath was made for man, and not man for the Sabbath. Therefore the Son of Man is also Lord of the Sabbath".
>
> Christ did not say that the Sabbath was made for the Jews—but for "man." He said the Sabbath (not Sunday) is the day He is "Lord of." Jesus did not give the slightest hint about abrogating the Sabbath commandment.

Genesis 2:23 begins to provide the answer in this argument.

"And on the seventh day God ended His work which He had done, and He rested on the seventh day from all His work which He had done. Then God *blessed* the seventh day and *sanctified* it, because in it He rested from all His work which God had created and made."

Notice that God "ended" or completed His work of creation by resting on the seventh day of the week. The word "Sabbath" is derived from the Hebrew word *Shabath*, which literally means "rest" or "cessation." God created the Sabbath by resting on this day and ceasing from creating material things. And He "blessed" and "sanctified"—that is, set apart for holy use—this day and no other! By blessing and sanctifying the seventh-day Sabbath, God showed that His presence is IN this day in a very special way. For of all the days of the week, this one ALONE points to Him in a unique way as the true God, the One who created and now governs the entire universe. [That it is the seal of the LORD God the Creator can be seen by the fact that "it is a sign" is joined to His identity as Creator by the logical connector "for" in Exodus 31:17.]

"For assuredly, I say to you, till heaven and earth pass away [and they still have not!], one jot or one tittle will by no means pass from the law till all is fulfilled. Whoever therefore breaks one of the LEAST of these commandments, and teaches men so, shall be called least in the kingdom of heaven; but whoever does and teaches them, he shall be called great in the kingdom of heaven" (Matthew 5:17–19).

Mark 7:7–9.

7 Howbeit in vain do they worship me, teaching for doctrines the commandments of men. 8 For laying aside the commandment of God, ye hold the tradition of men, as the washing of pots and cups: and many other such like things ye do. 9 And he said unto them, Full well ye reject the commandment of God, that ye may keep your own tradition. (Keohane, "Sabbath Changed to Sunday," Bible Probe, http://1ref.us/4m)

We find more about the change from Saturday to Sunday in a sermon by evangelist Joe Crews:

History Gives Some Clues. If the change did not take place in the Scriptures or through the influence of the apostles, when and how did it happen? In order to understand this, we must understand what happened in that early church soon after the apostles passed off the stage of action. Paul had prophesied that apostasy would take place soon after his departure.

He said there would be a falling away from the truth. One doesn't have to read very far in early church history to see just how that prophecy was fulfilled. Gnosticism began to rise up under the influence of philosophers who sought to reconcile Christianity with Paganism. At the same time, a strong anti-Jewish sentiment became more widespread. Very speculative interpretations began to appear regarding some of the great doctrines of Christ and the apostles.

The Conversion of Constantine. By the time Constantine was established as the emperor of Rome in the early fourth century, there was a decided division in the church as a result of all these factors. I think most of you know that Constantine was the first so-called Christian emperor of the Roman Empire. The story of his conversion has become very well known to students of ancient history.

He was marching forth to fight the battle of Milvian Bridge when he had some kind of vision, and saw a flaming cross in the sky.

Underneath the cross were the Latin words meaning "In this sign conquer." Constantine took this as an omen that he should be a Christian, and his army as well. He declared all his pagan soldiers to be Christians, and became very zealous to build up the power and prestige of the church. Through his influence great blocks of pagans were taken into the Christian ranks.

But, friends, they were still pagan at heart, and they brought in much of the paraphernalia of sun-worship to which they continued to be devoted.... At the same time, many other customs were Christianized and appropriated into the practice of the church as well.

Sun Worship. You see, at that time the cult of Mithraism or sun-worship was the official religion of the Roman Empire. It stood as the greatest competitor to the new Christian religion. It had its own organization, temples, priesthood, robes—everything. It also had an official worship day on which special homage was given to the sun. That day was called "The Venerable Day of the Sun." It was the first day of the week, and from it we get our name Sunday. When Constantine pressed his pagan hordes into the church they were observing the day of the sun for their adoration of the sun god. It was their special holy day. In order to make it more convenient for them to make the change to the new religion, Constantine accepted their day of worship, Sunday, instead of the Christian Sabbath which had been observed by Jesus and His disciples. Remember that the way had been prepared for this already by the increasing anti-Jewish feelings against those who were accused of putting Jesus to death. Those feelings would naturally condition many Christians to swing away from something which was held religiously by the Jews. It is therefore easier to understand how the change was imposed on Christianity through a strong civil law issued by Constantine as the Emperor of Rome. The very wording of that law, by the way, can be found in any reliable encyclopedia. Those early Christians, feeling that the Jews should not be followed any more than necessary, were ready to swing away from the Sabbath which was kept by the Jews.

Historical Accounts. Some of you may be greatly surprised by the explanation

I've just made, and I'm not going to ask you to believe it blindly. I have before me a multitude of authorities to verify what has been said. Here are historians, Catholics and Protestants, speaking in harmony about what actually took place in the fourth century. After Constantine made the initial pronouncement and legal decree about the change, the Catholic Church reinforced that act in one church council after another. For this reason, many, many official statements from Catholic sources are made, claiming that the church made the change from Saturday to Sunday. But before I read those statements I shall refer to one from the *Encyclopedia Britannica* under the article, "Sunday." Notice: "It was Constantine who first made a law for the proper observance of Sunday; and who appointed that it should be regularly celebrated throughout the Roman Empire" (Crews, "How the Sabbath Was Changed," SabbathTruth.com, http://1ref.us/4n)

Distinguished scholar Edwyn Robert Bevan also described the Sabbath's replacement:

> Now, since Mithras was "The Sun, the Unconquered", and the Sun was "the royal Star", the religion looked for a King whom it could serve as the representative of Mithras upon earth ... the Roman Emperor seemed to be clearly indicated as the true King. In sharp contrast to Christianity, Mithraism recognized Caesar as the bearer of divine Grace, and its votaries filled the legions and the civil service.... It had so many acceptances that it was able to impose on the Christian world its own Sun-Day in place of the Sabbath; its Sun's birthday, 25th December, as the birthday of Jesus ... (Bailey, *The History of Christianity in the Light of Modern Knowledge*, pp. 73, 74)

> **Mithras was "The Sun, the Unconquered", and the Sun was "the royal Star", the religion looked for a King whom it could serve as the representative of Mithras upon earth.**

In another historical statement, Dr. William Frederick wrote:

> ... The Gentiles were an idolatrous people who worshipped the sun, and Sunday was their most sacred day. Now, in order to reach the people in this new field, it seems but natural as well as necessary to make Sunday the rest day of the church.... At this time it became necessary for the church to either adopt the Gentile's day or else have the Gentile's change their day. To change the Gentile's day would have been an offense and a stumbling block to them. The church could naturally reach them better by keeping

their day. (*Three Prophetic Days*, pp. 169, 170)

The Catholic Encyclopedia states: "The Church, on the other hand, after changing the day of rest from the Jewish Sabbath, or seventh day of the week, to the first, made the Third Commandment refer to Sunday as the day to be kept holy as the Lord's day" (*The Catholic Encyclopedia*, vol. 4, p. 153).

Add to this what a Catholic newspaper in Sidney, Australia said at the turn of the twentieth century: "Sunday is a Catholic institution and its claims to observance can be defended only on Catholic principles. From the beginning to end of Scripture there is not a single passage that warrants the transfer of weekly public worship from the last day of the week to the first" (*Catholic Press*, August 25, 1900).

Previous to this, the September 23, 1894 *Catholic Mirror* had put it this way: "The Catholic Church for over one thousand years before the existence of a Protestant, by virtue of her divine mission, changed the day from Saturday to Sunday."

Various Catholic catechisms confirm this claim:

Q. Which is the Sabbath day?
A. Saturday is the Sabbath day.
Q. Why do we observe Sunday instead of Saturday?
A. We observe Sunday instead of Saturday because the Catholic Church, in the Council of Laodicea [AD 365], transferred the solemnity from Saturday to Sunday. (Giermann, *The Convert's Catechism of Catholic Doctrine*, p. 50)

Q. How prove you that the Church hath power to command feasts and holy-days?
A. By the very act of changing the sabbath into Sunday which Protestants allow of; and therefore they fondly contradict themselves, by keeping Sunday strictly, and breaking most other feasts commanded by the same church." (Tuberville, *An Abridgment of the Christian Doctrine*, p. 56)

Question: Have you any other way of proving that the Church has power to institute festivals of precept?
Answer: Had she not such power, she could not have done that in which all modern religionists agree with her;—she could not have substituted the observance of Sunday, the first day of the week, for the observance of Saturday, the seventh day, a change for which there is no Scriptural authority." (Keenan, *Doctrinal Catechism*, p. 174)

Then from Bertrand L. Conway we read: "If the Bible is the only guide for the Christian, then the Seventh Day Adventist is right in observing Saturday with the Jew.... Is it not strange that those who make the Bible their only teacher should inconsistently follow in this matter the tradition of the

Catholic Church?" (*The Question-Box Answers*, pp. 254, 255).

These are most interesting statements. In concluding his sermon, Joe Crews said:

> There is some inconsistency somewhere along the line, because we have examined the statements of history, and you can check them for yourself in any library [or, today, on the Internet]. I'm not reading anything one-sided here at all. I've tried to give you an unbiased picture. Although we have seen the claims made by the Catholic Church in their publications, we are not reading them to cast any reflection upon anyone, by any means. We are simply bringing you a recital of what has been written and what claims have been made. ("How the Sabbath Was Changed," SabbathTruth.com, http://1ref.us/4n)

In answer to the question, "Who made the claim?" the clear answer is that it was the Catholic Church and the Catholic Church alone. There are no biblical statements that transfer Sabbath observance from the seventh day of the week to the first day of the week; it is only the Catholic Church's tradition.

Chapter 16

Protestants Come to America

Steve Keohane describes Protestantism's crossing of the Atlantic:

> As Christianity headed west, the earliest settlers to America included both Sunday-keepers—such as the Puritans who landed at Plymouth, Mass., in 1620—and Sabbath-observers like the Seventh Day Baptists, whose first church was founded in Newport, R.I., in 1671.
>
> When the Puritan Christians used the word Sabbath, they would mean Sunday—"the Lord's Day"—and passed rules enforcing its observance from sunset Saturday to sunset Sunday. (Keohane, "Sabbath Changed to Sunday," Bible Probe, http://1ref.us/4m)

Most Protestant churches accept the Catholic tradition that "the Lord's Day" is Sunday. Yet, in the biblical account, the term "Lord's Day" is plainly referring to the seventh-day Sabbath. The fourth commandment identifies the seventh day as "the sabbath of the Lord thy God" (Exodus 20:10), and God refers to the seventh-day Sabbath as "my holy day" (Isaiah 58:13). Moreover, Jesus claimed the title of "Lord of the sabbath" (Mark 2:28).

In chapter 15 I quoted a sampling of authoritative statements on who made the claim about abandoning the Sabbath for worship in favor of Sunday. Most Sunday-observing believers in the world today do not really know why they go to church on Sunday. They believe that it is to commemorate the resurrection of Jesus. They rest in the assurance that the traditional day of worship is correct.

Their basis for Sunday is similar to the response I received when I asked a person why he was a Methodist. He answered that it was because his parents and grandparents were Methodist. I then ask

> **Most Sunday-observing believers in the world today do not really know why they go to church on Sunday.**

him how much he knew about the beliefs of the Methodist Church. He responded, "Oh, not much, but, if it was good enough for my folks, it is good enough for me." (I intend no denigration of Methodists in quoting this person.)

Could it be that people do not care enough about what will happen to them when this life is over to uncover the foundation of their beliefs or to find out from the Bible what is the truth? How difficult it is to change our way of thinking! The devil knows this, and it serves his purposes for us to believe some error even though it may be only a small amount.

How much do we know about the teachings and beliefs of the church we attend? Have we ever compared those beliefs with the teachings of the Bible? Are we satisfied with just accepting the little we know from what the preachers have told us? Think about Jesus' warning to His followers: "Take heed that no man deceive you. For many shall come in my name, saying, I am Christ; and shall deceive many" (Matthew 24:4, 5). If what preachers are telling us is all Bible truth, then why are there so many different beliefs?

Jesus also said: "For there shall arise false Christs, and false prophets, and shall shew great signs and wonders; insomuch that, if it were possible, they shall deceive the very elect" (Matthew 24:24). Are any of us so sure of what the Bible teaches that we can say with certainty, "I am part of the elect; there is no way I can be deceived"? Are we willing to gamble eternity on someone else's beliefs?

The different teachings discussed so far in this book are only a sampling of the large number of differences in belief within the wide spectrum of Christian denominations in the world today. Just how many different denominations are there? As of 2014 Wiki.ask.com asserts that there are approximately 38,000 Christian denominations, although many of these cannot be verified as being significant. David Barrett's editorial in "World Christian Encyclopedia" estimates that there are approximately 34,000 separate Christian groups around the world. All claim to derive their beliefs from Scripture, but how can this be so? It may be helpful here to look at a list of beliefs that are considered to be mainstream within Christianity as well as the greatest differences in belief between denominations. None of these differences are mentioned to bash any group or to promote error. Each person is free to make his or her own decision about what to believe and about what is useful in their relationship to God.

> **If what preachers are telling us is all Bible truth, then why are there so many different beliefs?**

Previously we have looked at the major differences between the Catholic Church and the Orthodox Church. At first glance, there may not be much difference between these two churches since they hold major beliefs in common. Nonetheless, the Orthodox Church can be considered the first "protestant" denomination in that it broke away from the Catholic Church before others. However, today its day of worship is the same as that of the Roman Catholic Church—Sunday.

The authority for Sunday observance is a difficulty to any true Protestant, as noted Catholic author John Anthony O'Brien has pointed out:

But since Saturday, not Sunday, is specified in the Bible, isn't it curious that non-Catholics who profess to take their religion directly from the Bible and not from the Church, observe Sunday instead of Saturday? Yes, of course, it is inconsistent; but this change was made about fifteen centuries before Protestantism was born, and by that time the custom was universally observed. They have continued the custom, even though it rests upon the authority of the Catholic Church and not upon an explicit text in the Bible. That observance [of Sunday] remains as a reminder of the Mother Church from which the non-Catholic sects broke away—like a boy running away from home but still carrying in his pocket a picture of his mother or a lock of her hair. (O'Brien, *The Faith of Millions: The Credentials of the Catholic Religion*, pp. 400, 401)

"That observing (Sunday) remains as a reminder of the Mother Church from which the non-Catholic sects broke away." Is Sunday worship ordained from God or a counterfeit of the devil? Of course, it's a counterfeit of the devil.

The Basic Beliefs of Mainline Christian Churches

What are the beliefs that most Christians hold in common? To answer that question is no simple matter. Christianity encompasses a wide range of denominations and faith groups, and each subscribes to its own set of doctrinal positions. Certain faith groups, who consider themselves to be within the framework of Christianity, do not accept some of the beliefs of the rest, and they hold slight variations, exceptions, and additions to the beliefs of other faith groups that fall beneath the broad umbrella of Christianity. Nonetheless, following are the core beliefs that mainline Christian faith groups hold in common:

1. There is only one God (Isa 43:10; 44:6, 8; John 17:3; 1 Cor 8:5–6; Gal 4:8–9).
2. God is three in one or a Trinity (Matthew 3:16–17, 28:19; John 14:16–17; 2 Cor 13:14; Acts 2:32–33, John 10:30; 17:11, 21; 1 Pet. 1:2).
3. God is omniscient or "knows all things" (Acts 15:18; 1 John 3:20).
4. God is omnipotent or "all-powerful" (Ps 115:3; Rev 19:6).
5. God is omnipresent or "present everywhere" (Jer 23:23, 24; Ps 139).
6. God is sovereign (Zech 9:14; 1 Tim 6:15–16).
7. God is holy (1 Pet 1:15).
8. God is just or "righteous" (Pss 19:9, 116:5, 145:17; Jer 12:1).
9. God is love (1 John 4:8).
10. God is true (Rom 3:4; John 14:6).
11. God is spirit (John 4:24).
12. God is the creator of everything that exists (Gen 1:1; Isa 44:24).
13. God is infinite and eternal. He has always been God (Ps 90:2; Gen 21:33; Acts 17:24).

14. God is immutable. He does not change (Jas 1:17; Mal 3:6; Isa 46:9, 10).
15. The Holy Spirit is God (Acts 5:3, 4; 1 Cor 2:11, 12; 2 Cor 13:14).
16. Jesus Christ is God (John 1:1, 14, 10:30–33, 20:28; Col 2:9; Phil 2:5–8; Heb 1:8).
17. Jesus became a man (Phil 2:1–11).
18. Jesus is fully God and fully man (Col 2:9; 1 Tim 2:5; Heb 4:15; 2 Cor 5:21).
19. Jesus was sinless (1 Pet 2:22; Heb 4:15).
20. Jesus is the only way to God the Father (John 14:6; Matt 11:27; Luke 10:22).
21. Man was created by God in the image of God (Gen 1:26, 27).
22. All people have sinned (Rom 3:23, 5:12).
23. Death came into the world through Adam's sin (Rom 5:12–15).
24. Sin separates us from God (Isa 59:2).
25. Jesus died for the sins of each and every person in the world (1 John 2:2; 2 Cor 5:14; 1 Pet 2:24).
26. Jesus' death was a substitutionary sacrifice. He died and paid the price for our sins, so that we might live (1 Pet 2:24; Matt 20:28; Mark 10:45).
27. Jesus resurrected from the dead in physical form (John 2:19–21).
28. Salvation is a free gift of God (Rom 4:5, 6:23; Eph 2:8, 9; 1 John 1:8–10).
29. The Bible is the "inspired" or "God-breathed," Word of God (2 Tim 3:16; 2 Peter 1:21).
30. Those who reject Jesus Christ, after they die, will go to hell forever (Rev 20:11–15, 21:8).
31. Those who accept Jesus Christ, after they die, will live for eternity with Him (John 11:25, 26; 2 Cor 5:6).
32. Hell is a place of punishment (Matt 25:41, 46; Rev 19:20).
33. Hell is eternal (Matt 25:46).
34. There will be a rapture of the church (Matt 24:30–36, 40–41; John 14:1–3; 1 Cor 15:51–52; 1 Thess 4:16–17; 2 Thess 2:1–12).
35. Jesus will return to the earth (Acts 1:11).
36. Christians will be raised from the dead when Jesus returns (1 Thess 4:14–17).
37. There will be a final judgment (Heb 9:27; 2 Pet 3:7).
38. Satan will be thrown into the lake of fire (Rev 20:10).
39. God will create a new heaven and a new earth (2 Pet 3:13; Rev 21:1).

(Blanc, "A Summary of the Gospel Message," Biblical Scholarship with a Global Perspective, http://1ref.us/4o)

Almost all denominations present their doctrines as groups of beliefs to make it simpler for people to manage in picking a church. The list omits one crucial belief that is assumed by the majority of Christian churches (and even used as a litmus test for shunning certain churches)—it is the observance of Sunday, the first day of the week, as the day of sacred assembly.

List of the Branches of Christianity

The following is a list of Christian churches taken from Wikipedia. To keep the list short, only the name of each church/denomination and the number of groups within that church structure [within brackets] will appear. As the Wikipedia article "List of Christian denominations" points out:

> This is not a complete list, but aims to provide a comprehensible overview of the diversity among denominations of Christianity. As there are reported to be approximately 41,000 Christian denominations (figure includes overlap between countries), many of which cannot be verified to be significant, only those denominations with Wikipedia articles will be listed in order to ensure that all entries on this list are notable and verifiable.
>
> Between denominations, theologians, and comparative religionists there are considerable disagreements about which groups can be properly called Christian, disagreements arising primarily from doctrinal differences between groups. For the purpose of simplicity, this list is intended to reflect the self-understanding of each denomination. Explanations of different opinions concerning their status as Christian denominations can be found at their respective articles.
>
> There is no official recognition in most parts of the world for religious bodies, and there is no official clearinghouse which could determine the status or respectability of religious bodies. Often there is considerable disagreement between various churches about whether other churches should be labeled with pejorative terms such as "cult", or about whether this or that group enjoys some measure of respectability. Such considerations often vary from place to place, where one religious group may enjoy majority status in one region, but be widely regarded as a "dangerous cult" in another part of the world. Inclusion on this list does not indicate any judgment about the size, importance, or character of a group or its members. ("List of Christian Denominations," Wikipedia, http://1ref.us/4p)

Catholicism. These include three main branches: the Latin Church [1], the Eastern Catholic Churches [22], and other independent Catholic churches, self-identified as "Catholic" [18]. "The Catholic Church considers itself the One Holy Catholic and Apostolic Church that Christ founded. As such, the Catholic Church does not consider itself a denomination, but as pre-denominational, the original Church of Christ" (Ibid.).

The Eastern Orthodox Church. "The Oriental Orthodox Churches [25] consider themselves collectively to be the One Holy Catholic and Apostolic Church that Christ founded" (Ibid.). There are other Orthodox Churches [6]. Some Orthodox Churches are not universally recognized by the Ecumenical Patriarchate of Constantinople.

Oriental Orthodoxy. "Oriental Orthodoxy comprises those Christians who did not accept the Council of Chalcedon (AD 451). Other denominations often erroneously label these Churches as 'Monophysite'; however, as the Oriental Orthodox do not adhere to the teachings of Eutyches, they themselves reject this label, preferring the term **Miaphysite**" [15] (Ibid.). "Historically, many of the Oriental Orthodox Churches consider themselves collectively to be the One Holy Catholic and Apostolic Church that Christ founded. Some have considered the Oriental Orthodox communion to be a part of the One Holy Catholic and Apostolic Church, a view which is gaining increasing acceptance in the wake of the ecumenical dialogues" (Ibid.).

Church of the East. "The Church of the East [2] is said to have been formed by St Thomas…. The Church did not attend the Council of Ephesus (AD 431). Historically, it has often been incorrectly referred to as the Nestorian Church" (Ibid.). Assyrian Christians do not consider themselves Nestorians, and "recent Christological agreements with the Roman Catholic Church and some of the Eastern and Oriental Orthodox Churches have substantially resolved this semantic debate permanently, clearing the way for ecumenical relations…. The Church of the East also considers itself to be a part of the One Holy Catholic and Apostolic Church that Christ founded" (Ibid.).

Protestantism

"These are the churches 'which repudiated the papal authority, and separated or were severed from the Roman communion in the Reformation of the 16th century and of any of the bodies of Christians descended from them'"(Ibid.).

Pre-Lutheran Protestants have two branches: the **Hussites** [3] and the **Waldensian Evangelical Church** [1]. **Protestantism** has four main branches: **Lutherans, Anglicanism, Calvinism,** and **Anabaptists.**

Lutheranism [65] is divided largely by country, but, in the United States has more than one denomination, the best known of which is the Evangelical Lutheran Church in America (ELCA), with over three million members, and Lutheran Church-Missouri Synod (LC-MS), with 2.28 million members ("Evangelical Lutheran Church in America," Wikipedia, http://1ref.us/4q). **Pietists and Holiness Churches** [16] derive from the Lutheran movement.

Anglican Communion. "Anglicanism has referred to itself as the via media between Catholicism and Protestantism. It considers itself to be both Catholic and Reformed. Although the use of the term 'Protestant' to refer to Anglicans was once common, it is controversial today, with some rejecting the label and others accepting it" ("List of Christian Denominations," Wikipedia, http://1ref.us/4p). [68] **Methodists** [18] derive from the Anglican tradition since John Wesley, who emphasized personal piety and ministry, was an Anglican priest. The various branches of the **Brethren** [21] also originate from Anglicanism.

Under **Calvinism** are the **Presbyterians** and **Reformed Churches. Continental Reformed churches** [55] and the churches under **Presbyterianism** [81] are also divided nationally. There are a number of churches that identify as Congregationalist [27]; a major denomination among these is the

United Church of Christ.

The Anabaptists exist today in three branches: the **Amish** [5], the **Mennonites** [22], and the **Shakers** [1].

Baptists [93]. "Modern Baptist churches trace their history to the English Separatist movement in the century after the rise of the original Protestant denominations. This view of Baptist origins has the most historical support and is the most widely accepted. Adherents to this position consider the influence of Anabaptists upon early Baptists to be minimal" ("Baptists," Wikipedia, http://1ref.us/56). "All Baptist associations are congregationalist affiliations for the purpose of cooperation, in which each local church is governmentally independent. The most prominent Baptist organizations in the United States are the American Baptist Association, tending to be more liberal, the National Baptist Convention, tending to be more moderate, and the Southern Baptist Convention, tending to be more conservative" ("List of Christian Denominations," Wikipedia, http://1ref.us/4p).

Spiritual Baptists [1], **Apostolic churches – Irvingites** [4], **Pentecostalism** [66], **Charismatics** [13], **Neo-Charismatic churches** [7], and **African initiated churches** [8] are grouped here, not because of direct relationships, but because of their more emotional elements in worship. To see their distinctive features and doctrines, see each individual Wikipedia article.

United and uniting churches [16]. "Churches that are the result of a merger between distinct denominational churches. Churches are listed here when their disparate heritage marks them as inappropriately listed in the particular categories above" (Ibid.).

"**The Religious Society of Friends (Quakers)** [9], is considered historically to be a Protestant Christian denomination. It has gone through a small number of doctrinal schisms in its history as a Christian church. Today, the Society exists as several distinct and separate Quaker branches, and it also has an emphasis on Christian belief and practice which ranges from evangelical to liberal" (Ibid.).

The **Stone-Campbell Restoration Movement** [7] sought to restore primitive Christianity built upon the New Testament. These include the **Disciples of Christ**, various **Christian Churches** and **Churches of Christ**.

Under the **Southcottites** [3], Wikipedia lists the **Christian Israelite Church**, which began in the UK and are now in Australia; the **House of David**, in Benton Harbor, Michigan; and the **Panacea Society** in England. It is puzzling how these groups are linked.

Millerites and comparable groups—Seventh-day Sabbath-keeping churches that are Adventist [8], **Sabbath-keeping churches that are non-Adventist** [12+], **Sunday-observing Adventists** [3], **sacred name groups** [8], **British-Israelism** [4], **Christian Identity** [4], miscellaneous/other [26], and non-trinitarian groups.

Non-trinitarians consider themselves Christians, such as the members of the Church of Christ, "who do not believe in the traditional hypothesis of a Triune God ('one God in three co-equal Persons')" (Ibid.). There are a number of unrelated non-trinitarian denominations. Most Latter Day Saint denominations, which derive from the Church of Christ, are non-trinitarian.

The Church of Jesus Christ of Latter Day Saints [1] was established by Joseph Smith in 1830.

"Most of the 'Prairie Saint' denominations ... were established after Smith's death by the remnants of the Latter Day Saints who did not go west with Brigham Young. Many of these opposed some or most of the 1840s theological developments in favor of 1830s theological understandings and practices" (Ibid.). The Rocky Mountain denominations are the Church of Jesus Christ of Latter-day Saints and various sects who broke from it after its settlement in the Rocky Mountains, many breaking after its abandonment of the practice of polygamy in 1890. Other denominations are defined by either a belief in Joseph Smith as a prophet, or acceptance of the Book of Mormon as scripture. Mormonism is generally considered "restorationist," believing that Smith, by inspiration and revelation, restored the original Church of Christ to the earth. "Some Latter Day Saint denominations are regarded by other Christians as being non-trinitarian or even non-Christian, but the Latter Day Saints are predominantly in disagreement with these claims" (Ibid.). The various church organizations within the Latter Day Saint movement are not recognized as orthodox Christian denominations. With the exception of the Community of Christ, which is a member of the communion of the National Council of Churches, they are rejected as Christian by many Protestants. Mormons, however, strongly oppose this rejection. Branches of the original denomination are the **"Prairie Saint" denominations** [10] and the **Rocky Mountain denominations** [5].

Other non-trinitarian denominations are **Oneness Pentecostalism** [11], **Unitarianism and Universalism** [12], **Bible Student groups** [6], **Swedenborgianism** [3], and other non-Trinitarians [21], which include groups that are linked to different branches of Pentecostalism.

Besides these branches of Christian Denominations there are a number of other categories, which include: **New Thought** [8], **Messianic Judaism** and **Jewish Christians** [8], **Esoteric Christianity** [6], and syncretistic religions [9], the last of which incorporate elements of Christianity, as in certain Afro-American religions. Describing these final categories, Wikipedia notes: "The relation of these movements to other Christian ideas can be remote. They are listed here because they include some elements of Christian practice or beliefs, within religious contexts which may be only loosely characterized as Christian" (Ibid.).

Sabbath-observing Church Organizations

There are several seventh-day Sabbath-observing church organizations. The web service topix.com has a list of more than five hundred of these, although some commented that all of those named in the list are not actual church organizations; some are ministries or funds of seventh-day Sabbath-observing organizations (http://1ref.us/4s). Before its "Directory of Sabbath Churches Worldwide," The Ten Commandments website gives an introductory essay on Sabbath-keeping Christians:

> Many say that Sabbath keeping is legalism, but legalism is something you do to earn your way to heaven. The hundreds of different Sabbath keeping Churches that know the blessings of keeping God's Sabbath do not keep the day to earn entrance into the kingdom but keep the day because they love God with all their heart, soul and might....

Salvation is a free gift and so there is nothing we can do to earn our entrance into the kingdom as we are justified by faith and not by works of the law. But does this mean we do not have to obey the law? Thankfully, Paul made the answer to this question clear and informs us that we do not make void the law through faith. Romans 3:31. For even further clarity, Romans 2:13 leaves no doubt as to who is justified before God. [It says: "For not the hearers of the law are just before God, but the doers of the law shall be justified."]

Sabbath keeping Churches know that keeping the Sabbath day is a SIGN that it is God we love and worship and that we are His children. It is also a SIGN that it is God that sanctifies us and makes us Holy. These are wonderful signs and very much a blessing. What happens when we devote a full day to God because we love Him so? What is the result of spending quality time with anyone you love? This of course is not legalism by any means and applies to any of the Ten Commandments. It is something we do because we love God and our fellow man. Even though we cannot earn our way into the kingdom by keeping the Ten Commandments, we are still judged by them and will not make it into the kingdom … [until we gain the victory over all our sins by the help that God will give us by asking and believing]. Jesus said in John 14:15, *"If you love me, keep my Commandments,"* and in John 15:10, *"If you keep my Commandments, you shall abide in my love; even as I have kept my Father's Commandments, and abide in his love."* Jesus obeyed the Father's Commandments and He asks us to demonstrate our love for Him by doing the same. We also find in 1 John 2:4, *"He that saith, I know him, and keepeth not his Commandments, is a liar, and the truth is not in him."* See also Matthew 7:21–23, Hebrews 10:26–29. [Jesus said to keep His Commandments not just try to keep them.]

Sabbath keeping Churches also know that God said we are to call His Holy day a delight, not legalism.

Isaiah 58:13–14 If you turn away your foot from the Sabbath, from doing your pleasure on my holy day; and call the Sabbath a DELIGHT, the holy of the Lord, honorable; and shall honour him, not doing thine own ways, nor finding thine own pleasure, nor speaking thine own words: Then shall you delight thyself in the Lord; and I will cause you to ride upon the high places of the earth, and feed you with the heritage of Jacob your father: for the mouth of the Lord has spoken it.

Some of the largest Sabbath keeping Churches would be the Seventh Day Baptist, Seventh-day Adventist, Church of God and the United Church of God but this last one still unnecessarily keeps the feast days that ended at the cross.… ("Sabbath Observing Denominations—Sabbath Churches," The Ten Commandments, http://1ref.us/4t)

A number of seventh-day Sabbath-keeping church organizations "trace their heritage back to"

Herbert W. Armstrong, who was at one time an 'apostle' within the Church of God (Seventh Day), and separated from that group over British Israelism." They believe "Christ revealed to Mr. Armstrong the Christian spiritual meaning of the Holy Days as kept by Old Testament Israel" and the "New Testament meanings of the Holy Days contain the details of the Plan of God for the salvation of all mankind. His crowning achievement was the book, *Mystery of the Ages*." What Armstrong started as the Radio Church of God expanded into the Worldwide Church of God. (The Reluctant Messenger, http://1ref.us/4u).

Spin-offs of the Worldwide Church of God include: Big Sandy Church of God; Christian Churches of God; Church of God; Church of God, a Christian Fellowship, Church of God, Berean Fellowship; Church of God News; Church of God, International; Church of God (Seventh Day); Church of the Great God; Friends and Helpers; GodWard.Org; Intercontinental Church of God; Like Minds; Living Church of God; Philadelphia Church of God; Restored Church of God; Triumph Prophetic Ministries; United Church of God; Worldwide Church of God; and Zion Ministry.

Other Sabbath-keeping churches, in alphabetical order, are: A Church of God Ministry, Abiding Faith in Truth Church Inc. Advent Fellowship of All Nations, All Nations Assembly House of Prayer for All People, Anointed Sabbath Ministries Inc, Anointed Ministry Temple, Association of 7th Day Pentecostal Assemblies, Church of Christ of Seventh Day, Church of Jesus Christ Sabbath Day, Church of the Remnant Hope, Evangelical Seventh Day Baptist Church, Father's House Sabbath Congregation, Finding Truth Ministries, Grace Cowboy Church, House Church of Jesus Christ, LifePointe, Seventh-Day Remnant Church, New Bethel House of Prayer, Reformation Church Sabbath Assembly of God, Free Seventh-day Adventist Church, Seventh Day Sabbatarian Mennonites, Seventh-day Adventist Reform Movement, the Seventh-day Adventist Church, Truth on The Web Ministries etc. There are many different Seventh Day Baptist Church branches as well as "Church of God" branches.

The author of the website The Ten Commandments issues the following statement and warning:

> The Seventh-day Adventist Church understands Bible prophecy better than any of the other churches I have investigated, and they are attacked by people more fiercely then you can ever imagine. I have not been able to substantiate any of the rumors or attacks on this church and they seem to be deliberate attacks inspired by Satan himself because they prove to be a huge threat to him. I often found the Christian web sites attacking it to be ex-Adventists that did not understand something so decided to turn on the whole Church instead and condemn it.
>
> Warning: The most accurate of these Churches is the one that has the most criticisms and attacks coming against it. Never underestimate the ability of the enemy to make a Church with the most Biblical truth and the best understanding on Bible Prophecy to be labeled falsely as a cult. It should be obvious to us that Satan will attack truth the hardest and has no trouble finding those he can deceive to accomplish his

task very convincingly. To find the most Biblically accurate Church, you will need to personally do your own research and not just read web sites. The exception to this would be reading the web site that belongs to the Church you have in question to find out what they believe and compare that against the Word of God. Even this can be challenging as some of the things that you may assume to be wrong may in fact be right.... If you see nothing else here, please note the following:

What is truth is not always popular and what is popular is not always truth. The Church with the most truth will more often than not be the Church with the most people and web sites attacking it.

It is interesting to note that the biggest and most Biblically inaccurate Church, which is none other than mystery Babylon (Revelation 17) and a woman riding a beast (a woman in prophecy is a Church) that has the blood of millions of Christian saints on her hands has almost nothing coming against it. Why is this so? Satan attacks the Church with the most truth with the equivalent fire power of Hydrogen bombs and almost all Christians just believe these attacks like they are Gospel truth without researching to find out if they are lies. On the other hand, Satan does not attack this Church mystery Babylon at all that is guilty of so much heresy and crimes against God's people that God is going to destroy it with plagues at the time of the Battle of Armageddon. This Church is none other than the Church that changed God's Sabbath to Sunday in favour of Sun worship. You will find that any Sabbath keeping denomination of any significant size will have Satan coming against it. It is important to Satan that he keeps Christians deceived on the truth about the Sabbath especially. ("Sabbath Observing Denominations—Sabbath Churches," The Ten Commandments, http://1ref.us/4t)

Chapter 17
Filtering a Long, Long List

As you can see, there are many organizations within Catholicism and Protestantism. If a person is serious about being a Christian and about finding the church that is closest to Scripture, he or she could spend a lifetime checking out the many different beliefs of the 4200 different organizations—or they can fast track the search by a simplified method I offer below.

First of all, to be a Christian, you have to believe what the Bible teaches and then practice its teachings. Keep the list of basic Christian beliefs found in chapter 16 in mind. All of these beliefs are based on texts found in the Bible and are a good place to start. Check out each topic and look up the Bible texts to see if the statement of belief lines up with the Bible. Here is the first one: "There is only one God" (Isaiah 43:10; 44:6, 8; John 17:3; 1 Corinthians 8:5, 6; Galatians 4:8, 9).

"Ye are my witnesses, saith the LORD, and my servant whom I have chosen: that ye may know and believe me, and understand that I am he: before me there was no God formed, neither shall there be after me" (Isaiah 43:10).

Do these texts support the idea of "only one God"? Yes they do. What about the others?

"Thus saith the LORD the King of Israel, and his redeemer the Lord of hosts; I am the first, and I am the last; and beside me there is no God" (Isaiah 44:6).

"Fear ye not, neither be afraid: have not I told thee from that time, and have declared it? Ye are even my witnesses. Is there a God beside me? Yea, there is no God; I know not any" (Isaiah 44:8).

"And this is life eternal, that they might know thee the only true God, and Jesus Christ, whom thou hast sent" (John 17:3).

"For though there be that are called gods, whether in heaven or in earth, (as there be gods many, and lords many,) But to us there is but one God, the Father, of whom are all things, and we in him; and one Lord Jesus Christ, by whom are all things, and we by him" (1 Corinthians 8:5, 6).

"Howbeit then, when ye knew not God, ye did service unto them which by nature are no gods. But now, after that ye have known God, or rather are known of God, how turn ye again to the weak and beggarly elements, whereunto ye desire again to be in bondage" (Galatians 4:8, 9).

Do all these texts support the belief of "only one God?" Yes, they do.

If a person compares all of the doctrines found in the list of common beliefs and agrees with the majority of them, then he or she will be ready for the next step, which is to determine whether the doctrines of different Christian church organizations are based on the Bible only or are the Bible mixed with tradition.

A person may not agree with all the beliefs of all the churches, but they should agree with most of them because you will have to make sure that the common beliefs, which are from the Bible, have been interpreted correctly. Now a person may think this requires much effort, which it does, but is this too much to ask when we are talking about the salvation of our soul and eternal life with Jesus Christ our Savior?

Let us separate the churches listed in the preceding chapters, which claim to base their beliefs on the Bible, from those which use tradition as the basis of their beliefs. We will consider the churches in the same order as listed before. First are the "Catholic" Churches, which number sixty-three different organizations and have somewhat common beliefs. They with others claim to be "Apostolic," which means: "A line of succession from Jesus Christ through the apostles." Their claim is through Simon Peter, whom they believe to have received the "keys of heaven" from Jesus Christ (Matthew 16:18, 19), and they believe that Peter was the first pope.

Was Peter the First Pope?

History and Scripture counter this belief. Christ commission to Peter is often very embarrassing to Catholics because Christ commissioned Peter to become the chief minister of the gospel to *the circumcised Jews*, not to the uncircumcised Gentiles. Paul wrote: "For He that wrought effectually in Peter to the apostleship of the circumcision, the same was mighty in me toward the Gentiles" (Galatians 2:8). Besides this, there is no mention throughout the book of Acts of the apostle Peter ever being in Rome, though tradition does assert that Peter was executed in Rome by crucifixion upside-down. The tradition claims to be supported by Jesus' prediction: "Verily, verily, I say unto thee, When thou wast young, thou girdedst thyself, and walkedst whither thou wouldest: but when thou shalt be old, thou shalt stretch forth thy hands, and another shall gird thee, and carry thee whither thou wouldest not" (John 21:18).

Countering the Catholic claim of Peter's supremacy over the church, is speaker at the Vatican Council of 1870 Catholic Bishop Joseph Strossmeyer:

> Therefore, to resume, I establish: (1) that Jesus has given to His apostles the same power that He gave to St. Peter. (2) That the apostles never recognized in St. Peter the vicar of Jesus Christ and the infallible doctor of the Church. (3) That St. Peter never thought of being pope, and never acted as if he were pope ... I conclude victoriously, with history, with reason, with logic, with good sense, and with a Christian conscience, that Jesus Christ did not confer any supremacy on St. Peter and that the bishops of Rome did not become sovereigns of the church, but only by confiscating one by one all the rights of the episcopate. (Schroeder, *Heresies of Catholicism... The Apostate Church*, p. 80)

Another Day of Worship

Another discrepancy between the Catholic Church and the Bible is in the day of worship. The Catholic Church has identified herself as having changed the day of worship from the seventh-day Sabbath to the first-day Sunday. Thus, every Christian organization that keeps the first day Sunday instead of the Sabbath is not following the teachings of Christ, but rather a tradition of an organization that has substituted its teachings for Christ's.

Orthodox churches make similar claims to those of the Roman Catholic Church. They claim to be the true apostolic church with lineage back to the Day of Pentecost and believe that the bishops of Byzantium date back to the apostle Andrew. They also make the traditional claim: "Every Sunday is especially dedicated to celebrating the Resurrection and the triune God, representing a mini-Pascha [Easter celebration] …" ("Eastern Orthodox Church," Wikipedia, http://1ref.us/4v). Since the Roman Catholic Church clearly claims to have changed the Sabbath to Sunday, it must be that the Orthodox churches are following the Roman Catholic Church, just as all other Sunday-keeping churches are.

When looking at the Protestant churches, there has to be a separation between those who worship on Sunday, the first day of the week, and those who worship on the Sabbath, the seventh day. Since all Sunday-keeping churches follow tradition and the Roman Catholic Church in this regard, they must be stricken from the list. They are not following the Bible and the Bible only, despite claims to the contrary. To find a church that follows the Bible and the Bible only, we can look no further than among the seventh-day Sabbath-keeping churches. Many Internet sources do not like the word "denomination" and eschew formal organization in a denominated group. They claim that the true church will only be made up of people in small groups. Since many of these are Sabbath keeping people, we need to include them with the seventh-day Sabbath-keeping denominations.

Again, we need to look at all of the teachings of the Bible. Just because a church keeps one Bible truth does not mean that it follows all Bible truth. So, how do we separate the true from the false? Again, it is by looking at the requirements of God's Word. We started our search with a list of Christian beliefs that most Protestant churches profess to believe, so let us take one Sabbath-keeping church at a time and compare it with that list.

The beliefs of the more prominent Sabbath-keeping churches listed in chapter 16 are available on the Internet for comparison with the Bible. Since there is not enough space in this book to include every Sabbath-keeping church, I will start with the oldest of the Sabbath-keeping denominations—the Seventh Day Baptists. Their statement of beliefs declares:

I. God

We believe in one God, infinite and perfect, the Creator and Sustainer of the universe who exists eternally in three persons—Father, Son, and Holy Spirit—and desires to share His love in a personal relationship with everyone.

1 Timothy 1:17; Deuteronomy 6:4; 1 Kings 8:27; 1 John 1:5; Genesis 1:1–2; Acts 17:24–25, 28; Psalm 90:1–2; Matthew 28:19; John 3:16; Isaiah 57:15; 2 Peter 3:9.

The Father

We believe in God the Father, who is sovereign over all, and is loving and just as He forgives the repentant and condemns the unrepentant.

1 Corinthians 8:6; Ephesians 4:6; Ezekiel 33:11; 2 Thessalonians 1:6-8; John 5:24; John 3:16–18.

The Son

We believe in God the Son, who became incarnate in Jesus Christ, our Lord and Savior. He gave Himself on the cross as the complete and final sacrifice for sin. As our Risen Lord, He is the mediator between God the Father and mankind.

John 1:34; Hebrews 1:3; John 1:14–18; Romans 1:3–4; 1 John 3:16; 1 Peter 2:24; Hebrews 10:10–14; 1 Corinthians 15:20–21; 1 Timothy 2:5; John 14:6; 1 John 2:1–2.

The Holy Spirit

We believe in God the Holy Spirit, the Comforter, who gives spiritual birth to believers lives within them, and empowers them for witnessing and service. We believe the Holy Spirit inspired the Scriptures, convicts of sin and instructs in righteousness.

John 14:16; 3:5–8; 14:17; Romans 5:5; 1 Corinthians 12:4–7; 2 Peter 1:20–21; John 16:7–11.

II. The Bible

We believe that the Bible is the inspired Word of God and is our final authority in matters of faith and practice. We believe that Jesus Christ, in His life and teachings as recorded in the Bible, is the supreme interpreter of God's will for mankind.

2 Peter 1:20–21; Romans 3:2; 2 Peter 3:1–2, 15–16; 2 Timothy 3:14–17; Matthew 5:17–19; Psalm 119:105; John 20:30–31; Hebrews 1:1–2.

III. Mankind

We believe that mankind was created in the image of God and is therefore the noblest work of creation. We believe that human beings have moral responsibility and are created to enjoy both divine and human fellowship as children of God.

Genesis 1:26–27; Psalm 8:3–9; Micah 6:8; Matthew 5:44–48; 1 John 1:3; John 1:12.

IV. Sin and Salvation

We believe that sin is disobedience to God and failure to live according to His will. Because of sin all people have separated themselves from God. We believe that because we are sinners, we are in need of a Savior.

We believe that salvation from sin and death is the gift of God by redeeming love accomplished by Christ's death and resurrection, and is received only by repentance and faith in Him. We believe that all who repent of their sin and receive Christ as Savior will not be punished at the final judgment but enjoy eternal life.

1 John 3:4–5; Romans 3:23-25; Isaiah 59:2; 1 John 1:8-10; Romans 5:6-8; Romans 6:23; Hebrews 10:10-14; 1 Peter 1:3; John 3:16-18, 36; Ephesians 2:8-9; John 14:6; Matthew 25:41-46; Romans 5:10.

V. Eternal Life

We believe that Jesus rose from the dead and lives eternally with the Father, and that He will come again with power and great glory. We believe that eternal life begins in knowing God through a commitment to Jesus Christ. We believe that because He died and lives again, resurrection with spiritual and imperishable bodies is the gift of God to believers.

1 Corinthians 15:3-4, 20-23; John 14:1-3; Matthew 24:30; Titus 2:13; John 17:3; 1 John 5:11-13; 1 Corinthians 15:42-44; John 10:27-28; John 6:40.

VI. The Church

We believe that the church of God is all believers gathered by the Holy Spirit and joined into one body, of which Christ is the Head. We believe that the local church is a community of believers organized in covenant relationship for worship, fellowship and service, practicing and proclaiming common convictions, while growing in grace and in the knowledge of our Lord and Savior Jesus Christ.

We believe in the priesthood of all believers and practice the autonomy of the local congregation, as we seek to work in association with others for more effective witness.

Acts 20:28; 1 Corinthians 12:13, 14, 27; Romans 12:4-5; Colossians 1:18; Acts 2:42; Ephesians 2:19-22; Romans 15:5-7; Ephesians 4:11-16; 2 Peter 3:18; 1 Peter 2:4-10; Matthew 18:20; Hebrews 10:24-25.

VII. Baptism

We believe that baptism of believers in obedience to Christ's command is a witness to the acceptance of Jesus Christ as Savior and Lord. We believe in baptism by immersion as a symbol of death to sin, and a pledge to a new life in Him.

Romans 6:3–4; Matthew 28:19–20; Acts 2:41; Colossians 2:12; Romans 6:11; Galatians 3:26–27.

VIII. The Lord's Supper

We believe that the Lord's Supper commemorates the suffering and death of our Redeemer until He comes, and is a symbol of union in Christ and a pledge of renewed allegiance to our risen Lord.

Mark 14:22–25; Matthew 26:26–29; 1 Corinthians 10:16–17, 11:23–30.

IX. Sabbath

We believe that the Sabbath of the Bible, the seventh day of the week, is sacred time, a gift of God to all people, instituted at creation, affirmed in the Ten Commandments and reaffirmed in the teaching and example of Jesus and the apostles.

We believe that the gift of Sabbath rest is an experience of God's eternal presence with His people.

We believe that in obedience to God and in loving response to His grace in Christ, the Sabbath should be faithfully observed as a day of rest, worship, and celebration.

Genesis 2:2–3; Exodus 16:23–30; Exodus 20:8–11; Matthew 5:17–19; Mark 2:27–28; Luke 4:16; Acts 13:14, 42–44; 16:11–13; 17:2–3; 18:4–11; Ezekiel 20:19–20; Hebrews 4:9–10; John 14:15; Isaiah 58:13–14; Luke 23:56.

X. Evangelism

We believe that Jesus Christ commissions us to proclaim the Gospel, to make disciples, to baptize and to teach observance of all that He has commanded. We are called to be witnesses for Christ throughout the world and in all human relationships.

Matthew 24:14; Acts 1:8; Matthew 28:18–20; 2 Corinthians 4:1–2, 5–6; 1 Peter 3:15; 2 Corinthians 5:17–20; Ephesians 6:14–20. ("Seventh Day Baptists," Wikipedia, http://1ref.us/4w)

These are the ten beliefs of the Seventh Day Baptist Church, as listed in the Wikipedia article "The Seventh Day Baptists." If we compare these ten beliefs with the list of thirty-seven common beliefs of Christians, we find certain differences. In the list of thirty-seven common beliefs, there is no statement regarding the day that should be used for worshipping God, which by now people should know without doubt. Yet, that day is part of the Seventh Day Baptists beliefs, as is baptism by immersion, which is a symbol of death to sin and a pledge to a new life through Jesus.

Are any of these beliefs not covered by Bible truth? Not as listed. However, another website reveals: "Seventh Day Baptists in general believe that, upon death, the body 'falls asleep' (figuratively), but the spirits of the righteous go to be with Christ in the Father's presence, and are not unconscious there. They believe that the redeemed will be given spiritual and glorified bodies at the resurrection" ("A Comparison of Seventh Day Baptists with Seventh-day Adventists," Seattle Area Seventh Day Baptist Church, http://1ref.us/4x). Thus, death is not a conscious state. You may have noticed that this subject has not been addressed in any set of Christian beliefs thus far. A person really needs to find out exactly what a church's belief is on that subject and whether it is supported in the Bible before joining.

The next church listed in chapter 16 was the Seventh-day Adventist Church. We can find their twenty-eight fundamental beliefs listed on the Internet as follows:

Seventh-day Adventists accept the Bible as their only creed and hold certain fundamental beliefs to be the teaching of the Holy Scriptures. These beliefs, as set forth here, constitute the church's understanding and expression of the teaching of Scripture.

1. Holy Scriptures:

The Holy Scriptures, Old and New Testaments, are the written Word of God, given by divine inspiration through holy men of God who spoke and wrote as they were moved by the Holy Spirit. In this Word, God has committed to man the knowledge necessary for salvation. The Holy Scriptures are the infallible revelation of His will. They are the standard of character, the test of experience, the authoritative revealer of doctrines, and the trustworthy record of God's acts in history. (2 Peter 1:20, 21; 2 Timothy 3:16, 17; Psalms 119:105; Proverbs 30:5, 6; Isaiah 8:20; John 17:17; 1 Thessalonians 2:13; Hebrews 4:12.)

2. Trinity:

There is one God: Father, Son, and Holy Spirit, a unity of three co-eternal Persons. God is immortal, all-powerful, all-knowing, above all, and ever present. He is infinite and beyond human comprehension, yet known through His self-revelation. He is forever worthy of worship, adoration, and service by the whole creation. (Deuteronomy 6:4; Matthew 28:19; 2 Corinthians 13:14; Ephesians 4:4-6; 1 Peter 1:2; 1 Timothy 1:17; Revelation 14:7.)

3. Father:

God the eternal Father is the Creator, Source, Sustainer, and Sovereign of all creation. He is just and holy, merciful and gracious, slow to anger, and abounding in steadfast love and faithfulness. The qualities and powers exhibited in the Son and the Holy Spirit are also revelations of the Father. (Genesis 1:1; Revelation 4:11; 1 Corinthians 15:28; John 3:16; 1 John 4:8; 1 Timothy 1:17; Exodus 34:6, 7; John 14:9.)

4. Son:

God the eternal Son became incarnate in Jesus Christ. Through Him all things were created, the character of God is revealed, the salvation of humanity is accomplished, and the world is judged. Forever truly God, He became also truly man, Jesus the Christ. He was conceived of the Holy Spirit and born of the virgin Mary. He lived and experienced temptation as a human being, but perfectly exemplified the righteousness and love of God. By His miracles He manifested God's power and was attested as God's promised Messiah. He suffered and died voluntarily on the cross for our sins and in our place, was raised from the dead, and ascended to minister in the heavenly sanctuary in our behalf. He will come again in glory for the final deliverance of His people and the restoration of all things. (John 1:1-3, 14; Colossians 1:15-19; John 10:30; 14:9; Romans 6:23; 2 Corinthians 5:17-19; John 5:22; Luke 1:35; Philippians 2:5-11; Hebrews 2:9-18; 1 Corinthians 15:3, 4; Hebrews 8:1, 2; John 14:1-3.)

5. Holy Spirit:

God the eternal Spirit was active with the Father and the Son in Creation, incarnation, and redemption. He inspired the writers of Scripture. He filled Christ's life with power. He draws and convicts human beings; and those who respond He renews and transforms into the image of God. Sent by the Father and the Son to be always with His children, He extends spiritual gifts to the church, empowers it to bear witness to Christ, and in harmony with the Scriptures leads it into all truth. (Genesis 1:1, 2; Luke 1:35; 4:18; Acts 10:38; 2 Peter 1:21; 2 Corinthians 3:18; Ephesians 4:11, 12; Acts 1:8; John 14:16–18, 26; 15:26, 27; 16:7–13.)

6. Creation:

God is Creator of all things, and has revealed in Scripture the authentic account of His creative activity. In six days the Lord made "the heaven and the earth" and all living things upon the earth, and rested on the seventh day of that first week. Thus He established the Sabbath as a perpetual memorial of His completed creative work. The first man and woman were made in the image of God as the crowning work of Creation, given dominion over the world, and charged with responsibility to care for it. When the world was finished it was "very good," declaring the glory of God. (Genesis 1; 2; Exodus 20:8–11; Psalms 19:1–6; 33:6, 9; 104; Hebrews 11:3.)

7. Nature of Man:

Man and woman were made in the image of God with individuality, the power and freedom to think and to do. Though created free beings, each is an indivisible unity of body, mind, and spirit, dependent upon God for life and breath and all else. When our first parents disobeyed God, they denied their dependence upon Him and fell from their high position under God. The image of God in them was marred and they became subject to death. Their descendants share this fallen nature and its consequences. They are born with weaknesses and tendencies to evil. But God in Christ reconciled the world to Himself and by His Spirit restores in penitent mortals the image of their Maker. Created for the glory of God, they are called to love Him and one another, and to care for their environment. (Genesis 1:26–28; 2:7; Psalms 8:4–8; Acts 17:24–28; Genesis 3; Psalms 51:5; Romans 5:12–17; 2 Corinthians 5:19, 20; Psalms 51:10; 1 John 4:7, 8, 11, 20; Genesis 2:15.)

8. Great Controversy:

All humanity is now involved in a great controversy between Christ and Satan regarding the character of God, His law, and His sovereignty over the universe. This conflict originated in heaven when a created being, endowed with freedom of choice, in self-exaltation became Satan, God's adversary, and led into rebellion a portion of the angels. He introduced the spirit of rebellion into this world when he led Adam and Eve into sin. This human sin resulted in the distortion of the image of God in humanity, the disordering of the created world, and its eventual devastation at the time of the worldwide flood. Observed by the whole creation, this world became the arena of the universal conflict, out of which the God of love will ultimately be vindicated. To assist His people in this controversy, Christ sends the Holy Spirit and the loyal angels to guide, protect, and sustain them in the way of salvation. (Revelation 12:4–9; Isaiah 14:12–14; Ezekiel 28:12–18; Genesis 3; Romans 1:19–32; 5:12–21; 8:19–22; Genesis 6–8; 2 Peter 3:6; 1 Corinthians 4:9; Hebrews 1:14.)

9. Life, Death, and Resurrection of Christ:

In Christ's life of perfect obedience to God's will, His suffering, death, and resurrection, God provided the only means of atonement for human sin, so that those who by faith accept this atonement may have eternal life, and the whole creation may better understand the infinite and holy love of the Creator. This perfect atonement vindicates the righteousness of God's law and the graciousness of His character; for it both condemns our sin and provides for our forgiveness. The death of Christ is substitutionary and expiatory, reconciling and transforming. The resurrection of Christ proclaims God's triumph over the forces of evil, and for those who accept the atonement assures their final victory over sin and death. It declares the Lordship of Jesus Christ, before whom every knee in heaven and on earth will bow. (John 3:16; Isaiah 53; 1 Peter 2:21, 22; 1 Corinthians 5:3, 4, 20–22; 2 Corinthians 5:14, 15, 19–21; Romans 1:4; 3:25; 4:25; 8:3, 4; 1 John 2:2; 4:10; Colossians 2:15; Philippians 2:6–11.)

10. Experience of Salvation:

In infinite love and mercy God made Christ, who knew no sin, to be sin for us, so that in Him we might be made the righteousness of God. Led by the Holy Spirit we sense our need, acknowledge our sinfulness, repent of our transgressions, and exercise faith in Jesus as Lord and Christ, as Substitute and Example. This faith which receives salvation comes through the divine power of the Word and is the gift of God's grace. Through Christ we are justified, adopted as God's sons and daughters, and delivered from the lordship of sin. Through the Spirit we are born again and sanctified; the Spirit renews our minds, writes God's law of love in our hearts, and we are given the power to live a holy life. Abiding in Him we become partakers of the divine nature and have the assurance of salvation now and in the judgment. (2 Corinthians 5:17–21; John 3:16; Galatians 1:4; 4:4–7; Titus 3:3–7; John 16:8; Galatians 3:13, 14; 1 Peter 2:21, 22; Romans 10:17; Luke 17:5; Mark 9:23, 24; Ephesians 2:5–10; Romans 3:21–26; Colossians 1:13, 14; Romans 8:14–17; Galatians 3:26; John 3:3–8; 1 Peter 1:23; Romans 12:2; Hebrews 8:7–12; Ezekiel 36:25–27; 2 Peter 1:3, 4; Romans 8:1–4; 5:6–10.)

11. Growing in Christ:

By His death on the cross Jesus triumphed over the forces of evil. He who subjugated the demonic spirits during His earthly ministry has broken their power and made certain their ultimate doom. Jesus' victory gives us victory over the evil forces that still seek to control us, as we walk with Him in peace, joy, and assurance of His love. Now the Holy Spirit dwells within us and empowers us. Continually committed to Jesus as our Saviour and Lord, we are set free from the burden of our past deeds. No longer do we live in the darkness, fear of evil powers, ignorance, and meaninglessness of our former way of life. In this new freedom in Jesus, we are called to grow into the likeness of His character, communing with Him daily in prayer, feeding on His Word, meditating on it and on His providence, singing His praises, gathering together for worship, and participating in the mission of the Church. As we give ourselves in loving service to those around us and in witnessing to His salvation, His constant presence with us through the Spirit transforms every moment and every task into a spiritual experience. (Psalms 1:1, 2; 23:4; 77:11, 12; Colossians 1:13, 14; 2:6, 14, 15; Luke 10:17–20; Ephesians 5:19, 20; 6:12–18; 1 Thessalonians 5:23; 2 Peter 2:9; 3:18; 2 Corinthians 3:17, 18; Philippians 3:7–14; 1 Thessalonians 5:16–18; Matthew 20:25–28; John 20:21; Galatians 5:22–25; Romans 8:38, 39; 1 John 4:4; Hebrews 10:25.)

12. Church:

The church is the community of believers who confess Jesus Christ as Lord and Saviour. In continuity with the people of God in Old Testament times, we are called out from the world; and we join together for worship, for fellowship, for instruction in the Word, for the celebration of the Lord's Supper, for service to all mankind, and for the worldwide proclamation of the gospel. The church derives its authority from Christ, who is the incarnate Word, and from the Scriptures, which are the written Word. The church is God's family; adopted by Him as children, its members live on the basis of the new covenant. The church is the body of Christ, a community of faith of which Christ Himself is the Head. The church is the bride for whom Christ died that He might sanctify and cleanse her. At His return in triumph, He will present her to Himself a glorious church, the faithful of all the ages, the purchase of His blood, not having spot or wrinkle, but holy and without blemish. (Genesis 12:3; Acts 7:38; Ephesians 4:11–15; 3:8–11; Matthew 28:19, 20; 16:13–20; 18:18; Ephesians 2:19–22; 1:22, 23; 5:23–27; Colossians 1:17, 18.)

13. Remnant and Its Mission:

The universal church is composed of all who truly believe in Christ, but in the last days, a time of widespread apostasy, a remnant has been called out to keep the commandments of God and the faith of Jesus. This remnant announces the arrival of the judgment hour, proclaims salvation through Christ, and heralds the approach of His second advent. This proclamation is symbolized by the three angels of Revelation 14; it coincides with the work of judgment in heaven and results in a work of repentance and reform on earth. Every believer is called to have a personal part in this worldwide witness. (Revelation 12:17; 14:6–12; 18:1–4; 2 Corinthians 5:10; Jude 3, 14; 1 Peter 1:16–19; 2 Peter 3:10–14; Revelation 21:1–14.)

14. Unity in the Body of Christ:

The church is one body with many members, called from every nation, kindred, tongue, and people. In Christ we are a new creation; distinctions of race, culture, learning, and nationality, and differences between high and low, rich and poor, male and female, must not be divisive among us. We are all equal in Christ, who by one Spirit has bonded us into one fellowship with Him and with one another; we are to serve and be served without partiality or reservation. Through the revelation of Jesus Christ in the Scriptures we share the same faith and hope, and reach out in one witness to all. This unity has its source in the oneness of the triune God, who has adopted us as His children. (Romans 12:4, 5; 1 Corinthians 12:12–14; Matthew 28:19, 20; Psalms 133:1; 2 Corinthians 5:16, 17; Acts 17:26, 27; Galatians 3:27, 29; Colossians 3:10–15; Ephesians 4:14–16; 4:1–6; John 17:20–23.)

15. Baptism:

By baptism we confess our faith in the death and resurrection of Jesus Christ, and testify of our death to sin and of our purpose to walk in newness of life. Thus we acknowledge Christ as Lord and Saviour, become His people, and are received as members by His church. Baptism is a symbol of our union with Christ, the forgiveness of our sins, and our reception of the Holy Spirit. It is by immersion in water and is contingent on an affirmation of faith in Jesus and evidence of repentance of sin. It follows instruction in the Holy Scriptures and acceptance of their teachings. (Romans 6:1–6; Colossians 2:12, 13; Acts 16:30–33; 22:16; 2:38; Matthew 28:19, 20.)

16. Lord's Supper:

The Lord's Supper is a participation in the emblems of the body and blood of Jesus as an expression of faith in Him, our Lord and Saviour. In this experience of communion Christ is present to meet and strengthen His people. As we partake, we joyfully proclaim the Lord's death until He comes again. Preparation for the Supper includes self-examination, repentance, and confession. The Master ordained the service of foot washing to signify renewed cleansing, to express a willingness to serve one another in Christlike humility, and to unite our hearts in love. The communion service is open to all believing Christians. (1 Corinthians 10:16, 17; 11:23–30; Matthew 26:17–30; Revelation 3:20; John 6:48–63; 13:1–17.)

17. Spiritual Gifts and Ministries:

God bestows upon all members of His church in every age spiritual gifts which each member is to employ in loving ministry for the common good of the church and of humanity. Given by the agency of the Holy Spirit, who apportions to each member as He wills, the gifts provide all abilities and ministries needed by the church to fulfill its divinely ordained functions. According to the Scriptures, these gifts include such ministries as faith, healing, prophecy, proclamation, teaching, administration, reconciliation, compassion, and self-sacrificing service and charity for the help and encouragement of people. Some members are called of God and endowed by the Spirit for functions recognized by the church in pastoral, evangelistic, apostolic, and teaching ministries particularly needed to equip the members for service, to build up the church to spiritual maturity, and to foster unity of the faith and knowledge of God. When members employ these spiritual gifts as faithful stewards of God's varied grace, the church is protected from the destructive influence of false doctrine, grows with a growth that is from God, and is built up in faith and love. (Romans 12:4–8; 1 Corinthians 12:9–11, 27, 28; Ephesians 4:8, 11–16; Acts 6:1–7; 1 Timothy 3:1–13; 1 Peter 4:10, 11.)

18. The Gift of Prophecy:

One of the gifts of the Holy Spirit is prophecy. This gift is an identifying mark of the remnant church and was manifested in the ministry of Ellen G. White. As the Lord's messenger, her writings are a continuing and authoritative source of truth which provide for the church comfort, guidance, instruction, and correction. They also make clear that the Bible is the standard by which all teaching and experience must be tested. (Joel 2:28, 29; Acts 2:14–21; Hebrews 1:1–3; Revelation 12:17; 19:10.)

19. Law of God:

The great principles of God's law are embodied in the Ten Commandments and exemplified in the life of Christ. They express God's love, will, and purposes concerning human conduct and relationships and are binding upon all people in every age. These precepts are the basis of God's covenant with His people and the standard in God's judgment. Through the agency of the Holy Spirit they point out sin and awaken a sense of need for a Saviour. Salvation is all of grace and not of works, but its fruitage is obedience to the Commandments. This obedience develops Christian character and results in a sense of well-being. It is an evidence of our love for the Lord and our concern for our fellow men. The obedience of faith demonstrates the power of Christ to transform lives, and therefore strengthens Christian witness. (Exodus 20:1–17; Psalms 40:7, 8; Matthew 22:36–40; Deuteronomy 28:1–14; Matthew 5:17–20; Hebrews 8:8–10; John 15:7–10; Ephesians 2:8–10; 1 John 5:3; Romans 8:3, 4; Psalms 19:7–14.)

20. Sabbath:

The beneficent Creator, after the six days of Creation, rested on the seventh day and instituted the Sabbath for all people as a memorial of Creation. The fourth commandment of God's unchangeable law requires the observance of this seventh-day Sabbath as the day of rest, worship, and ministry in harmony with the teaching and practice of

Jesus, the Lord of the Sabbath. The Sabbath is a day of delightful communion with God and one another. It is a symbol of our redemption in Christ, a sign of our sanctification, a token of our allegiance, and a foretaste of our eternal future in God's kingdom. The Sabbath is God's perpetual sign of His eternal covenant between Him and His people. Joyful observance of this holy time from evening to evening, sunset to sunset, is a celebration of God's creative and redemptive acts. (Genesis 2:1-3; Exodus 20:8-11; Luke 4:16; Isaiah 56:5, 6; 58:13, 14; Matthew 12:1-12; Exodus 31:13-17; Ezekiel 20:12, 20; Deuteronomy 5:12-15; Hebrews 4:1-11; Leviticus 23:32; Mark 1:32.)

21. Stewardship:

We are God's stewards, entrusted by Him with time and opportunities, abilities and possessions, and the blessings of the earth and its resources. We are responsible to Him for their proper use. We acknowledge God's ownership by faithful service to Him and our fellow men, and by returning tithes and giving offerings for the proclamation of His gospel and the support and growth of His church. Stewardship is a privilege given to us by God for nurture in love and the victory over selfishness and covetousness. The steward rejoices in the blessings that come to others as a result of his faithfulness. (Genesis 1:26-28; 2:15; 1 Chronicles 29:14; Haggai 1:3-11; Malachi 3:8-12; 1 Corinthians 9:9-14; Matthew 23:23; 2 Corinthians 8:1-15; Romans 15:26, 27.)

22. Christian Behavior:

We are called to be a godly people who think, feel, and act in harmony with the principles of heaven. For the Spirit to recreate in us the character of our Lord we involve ourselves only in those things which will produce Christlike purity, health, and joy in our lives. This means that our amusement and entertainment should meet the highest standards of Christian taste and beauty. While recognizing cultural differences, our dress is to be simple, modest, and neat, befitting those whose true beauty does not consist of outward adornment but in the imperishable ornament of a gentle and quiet spirit. It also means that because our bodies are the temples of the Holy Spirit, we are to care for them intelligently. Along with adequate exercise and rest, we are to adopt the most healthful diet possible and abstain from the unclean foods identified in the Scriptures. Since alcoholic beverages, tobacco, and the irresponsible use of drugs and narcotics are harmful to our bodies, we are to abstain from them as well. Instead, we are to engage in whatever brings our thoughts and bodies into the discipline of Christ, who desires our wholesomeness, joy, and goodness. (Romans 12:1, 2; 1 John 2:6; Ephesians 5:1-21; Philippians 4:8; 2 Corinthians 10:5; 6:14-7:1; 1 Peter 3:1-4; 1 Corinthians 6:19, 20; 10:31; Leviticus 11:1-47; 3 John 2.)

23. Marriage and the Family:

Marriage was divinely established in Eden and affirmed by Jesus to be a lifelong union between a man and a woman in loving companionship. For the Christian a marriage commitment is to God as well as to the spouse, and should be entered into only between partners who share a common faith. Mutual love, honor, respect, and responsibility are the fabric of this relationship, which is to reflect the love, sanctity, closeness, and permanence of the relationship between Christ and His church. Regarding divorce, Jesus taught that the person who divorces a spouse, except for fornication, and marries another, commits adultery. Although some family relationships may fall short of the ideal, marriage partners who fully commit themselves to each other in Christ may achieve loving unity through the guidance of the Spirit and the nurture of the church. God blesses the family and intends that its members shall assist each other toward complete maturity. Parents are to bring up their children to love and obey the Lord. By their example and their words they are to teach them that Christ is a loving disciplinarian, ever tender and caring, who wants them to become members of His body, the family of God. Increasing family closeness is one of the earmarks of the final gospel message. (Genesis 2:18–25; Matthew 19:3–9; John 2:1–11; 2 Corinthians 6:14; Ephesians 5:21–33; Matthew 5:31, 32; Mark 10:11, 12; Luke 16:18; 1 Corinthians 7:10, 11; Exodus 20:12; Ephesians 6:1–4; Deuteronomy 6:5–9; Proverbs 22:6; Malachi 4:5, 6.)

24. Christ's Ministry in the Heavenly Sanctuary:

There is a sanctuary in heaven, the true tabernacle which the Lord set up and not man. In it Christ ministers on our behalf, making available to believers the benefits of His atoning sacrifice offered once for all on the cross. He was inaugurated as our great High Priest and began His intercessory ministry at the time of His ascension. In 1844, at the end of the prophetic period of 2300 days, He entered the second and last phase of His atoning ministry. It is a work of investigative judgment which is part of the ultimate disposition of all sin, typified by the cleansing of the ancient Hebrew sanctuary on the Day of Atonement. In that typical service the sanctuary was cleansed with the blood of animal sacrifices, but the heavenly things are purified with the perfect sacrifice of the blood of Jesus. The investigative judgment reveals to heavenly intelligences who among the dead are asleep in Christ and therefore, in Him, are deemed worthy to have part in the first resurrection. It also makes manifest who among the living are abiding in Christ, keeping the commandments of God and the faith of Jesus, and in Him, therefore, are ready for translation into His everlasting kingdom. This judgment vindicates the justice of God in saving those who believe in Jesus. It declares that those who have remained loyal to God shall receive the kingdom. The completion of this ministry of Christ will mark the close of human probation before the Second Advent. (Hebrews 8:1–5; 4:14–16; 9:11–28; 10:19–22; 1:3; 2:16, 17; Daniel 7:9–27; 8:13, 14; 9:24–27; Numbers 14:34; Ezekiel 4:6; Leviticus 16; Revelation 14:6, 7; 20:12; 14:12; 22:12.)

25. Second Coming of Christ:

The second coming of Christ is the blessed hope of the church, the grand climax of the gospel. The Saviour's coming will be literal, personal, visible, and worldwide. When He returns, the righteous dead will be resurrected, and together with the righteous living will be glorified and taken to heaven, but the unrighteous will die. The almost complete fulfillment of most lines of prophecy, together with the present condition of the world, indicates that Christ's coming is imminent. The time of that event has not been revealed, and we are therefore exhorted to be ready at all times. (Titus 2:13; Hebrews 9:28; John 14:1–3; Acts 1:9-11; Matthew 24:14; Revelation 1:7; Matthew 24:43, 44; 1 Thessalonians 4:13–18; 1 Corinthians 15:51–54; 2 Thessalonians 1:7–10; 2:8; Revelation 14:14–20; 19:11–21; Matthew 24; Mark 13; Luke 21; 2 Timothy 3:1–5; 1 Thessalonians 5:1–6.)

26. Death and Resurrection:

The wages of sin is death. But God, who alone is immortal, will grant eternal life to His redeemed. Until that day death is an unconscious state for all people. When Christ, who is our life, appears, the resurrected righteous and the living righteous will be glorified and caught up to meet their Lord. The second resurrection, the resurrection of the unrighteous, will take place a thousand years later. (Romans 6:23; 1 Timothy 6:15, 16; Ecclesiastes 9:5, 6; Psalms 146:3, 4; John 11:11–14; Colossians 3:4; 1 Corinthians 5:51–54; 1 Thessalonians 4:13–17; John 5:28, 29; Revelation 20:1–10.)

27. Millennium and the End of Sin:

The millennium is the thousand-year reign of Christ with His saints in heaven between the first and second resurrections. During this time the wicked dead will be judged; the earth will be utterly desolate, without living human inhabitants, but occupied by Satan and his angels. At its close Christ with His saints and the Holy City will descend from heaven to earth. The unrighteous dead will then be resurrected, and with Satan and his angels will surround the city; but fire from God will consume them and cleanse the earth. The universe will thus be freed of sin and sinners forever. (Revelation 20; 1 Corinthians 6:2, 3; Jeremiah 4:23–26; Revelation 21:1–5; Malachi 4:1; Ezekiel 28:18, 19.)

28. New Earth:

On the new earth, in which righteousness dwells, God will provide an eternal home for the redeemed and a perfect environment for everlasting life, love, joy, and learning in His presence. For here God Himself will dwell with His people, and suffering and death will have passed away. The great controversy will be ended, and sin will be no more. All things, animate and inanimate, will declare that God is love; and He shall reign forever. Amen. (2 Peter 3:13; Isaiah 35; 65:17–25; Matthew 5:5; Revelation 21:1–7; 22:1–5; 11:15.) ("28 Fundamental Beliefs," Seventh-day Adventist Church, http://1ref.us/4y)

If we compare the list of Seventh-day Adventist beliefs with the general mainline Christian beliefs, what are the major differences? Several of the beliefs are merely combined rather than being listed individually, such as the qualities of God. One of the biggest differences is the view of the nature of hell. Some interpret Revelation 20:11–15 as pointing to an "eternal living hell." However, the Greek word translated "hell" (*hadēs*) is the equivalent of the word *sheol* in Hebrew, which simply means "the grave" (compare Psalm 16:10 with Acts 2:27 and Hosea 13:14 with 1 Corinthians 15:55). Everyone should know that there are no living people in the grave, so, without the resurrection, "hell" would mean eternal death. Revelation 20:13 says: "And the sea gave up the dead which were in it; and death and hell [the grave] delivered up the dead that were in them." Paul added: " … the dead shall be raised incorruptible" (1 Corinthians 15:52), and Jesus described the destruction of the wicked "at the end of the world" (Matthew 13:49). The most well-known verse of Scripture contrasts the reward of those who believe in Christ—everlasting life—with the reward of those who do not—they will perish. The Greek dictionary for *Strong's Exhaustive Concordance* shows that the Greek word behind "perish," *apollumi*, means "to destroy" or "to abolish." Thus, those who end up in hell will be utterly destroyed. This is a teaching reflected many places in Scripture (e.g. Malachi 4:3; Ezekiel 28:19; 2 Peter 2:12).

So far, the two churches that we have looked at do not seem to believe in an "eternal living hell." This is something that is from tradition and not from the Bible.

Another difference from the list of thirty-six common beliefs has to do with the word "rapture." The first text in the list used to support the rapture is Matthew 24:30–36. A careful reading of this passage reveals that it is talking about the second coming of Jesus. It declares: "the Son of man is coming in the clouds of heaven with power and great glory" and all the people who are alive, both the wicked and the redeemed, will see His coming. There is no secret rapture—every eye shall see Him.

The second passage, John 14:1–3, is Jesus' announcement about the place that He is preparing in heaven for the redeemed saints. He promises to return for His saints, but says nothing about it being a "secret rapture" or a two-phased return.

The third passage, 1 Corinthians 15:52, pictures the event when people will be transformed and taken away from the earth. It is pure imagination to impose upon this verse a secret rapture and a visible return, as people do, because it clearly points to one event, which occurs "at the last trump" when Jesus returns.

The fourth passage, 1 Thessalonians 4:16, 17, also clearly portrays the visible, audible, literal second coming of Jesus. It tells the order in which the saints will be taken up "to meet the Lord in the air"—the resurrected dead will rise first, then the saints who are alive will be next.

In the final supporting passage, 2 Thessalonians 2:1–12, the apostle Paul is describing the condition of the church prior to the second coming of Jesus and how the "man of sin," "whose coming is after the working of Satan," will be revealed. I have known preachers who refer to the second coming of Jesus as a "rapture" when all the saints are "caught up to meet the Lord in the air," however, the most common belief is that people will be snatched up individually, as certain popular books have indicated. Yet, there is no biblical backing for such a belief.

Now consider the next group of churches in the list—the Church of God and the United Church of God. "Church of God is a name used by numerous, mostly unrelated Christian denominational bodies, most of which descend from either Pentecostal/Holiness or Adventist traditions" ("Church of God," Wikipedia, http://1ref.us/4z). Wikipedia lists fifty-nine different organizations using the name "Church of God," as well as one listing for the "Mormons," who were once called the "Church of God" in their origination period.

The biggest difference among the various denomination that go by "Church of God" is that some believe in the Trinity while others do not, and some worship on Sunday while others worship on Saturday and seek to practice an adapted form of the Old Testament feasts days required of the nation of Israel.

> The Church of God, The Eternal is a remnant of the Worldwide Church of God still teaching the original doctrines first proclaimed by Mr. Herbert W. Armstrong. We accept these doctrines as the divine revelation of Jesus Christ to His Church of the last days, given through the inspiration of a chosen servant; teachings that were blessed by God, producing an annual growth of 30% over four decades, with incredible blessings in the lives of those who practiced the same in faith. ("Church of God, The Eternal." Church of God, The Eternal. http://1ref.us/50)

Though nice to have, the amount of a church's growth is not a matter of belief. A bigger question is Armstrong's British-Israelism and insistence on observance of feasts that are biblically tied to a temple in Jerusalem that no longer exists. The other major branch of the original Worldwide Church of God is non-trinitarian:

> The United Church of God, *an International Association* (UCGIA or simply UCG), is a religious denomination based in the United States, an offshoot of the Worldwide Church of God (WCG) founded by Herbert W. Armstrong. It is one of many Sabbatarian Churches of God to split from WCG.... After Armstrong's death in 1986, the subsequent WCG leadership introduced a series of major doctrinal changes starting in 1994, which substantially altered the fundamental beliefs and goals of the original WCG in the direction of historic Christian orthodoxy. A large segment of the membership wished to retain what they allege to be fundamental or first-century Christian teachings and consequently left WCG to start their own organizations UCG was established in May 1995 and is the largest of these offshoot organizations.... It identifies itself as Christian but denies some central teachings of historic Christianity, such as the Trinity (although it accepts and teaches the full divinity and pre-existence of Jesus Christ, and rejects all forms of Arianism), and the supersession of Old Testament law such as keeping the Seventh-day Sabbath. ("United Church of God," Wikipedia, http://1ref.uj106)

I personally do not see that these churches' beliefs agree with the entire Bible.

Chapter 18
A True Church

Is there a true church—one that is squarely founded on the Bible? We touched on this subject somewhat in chapter 17, when we recognized that many Protestant churches do not consider "The Church of Jesus Christ of Latter Day Saints," commonly known as "Mormons," as being a Protestant church because of their beliefs. Like most of the Sunday-keeping churches and their congregations, most Mormon believers do not understand what their church really adheres to in its basic beliefs. This is one of the ways the devil uses to deceive the whole world, as predicted in Revelation 12:9. Many modern Protestants consider the Mormon religion to be a cult. I will list some of their beliefs here and let the reader decide which category they should be placed in. There are many conscientious, good people within the Mormon church.

Christians believe the life, death and resurrection of Jesus, and the shedding of His blood paid the penalty for all the sins of those who accept His sacrifice. There is evidence that Mormons may still believe that some sins are so terrible that a person has to shed his or her own blood in order to be saved from that sin. The doctrine was known as "blood atonement."

I have also been told that Mormons believe that God is not capable of producing bodies to put His spirits in and that they must produce those bodies for Him. This accounts for the many children Mormons often have.

A Mormon once told me, "As God now is, we can become. As we now are, God once was." This sounds similar to what the devil said he would do: "I will ascend above the heights of the clouds; I will be like the most High" (Isaiah 14:14).

Mormons have told me they believe in the Bible, but when questioned about many beliefs they place *The Book of Mormon* above the Bible, claiming that the Bible was incorrectly translated and that *The Book of Mormon* gives the correct translation.

Mormons also worship on Sunday the first day of the week and by doing this they are following the Roman Catholic Church as are all other Sunday-keeping churches. (They will tell you that they do so because Joseph Smith had a revelation telling them to observe Sunday rather than the Sabbath.) We addressed this subject earlier. (To get a realistic view of the Mormon doctrine, get the book, *Mormonism, Momma and Me*, written by an author who was raised a devout Mormon.)

Now that we have looked at several different churches, denominations, and individual groups, I will make the statement that I have not found any one church who follows all the correct teachings of the Bible, and I am sure they will all disagree with me. However, can there be any one of them who can truthfully say that they follow the Bible and the Bible only?

Please note that I said that I did not find any church that I believe follows all the correct teachings of the Bible. This is because I do not believe that there is any church organization in which the whole church membership is going to make it to heaven. No church can assure its membership of salvation. Only Jesus can do that, when, as individuals, we accept His sacrifice. Why do I say this? It is because no Scripture says that the followers of Jesus Christ will be called by a certain name. People become followers of Jesus Christ by hearing the Word and then reading the Bible and receiving understanding through prayer and the guidance of the Holy Spirit for its proper interpretation.

The apostle Paul makes it clear that the original church was made up of believers who fulfilled the words of Jesus found in Matthew 28:18–20:

> And Jesus came and spake unto them, saying, All power is given unto me in heaven and in earth. Go ye therefore, and teach all nations, baptizing them in the name of the Father, and of the Son, and of the Holy Ghost: teaching them to observe all things whatsoever I have commanded you: and, lo, I am with you alway, even unto the end of the world. Amen.

The first thing Jesus told His followers to do was to teach. And what were they instructed to teach? He taught his disciples: "Think not that I am come to destroy the law, or the prophets: I am not come to destroy, but to fulfil" (Matthew 5:17). Here Jesus was teaching about the observance of the Old Testament teachings, which included the complete Ten Commandment law given by God to His chosen people, Israel. Jesus proclaimed it His duty to teach His followers to keep the law and believe what the prophets said. "Search the scriptures; for in them ye think ye have eternal life: and they are they which testify of me" (John 5:39).

> **No church can assure its membership of salvation. Only Jesus can do that, when, as individuals, we accept His sacrifice.**

Jesus said "search the scriptures," and, when we do, we will learn who Jesus is and what He wants us to do so we can receive eternal life. The entire Bible is a testimony of Jesus. It shows us the way we need to live to be a complete Christian, to pattern our lives after His example.

When Jesus was on the earth, the only Scriptures available were the Old Testament, yet Jesus knew that the word "Scriptures" would someday include the New Testament as well. Why do we need to search the Scriptures? It is to know Jesus and all the Bible teachings that point to Him and to do as He has commanded, being taught by the Word of God and not by tradition.

Did Jesus have a church when He was here on earth? Yes, it was composed of twelve disciples. Did it have a name? No, it did not. Did anyone of them apostatize? Yes, Judas Iscariot did. Should we look for an organization, denomination, church, or group of believers when I admitted that I do not find any one church that I believe follows all the correct teachings of the Bible? Yes, we should. We should look for the church that has the most truth as taught in the Bible. That it is lacking in some truth should not keep us from fellowshipping, as Hebrews says: "Not forsaking the assembling of ourselves together, as the manner of some is; but exhorting one another: and so much the more, as ye see the day approaching" (Hebrews 10:25).

The meaning of "exhort" from The Free Dictionary is: "To urge by strong, often stirring argument, admonition, advice, or appeal" ("Exhort," The Free Dictionary by Farlex, http://1ref.us/52). This is a perfect description of group Bible study, comparing different understandings of what the Bible teaches.

Consider the summary of church beliefs and find one that most closely agrees with the Bible texts listed in support of each statement of faith. The first thing I would look for in considering different church beliefs is the number of Bible texts given in support of each individual belief, affirming it to be true. After all, what we are seeking is Bible truths. Any church that claims to be the true church of Christ and to follow the teachings of the Bible must be a seventh-day Sabbath-keeping church. All Sunday-keeping churches follow the Roman Catholic Church and tradition rather than Scripture on this point.

Of the seventh-day Sabbath-keeping church called the Church of God, we found many that follow teachings out of sync with the Bible. The Seventh Day Baptists hold a view of death that contradicts the testimony of Jesus and Paul. The church with the most Scriptural references for each belief is the Seventh-day Adventist Church. Their twenty-eight Bible-based beliefs had nine hundred eighty-nine Scriptural texts and nine complete chapters in their support.

At the close of chapter 16, I shared an important article from the-ten-commandments.org that I believe all who are looking to follow God's will should review. It begins with the words:

> Many say that Sabbath keeping is legalism, but legalism is something you do to earn your way to heaven. The hundreds of different Sabbath keeping Churches that know the blessings of keeping God's Sabbath do not keep the day to earn entrance into the kingdom but keep the day because they love God with all their heart, soul and might.... ("Sabbath Observing Denominations—Sabbath Churches," The Ten Commandments, http://1ref.us/4t)

Sadly, some who keep the seventh-day Sabbath do keep it to gain entrance into heaven. They have never known the joy of observing the day out of love for their Lord. Jesus said:, "Not every one that saith unto me, Lord, Lord, shall enter into the kingdom of heaven; but he that doeth the will of my Father which is in heaven. Many will say to me in that day, Lord, Lord, have we not prophesied in thy name? and in thy name have cast out devils? and in thy name done many wonderful works?" (Matthew 7:21, 22). What was the answer that Jesus gave to them? He said, "Depart from me" (Matthew 7:23).

The author of the The Ten Commandments website said, "I have not been able to substantiate any of the rumors or attacks on this church." For those who really seek to find the truth, answers to the deliberate attacks on the Seventh-day Adventist Church can be found in various places on the Internet.

My intent is not to condemn other churches, but that people sincerely walk before God in whatever church they are in, following the truth of God's Word. God will be the judge. After people have received the truth about the Sabbath, I do not understand why they would not want to honor God by worshipping Him on the day He set aside to remember Him as our Creator. What is truth is not always popular, and what is popular is not always truth.

Do these statements then give credit to the Seventh-day Adventist Church as the truth church? One of the most astounding statements I have found on the Internet is from a Catholic theologian, writing about the Seventh-day Adventist Church. Cardinal Gibbons wrote in his book *The Question Box*: "If the Bible is the only guide for the Christian, then the Seventh-day Adventist is right in observing Saturday with the Jew. Is it not strange that those who make the Bible their only teacher should inconsistently follow in this matter the tradition of the Catholic Church?" (Crews, "How the Sabbath Was Changed," SabbathTruth.com, http://1ref.us/4n). Then there is the statement from Peter R. Tramer, editor of *the Catholic Extension Magazine*: "We also say that of all Protestants, the Seventh-day Adventists are the only group that reason correctly and are consistent with their teachings."

Such statements are interesting since they come from authorities within the Roman Catholic Church and they give credit to another church not their own. Are these statements a witness to the Seventh-day Adventist Church as being the true church?

Is there such a thing as an almost perfect church without fault? Jesus said, "Ye shall know them by their fruits. Do men gather grapes of thorns, or figs of thistles? Even so every good tree bringeth forth good fruit; but a corrupt tree bringeth forth evil fruit" (Matthew 7:16, 17). Is a church not actually just a building that cannot bring forth any fruit? "Wherefore by their fruits ye shall know them" (Matthew 7:20). This verse refers to the people who claim to belong to an organization or group. Evaluating the Seventh-day Adventist Church in this way, we are, in actuality, comparing the people's activities to the Bible's teachings as well as the doctrines of the church. The statement, "The Seventh-day Adventists are the only group that reason correctly and are consistent with their teachings," addresses doctrines. Are there not people in every organization who are true Christians? Likely so, because true Christians are people who have a true desire to do what God wants them to do and they have accepted Jesus' sacrifice for the forgiveness of their sin and have faith in Jesus as their Savior, producing works befitting true repentance.

Salvation is a free gift; there is nothing we can do to earn our entrance into the kingdom as we are justified by faith and not by the works of the law. Does this mean we do not have to obey the law? Thankfully, Paul made the answer to this question clear, and he informs us that we do not make void the law through faith. Romans 3:31 says, "Do we then make void the law through faith? God forbid: yea, we establish the law." "For not the hearers of the law are just before God, but the doers of the law shall be justified" (Romans 2:13). This leaves no doubt as to who is justified before God. It is those who have faith and produce good works.

There is one more qualification of a true Christian: as God reveals his will to His people through His Word by the Holy Spirit, they will gladly accept His instructions and depend on Jesus to give them the help they need to make the changes He points out. They will have a joyful spirit and rejoice that God loves them enough to show them the changes they need to make so they can have a closer relationship with Him. By obeying what Jesus has asked us to do, we show that we love Him. He said, "If ye love me, keep my commandments" (John 14:15). "He that hath my commandments, and keepeth them, he it is that loveth me: and he that loveth me shall be loved of my Father, and I will love him, and will manifest myself to him" (John 14:21).

Now what about the statement I made that I did not believe there is any church that keeps all the principles in the Bible? A church is made up of many people, and you will likely find no church in which all of its members sincerely believe the entire Bible. The devil has his people in every church, organization or group. I agree with the statements about the Seventh-day Adventist Church made by Catholic representatives: "If the Bible is the only guide for the Christian, then the Seventh-day Adventist is right in observing Saturday with the Jew"; and "Seventh-day Adventists are the only group that reason correctly and are consistent with their teachings."

The Bible depicts a remnant of God's people in this world at the very end who "keep the commandments of God, and have the testimony of Jesus Christ" (Revelation 12:17), and "worship God: for the testimony of Jesus is the spirit of prophecy" (Revelation 19:10). There is only one church in the world today that meets the qualifications given in this Scripture and that church is the Seventh-day Adventist Church. It is the only church that has all of their beliefs based on the Bible and can rightfully claim the testimony of Jesus in the spiritual gift of prophecy (Revelation 19:10). "Even so ye, forasmuch as ye are zealous of spiritual gifts, seek that ye may excel to the edifying of the church." "Follow after charity, and desire spiritual gifts, but rather that ye may prophesy" (1 Corinthians 14:1).

Again I wish to remind all that individuals are saved, not whole churches. For an entire church to be saved would require that every member of that church be saved. This is a wonderful thought, though it will never happen, as only a remnant will be saved (Romans 9:27).

Chapter 19
Receiving God's Guidance

Even in claiming that a church is the one true church for the last days of earth's history, there can be people within that church who have joined simply for what they can get. Those who are a genuine part of the true church must meet all of the Bible requirements, including loving their neighbor as themselves and reaching out in practical ways to the community.

Jesus was very clear about the foundation of commandment keeping. One day He was asked which was "the great commandment in the law," a common topic of discussion among the Jews at that time:

> Jesus said unto him, Thou shalt love the Lord thy God with all thy heart, and with all thy soul, and with all thy mind. This is the first and great commandment. And the second is like unto it. Thou shalt love thy neighbour as thyself. On these two commandments hang all the law and the prophets. (Matthew 22:37–40)

In reality, the whole Bible expresses the love of God for His created beings. It is found first in the Genesis account of creation, where God made a perfect world with everything in it that the human family would ever need, plus all the things that would add to their happiness.

Sin originated when Lucifer targeted the angels in heaven with his deceptions. Scripture indicates that he was successful in deceiving a third of them: "And his tail drew the third part of the stars of heaven, and did cast them to the earth" (Revelation 12:4).

After being expelled from heaven for his rebellion, where did he take his deceptions next? "And the great dragon was cast out, that old serpent, called the Devil, and Satan, which deceiveth the whole world: he was cast out into the earth, and his angels were cast out with him" (Revelation 12:9).

Thus, Lucifer, which means "light bearer," became Satan, which means "adversary," and has continued on earth what he had done in heaven, deceiving as many as he can. Time continued and "GOD saw that the wickedness of man was great in

> **Those who are a genuine part of the true church must meet all of the Bible requirements, including loving their neighbor as themselves ...**

the earth, and that every imagination of the thoughts of his heart was only evil continually" (Genesis 6:5). He determined to destroy mankind and the beasts of the earth for their violence through a worldwide flood (Genesis 6:11–13, 17). How was God's love expressed in the great flood of Noah's time? God destroyed all the wicked so that the eight righteous people could live without sin all around them. However, their descendants again turned to evil. What was God's response? "The Lord said in his heart, I will not again curse the ground any more for man's sake; for the imagination of man's heart is evil from his youth; neither will I again smite any more every thing living, as I have done" (Genesis 8:21).

God wanted people to live righteously, and He called Abram (later called "Abraham") into close friendship with Him, promising him that his descendants would be as many in number as the sands of the sea. God wanted a chosen people who would testify of His great love to the inhabitants of this world. However, the descendants of Abraham, through his grandson Jacob, failed to follow the commandments that God gave them, and even the chosen people sinned against God.

After many centuries, according to His original promise in Eden (Genesis 3:15), God sent His very own Son to the descendants of Abraham to get them to turn from sin and do what is right. How did the people show their gratitude to God for this great gift? They killed His Son on a cross and returned to their religious traditions.

All people who are not Abraham's descendants by birth are Gentiles. When the leaders of the Jews rejected God's Son, God sent apostles into the world to teach what Jesus had taught them and to show His great love and power to save, as the apostle Paul puts it, "to the Jew first, and also to the Greek" (Romans 1:16). So by the death and resurrection of Jesus, all the people of the world can be restored to God by accepting His sacrifice for their sins.

Church traditions are fine if they are based on the Bible and the Bible only (2 Thessalonians 2:15; 3:6). However, when the doctrines of a church are traditions that do not agree with Scripture, we recognize that the leaders of that church do not care enough about their members to teach only Bible truths. There are many people who attend churches with false doctrines who do love God, yet they do not know the truths in God's Word because they have been told to believe what they were taught and they have not compared their church's doctrines with Scripture.

Who is responsible for their believing false doctrine? It is the preachers and leaders of each church organization who claim to be teaching Bible truths when they are not. Does the Bible warn us of such things? Peter wrote: "But there were false prophets also among the people, even as there shall be false teachers among you, who privily shall bring in damnable heresies, even denying the Lord that bought them, and bring upon themselves swift destruction" (2 Peter 2:1). Paul declared: "For I know this, that after my departing shall grievous wolves enter in among you, not sparing the flock. Also of your own selves shall men arise, speaking perverse things, to draw away disciples after them" (Acts 20:29, 30). And Jesus Himself warned: "Beware of false prophets, which come to you in sheep's clothing, but inwardly they are ravening wolves" (Matthew 7:15).

Look at Peter and Paul's statements carefully and you will discover where the false prophets and preachers are coming from—they are coming from within the church. Jesus warned us about people who teach false doctrine while claiming to present truth. How many churches today assume that Sunday is the day to worship God? How many preachers today tell their congregations that people either go to heaven or hell when they die, thereby perpetuating the lie the devil told Eve in the Garden of Eden, "Ye shall not surly die"? If people never really die, then they are immortal, and the righteous and the wicked live on eternally without the need of a Savior. However, the same preachers who teach that we go to heaven or hell when we die also teach salvation through the death and resurrection of Jesus and the need of Jesus as a Savior. Perhaps they do not see the contradiction in the two messages. The deception comes when the devil works through people who claim to be biblical teachers.

Paul wrote, "That we henceforth be no more children, tossed to and fro, and carried about with every wind of doctrine, by the sleight of men, and cunning craftiness, whereby they lie in wait to deceive" (Ephesians 4:14). He also forecast, "But evil men and seducers shall wax worse and worse, deceiving, and being deceived" (2 Timothy 3:13). And Paul identified these among the believers: "For there are many unruly and vain talkers and deceivers, specially they of the circumcision" (Titus 1:10). These were preachers within the church. The apostle Paul is warning Titus about those who were supposedly believers but were an impediment to the message of Jesus. These were influential Jewish believers in the churches, who needed to be discerned by the Word of God, just as preachers need to be judged by the Bible today. All the devil wants is to get a little falsehood mixed in with the truth.

John wrote about antichrists: "For many deceivers are entered into the world, who confess not that Jesus Christ is come in the flesh. This is a deceiver and an antichrist" (2 John 1:7).

People talk a lot about the "antichrist." Putting it very simply, the antichrist is anyone who goes against the teachings we find in the Bible and in the teachings of Jesus. An organization can also bear the title of antichrist. If we do not believe all the teachings in the Bible, any one of us can also have the spirit of antichrist. Several texts support this conclusion: "Little children, it is the last time: and as ye have heard that antichrist shall come, even now are there many antichrists; whereby we know that it is the last time.... Who is a liar but he that denieth that Jesus is the Christ? He is antichrist, that denieth the Father and the Son" (1 John 2:18, 22). "And every spirit that confesseth not that Jesus Christ is come in the flesh is not of God: and this is that spirit of antichrist, whereof ye have heard that it should come; and even now already is it in the world" (1 John 4:3).

In 1 John 4:1, the apostle John refers to false prophets as "spirits" and he says that these false prophets claim to preach the Word of God but mix truth with falsehood. "Beloved, believe not every spirit, but try the spirits whether they are of God: because many false prophets are gone out into the world" (1 John 4:1). A person needs to compare all their teachings to the Bible. John declared that we must know what spirit a person is of. John's statement, "try the spirits" (1 John 4:1), is explained in the next two verses.

> Hereby know ye the Spirit of God: Every spirit that confesseth that Jesus Christ is come in the flesh is of God: And every spirit that confesseth not that Jesus Christ is come in the flesh is not of God: and this is that spirit of antichrist, whereof ye have heard that it should come; and even now already is it in the world. (1 John 4:2, 3)

A trustworthy "spirit" holds that Jesus is the Son of God and that He dwelt in the flesh while here on earth. The teaching that Jesus did not come in the flesh is very prominent in many of today's churches. The Contemporary English Version says it well:

> Dear friends, don't believe everyone who claims to have the Spirit of God. Test them all to find out if they really do come from God. Many false prophets have already gone out into the world, and you can know which ones come from God. His Spirit says that Jesus Christ had a truly human body. But when someone doesn't say this about Jesus, you know that person has a spirit that doesn't come from God and is the enemy of Christ. You knew that this enemy was coming into the world and now is already here. (1 John 4:1–3, CEV)

And how do we test them? By comparing their teachings with the teachings of the Bible.

In these latter days of earth's history, there is an ever growing belief that Jesus was only a spirit. The apostle John was one of Jesus' twelve disciples, and he knew for a certainty that Jesus had a physical body. All who choose to believe that He was only a spirit are allowing themselves to be deceived. The only way we can keep from being deceived is to know what the truth of God's Word is and trust that God knows what is best for everyone. That is what faith is: "Now faith is the substance of things hoped for, the evidence of things not seen.… Through faith we understand that the worlds were framed by the word of God, so that things which are seen were not made of things which do appear" (Hebrews 11:1, 3).

Philosophical naturalists, commonly called "evolutionists," have tried to undermine the Word of God with their theory of origins, which requires millions and millions of years for life to evolve from nothing to what now is. The Bible clearly tells us that God's creation was not dependent on preexisting matter but that He only had to speak for the things we see to come into existence: "By the word of the Lord were the heavens made; and all the host of them by the breath of his mouth" (Psalms 33:6).

Were any of us present to witness the wonders of creation? Of course not, but the Bible tells us that we can know it took place by faith through the evidence that we see around us in all the exquisitely designed things of nature.

Likewise, we grasp salvation when, by faith we accept the good news, called the gospel, that Jesus came as a baby, grew into manhood, taught salvation, and shed His blood for the forgiveness of our sins and gave His life for our reconciliation to God. It is by faith. "For therein is the righteousness of God revealed from faith to faith: as it is written, The just shall live by faith" (Romans 1:17). "Therefore being justified by faith, we have peace with God through our Lord Jesus Christ" (Romans 5:1). "What shall we say then? That the Gentiles, which followed not after righteousness, have attained to righteousness, even the righteousness which is of faith" (Romans 9:30). "So then faith cometh by hearing, and hearing by the word of God" (Romans 10:17).

It is important to see who preachers give the glory to. If they seek glory for themselves by some great outward show, they are false teachers. A true preacher will follow the words of Paul: "Whether therefore ye eat, or drink, or whatsoever ye do, do all to the glory of God" (1 Corinthians 10:31). No human being deserves credit for what he does. It is only through the grace of God that we are capable of doing anything, and we should always give our praise to God. Peter wrote: "If any man speak, let him speak as the oracles of God; if any man minister, let him do it as of the ability which God giveth: that God in all things may be glorified through Jesus Christ, to whom be praise and dominion for ever and ever" (1 Peter 4:11).

Chapter 20
The End

After learning from Scripture what we need to know and following what God has shown us, our next step is to prepare to be among those who God will save in the last days at the second coming of Jesus. We need to establish some important time lines from the books of prophecy, Daniel and Revelation, and apply this knowledge to the people who have accepted Jesus as their Savior. "Neither is there salvation in any other: for there is none other name under heaven given among men, whereby we must be saved" (Acts 4:12).

Daniel 2 describes the dream of a great statue that God gave Babylonian King Nebuchadnezzar to show him what would come to pass down to the end of time. The king could not remember what the dream was, so he called all the wise men in the province to tell him what it was. However, they could not tell him, so he ordered them all to be killed. Daniel was one of the wise men, so the death decree also applied to him. Yet, when he heard about it, he did not know why the order was given. So he asked the king for more time, and the king granted it to him because he liked Daniel. Daniel then went to his house and told his three friends what the king had decreed. The four of them prayed to God to reveal the dream and the interpretation, and God answered their prayer in a dream given to Daniel at night.

> **Neither is there salvation in any other: for there is none other name under heaven given among men, whereby we must be saved" (Acts 4:12).**

Daniel then went to the king and revealed the dream to the king and told him about the huge statute that he had seen in his dream:

> This image's head was of fine gold, his breast and his arms of silver, his belly and his thighs of brass, His legs of iron, his feet part of iron and part of clay, Thou sawest till that a stone was cut out without hands, which smote the image upon his feet that were of iron and clay, and brake them to pieces.
>
> Then was the iron, the clay, the brass, the silver, and the gold, broken to pieces

together, and became like the chaff of the summer threshingfloors; and the wind carried them away, that no place was found for them: and the stone that smote the image became a great mountain, and filled the whole earth. (Daniel 2: 32–35)

Daniel's interpretation of the dream starts in verse 38. King Nebuchadnezzar's kingdom was represented by the head of gold. After his kingdom, another kingdom would arise. It would be inferior to King Nebuchadnezzar's kingdom, for the breast and arms of silver are inferior to the image's head of gold.

Daniel 5 tells who this second kingdom was—Medo-Persia: "In that night was Belshazzar the king of the Chaldeans slain. And Darius the Median took the kingdom, being about threescore and two years old" (Daniel 5:30, 31).

The Third and Fourth Kingdoms

Daniel's explanation continues:

> And another third kingdom of brass, which shall bear rule over all the earth. And the fourth kingdom shall be strong as iron: forasmuch as iron breaketh in pieces and subdueth all things: and as iron that breaketh all these, shall it break in pieces and bruise....
>
> And whereas thou sawest the feet and toes, part of potters' clay, and part of iron, the kingdom shall be divided; but there shall be in it of the strength of the iron, forasmuch as thou sawest the iron mixed with miry clay. And as the toes of the feet were part of iron, and part of clay, so the kingdom shall be partly strong, and partly broken. And whereas thou sawest iron mixed with miry clay, they shall mingle themselves with the seed of men: but they shall not cleave one to another, even as iron is not mixed with clay. And in the days of these kings shall the God of heaven set up a kingdom, which shall never be destroyed: and the kingdom shall not be left to other people, but it shall break in pieces and consume all these kingdoms, and it shall stand for ever. Forasmuch as thou sawest that the stone was cut out of the mountain without hands, and that it brake in pieces the iron, the brass, the clay, the silver, and the gold; the great God hath made known to the king what shall come to pass hereafter: and the dream is certain, and the interpretation thereof sure. (Daniel 2:39–45)

The dream that God gave King Nebuchadnezzar told of all the earth's history from 605 BC to the end of time. History substantiates the exact dates and can be found in many King James Bibles at the beginning of each chapter.

The next timeframe given to Daniel is found in Daniel 7:

> In the first year of Belshazzar king of Babylon Daniel had a dream and visions of his head upon his bed: then he wrote the dream, and told the sum of the matters. Daniel spake and said, I saw in my vision by night, and, behold, the four winds of the heaven strove upon the great sea. And four great beasts came up from the sea, diverse one from another. (Daniel 7:1–3)

The "four great beasts" (Daniel 7:3) are interpreted in the vision itself: "These great beasts, which are four, are four kings, which shall arise out of the earth" (Daniel 7:17). Thus, beasts represent kings or kingdoms. The sea, or waters, represents "peoples, and multitudes, and nations, and tongues" (Revelation 17:15). That the winds "strove upon the great sea" represents unrest, wars, and conflict over the whole earth. The four winds of heaven are the four points of the compass—north, south, east, and west (Revelation 7:1). Verse 4 of Daniel 7 begins to describe what the four beasts looked like:

> The first was like a lion, and had eagle's wings: I beheld till the wings thereof were plucked, and it was lifted up from the earth, and made to stand upon the feet as a man, and a man's heart was given to it. (Daniel 7:4)

This first beast represents Babylon and King Nebuchadnezzar and his reign. Daniel continued: "And behold another beast, a second, like to a bear, and it raised up itself on one side, and it had three ribs in the mouth of it between the teeth of it: and they said thus unto it, Arise, devour much flesh" (Daniel 7:5). Just as the silver in the image is inferior to gold, so a bear is inferior to a lion. "It raised up itself on one side," indicating a division of power between the Medes and the Persians. "Three ribs in the mouth of it between the teeth of it." In the same time era that the Medo-Persians defeated Babylon, they also conquered three other nations: Lydia, Egypt, and Ethiopia. "Devour much flesh" signifies that the Medo-Persian soldiers had no mercy on anyone—men or women, old or young, or even children.

Daniel went on: "After this I beheld, and lo another, like a leopard, which had upon the back of it four wings of a fowl; the beast had also four heads; and dominion was given to it" (Daniel 7:6). This third kingdom was represented in the image as brass. "And another third kingdom of brass, which shall bear rule over all the earth" (Daniel 2:39). The four wings represent speed and the four heads represent the four generals of Alexander the great under the kingdom of Greece.

"After this I saw in the night visions, and behold a fourth beast, dreadful and terrible, and strong exceedingly; and it had great iron teeth: it devoured and brake in pieces, and stamped the residue with the feet of it: and it was diverse from all the beasts that were before it; and it had ten horns" (Daniel 7:7). The fourth kingdom in the image was made of iron, and, like the fourth beast, it represents Rome. The first part of the Roman Empire was pagan Rome, whose citizens practiced every kind of idolatry and devil worship there was, including sun worship and human sacrifice.

"I considered the horns, and, behold, there came up among them another little horn, before whom there were three of the first horns plucked up by the roots: and, behold, in this horn were eyes like the eyes of man, and a mouth speaking great things" (Daniel 7:8). Daniel is looking at the horns that were upon the head of the fourth beast and, as he does, a little horn pushed out three of the original ten horns and took on the likeness of a man with eyes and a mouth speaking great things.

There is a very interesting part in the chapter that we need to call attention to so we will be able to fit it into the right part of Revelation and other texts in the Bible. It reads: "I beheld till the thrones were cast down, and the Ancient of days did sit, whose garment was white as snow, and the hair of his head like the pure wool: his throne was like the fiery flame, and his wheels as burning fire. A fiery stream issued and came forth from before him: thousand thousands ministered unto him, and ten thousand times ten thousand stood before him: the judgment was set, and the books were opened" (Daniel 7:9, 10). Here Daniel talks about judgment—the same judgment that will be described in Revelation 20.

The four beasts of Daniel 7 are clearly correlated to the parts of the image in Daniel 2, and they relate to the history of this earth from shortly after the flood, in Genesis 7, to the end of the world at the second coming of Jesus.

In chapters 11 and 12, we surveyed the history of the nations up to the "little horn," which is papal Rome. Now we need to compare the words of Daniel 7:11 to those of Revelation 13:1–3.

Daniel described what he saw: "I beheld then because of the voice of the great words which the horn spake: I beheld even till the beast was slain, and his body destroyed, and given to the burning flame" (Daniel 7:11). John also described what he saw:

> And I stood upon the sand of the sea, and saw a beast rise up out of the sea, having seven heads and ten horns, and upon his horns ten crowns, and upon his heads the name of blasphemy. And the beast which I saw was like unto a leopard, and his feet were as the feet of a bear, and his mouth as the mouth of a lion: and the dragon gave him his power, and his seat, and great authority. And I saw one of his heads as it were wounded to death. (Revelation 13:1–3)

Daniel continued writing: "And the ten horns out of this kingdom are ten kings that shall arise: and another shall rise after them; and he shall be diverse from the first, and he shall subdue three kings. And he shall speak great words against the most High, and shall wear out the saints of the most High, and think to change times and laws: and they shall be given into his hand until a time and times and the dividing of time" (Daniel 7:24, 25).

These verses in Daniel 7, compared to those in Revelation 13, describe a kingdom that will "think to change times and laws." This description fits the Catholic papal system perfectly and helps us to identify the little horn as the Papacy.

Daniel mentions a specific time period—"until a time and times and the dividing of time." Revelation also mentions a time period of the same duration in Revelation 12:6: "And the woman fled into the wilderness, where she hath a place prepared of God, that they should feed her there a thousand two hundred and threescore days." Revelation 13:5 also mentions the time period in different terms:

"And there was given unto him a mouth speaking great things and blasphemies; and power was given unto him to continue forty and two months." Time, times, and half a time equals forty-two months, which also equals 1260 days, or 1260 years, in Bible prophecy.

The prophecy of Daniel 8 describes the same kingdoms but begins with Medo-Persia, represented by a ram with two horns. After that, it depicts the kingdom of Grecia, represented by a he goat, which conquers the ram. It then goes on to describe a "little horn" that does the same things as the "little horn" of the beast power. Consider the activities of the little horn: "And an host was given him against the daily sacrifice by reason of transgression, and it cast down the truth to the ground; and it practiced, and prospered. Then I heard one saint speaking, and another saint said unto that certain saint which spake, How long shall be the vision concerning the daily sacrifice, and the transgression of desolation, to give both the sanctuary and the host to be trodden under foot? And he said unto me. Unto two thousand and three hundred days; then shall the sanctuary be cleansed" (Daniel 8:12–14). Again, we have a specific time period—2300 prophetic days, or 2300 years—"then shall the sanctuary be cleansed."

To understand this time period we need to go to Daniel 9, where Daniel is praying to God and asking God to forgive the sins of the people of Israel and to restore Jerusalem and Judah for God's sake and not for the people's.

Daniel 9:2 points to a different time frame as Daniel is studying Jeremiah's prophecy. Daniel is studying so that he might be able to figure out when it would end. "The word of the LORD came to Jeremiah the prophet, that he would accomplish seventy years in the desolations of Jerusalem" (Daniel 9:2; see also Jeremiah 25:11, 12).

However, the angel points to a different time frame, and he gives a starting date:

> Know therefore and understand, that from the going forth of the commandment to restore and to build Jerusalem unto the Messiah the Prince shall be seven weeks, and threescore and two weeks: the street shall be built again, and the wall, even in troublous times. And after threescore and two weeks shall Messiah be cut off, but not for himself: and the people of the prince that shall come shall destroy the city and the sanctuary. (Daniel 9:25, 26)

The numbers thus far add up to sixty-nine weeks. For the starting date for these sixty-nine weeks, we turn to Ezra 7 (verses 12–26), which records "the commandment to restore and to build Jerusalem" (Daniel 9:25). This commandment was given by King Artaxerxes in 457 BC. Notice that the first section of the prophecy is a seven-week period, followed by threescore and two weeks—sixty-two more weeks. This seven weeks, or forty-nine years, was the period during which the actual rebuilding of Jerusalem was accomplished.

Now we have to see what will take place at the end of the sixty-nine weeks (or 483 years). These sixty-nine weeks begin at the same time as the seven-week period and takes us down to the year of the anointing of the Messiah ("Messiah" means anointed one). Jesus is the Messiah of Daniel 9:26. Acts describes Jesus' anointing as occurring at His baptism (Acts 10:38). This means that the prophecy points to the year of the baptism of Jesus, the start of His earthly ministry. Luke 3:1–22 records the baptism of Jesus in connection with the fifteenth year of Tiberius Caesar, which gives us the contemporary date for the event, identifying Jesus' baptism as occurring in AD 27. Now we can put that information into the prophecy of Daniel. This is where we left off at the end of the sixty-nine-week period. But this is only sixty-nine out of seventy weeks. There is one week more.

Daniel described that final week of the prophecy: "After threescore and two weeks shall Messiah be cut off, but not for himself … And he shall confirm the covenant with many for one week: and in the midst of the week he shall cause the sacrifice and the oblation to cease" (Daniel 9:26, 27).

This one week is the seventieth week of the prophecy. Daniel 9:27 points to "the midst," or the middle, of the week for Messiah to be "cut off," which would place Jesus' death three and a half years after He started His earthly ministry—in the year AD 31.

What was the objective of this final week? "And he shall confirm the covenant with many for one week …" (Daniel 9:27). Jesus started His earthly ministry in AD 27 just after His baptism, and He began expounding upon the "new covenant" or "new testament" (Matthew 26:28), marking the end of the symbolic use of the blood of animals for the forgiveness of sin. It would be His own blood that would be shed for all who would accept His sacrifice by faith and obey His commandments.

After Jesus' death, His disciples and apostles preached the good news, which is the gospel, beginning with the Jews until the close of the seventy weeks in AD 34. At that time, there was a great exodus of Jewish believers from Jerusalem when persecution under Saul became severe. Ironically, it was this same Saul who would be instrumental in taking the gospel to the Gentiles within the Roman world. The apostle Peter continued to preach to the Jews.

This sums up the seventy-week prophecy. Yet, there is still another time period mentioned in Daniel, chapter 8: "And he said unto me, Unto two thousand and three hundred days; then shall the sanctuary be cleansed" (Daniel 8:14).

Since the prophecy of Daniel 9 was the explanation of the strange "vision" of Daniel 8 (Daniel 8:27; 9:23), and Daniel 9:24 declared the seventy-weeks to be "determined upon"—or, literally, "cut off" for—the people, it only makes sense that the two prophecies have the same starting point—457 BC. By beginning in 457 BC and going forward 2300 years, we come to AD 1844, when, the prophecy said that the sanctuary would "be cleansed" (Daniel 8:14).

The earthly sanctuary was destroyed by the Roman army in AD 70, so what sanctuary could this be talking about? To get the answer to this question, we need to go to the book of Hebrews, where the apostle Paul explains the essence of the heavenly sanctuary and how Jesus is our High Priest:

> Seeing then that we have a great high priest, that is passed into the heavens, Jesus the Son of God, let us hold fast our profession. For we have not an high priest which cannot be touched with the feeling of our infirmities; but was in all points tempted like as we are, yet without sin. Let us therefore come boldly unto the

throne of grace, that we may obtain mercy, and find grace to help in time of need. (Hebrews 4:14–16)

Hebrews gives us three facts: "Seeing then that we have a great high priest" tells us that we have someone who is our High Priest; "that is passed into the heavens" tells us where He has gone; and "Jesus the Son of God" tells us who our High Priest is.

Since there is no earthly sanctuary when this prophecy comes to fulfillment, there should be no question which sanctuary Daniel 8 is talking about. Yet, let us look at what Hebrews 8 says:

> Now of the things which we have spoken this is the sum: We have such an high priest, who is set on the right hand of the throne of the Majesty in the heavens. A minister of the sanctuary, and of the true tabernacle, which the Lord pitched, and not man. For every high priest is ordained to offer gifts and sacrifices: wherefore it is of necessity that this man have somewhat also to offer. For if he were on earth, he should not be a priest, seeing that there are priests that offer gifts according to the law. (Hebrews 8:1–4)

In heaven is "the sanctuary" (literally "holy places"). In the most holy place, is the throne of the "Majesty in the heavens," which is God the Father. Paul is explaining that Jesus would not have been a priest on earth since He was not a descendant of Aaron, the family of the priests. The next verse points to the correlation between the heavenly and earthly "holy places": "Who serve unto the example and shadow of heavenly things, as Moses was admonished of God when he was about to make the tabernacle for Israel, for, See, saith he, that thou make all things according to the pattern shewed to thee in the mount" (Hebrews 8:5).

Here, Paul confirms that the earthly sanctuary had to be made after the pattern of the one in heaven, and that is why we can look at the services in the earthly sanctuary and know what was and is being done in the heavenly sanctuary. The earthly sanctuary services are all recorded in the book of Leviticus.

Still, we are not through with all the time prophecies in the book of Daniel, for there is another in chapter 7:

> And the ten horns out of this kingdom are ten kings that shall arise: and another shall rise after them; and he shall be diverse from the first, and he shall subdue three kings. And he shall speak great words against the most High, and shall wear out the saints of the most High, and think to change times and laws: and they shall be given into his hand until a time and times and the dividing of time. (Daniel 7:24, 25)

This time period equals 1260 prophetic days, or 1260 years, but we need to know when it starts to be able to calculate where it ends. Of the beasts in Daniel 7, the fourth was different from the rest and had ten horns, which represent ten kingdoms. Among those ten horns came up a little horn which uprooted three of the original horns. History reveals that it was papal Rome that uprooted from Italy three German tribes. Thus, papal Rome is the little horn. The prophecy states that the little horn would rule for "a time and times and the dividing of time." This equals 1260 years from beginning to end. The year AD 538 is when the Romans in Rome essentially defeated the Goths and set up the pope as ruler of church and state. Prior to this the pope did not hold power in the secular world. Distinguished French historians Charles Bémont and Gabriel Monod wrote:

> Down to the sixth century all popes are declared saints in the martyrologies. Vigilius (537–555) is the first of a series of popes who no longer bear this title, which is henceforth sparingly conferred. From this time on the popes, more and more involved in worldly events, no longer belong solely to the Church; they are men of the state, and then rulers of the state. (*Medieval Europe from 395 to 1270*, pp. 120, 121)

Twelve hundred and sixty years from AD 538 brings us to AD 1798, and this is the very year that the French General took the pope captive and placed him in exile. Is this 1260-year period mentioned elsewhere in the Bible? Yes, it is mentioned as 1260 days (Daniel 11:3; 12:14) and as forty-two months, which equal 1260 day or years (Daniel 7:25; 12:7; Revelation 11:2; 13:5).

Let us see if the parallel passages mentioning the same time period shed light on the subject:

> And there was given me a reed like unto a rod: and the angel stood, saying, Rise, and measure the temple of God, and the altar, and them that worship therein. But the court which is without the temple leave out, and measure it not; for it is given unto the Gentiles: and the holy city shall they tread under foot forty and two months. And I will give power unto my two witnesses, and they shall prophesy a thousand two hundred and threescore days, clothed in sackcloth. (Revelation 11:1–3)

The apostle John was given a rod to measure the temple, the altar, and the worshippers in the temple, signifying the true followers of God. The messenger said: "But the outer court is given unto the Gentiles." In the days of Rome there were only two recognized groups of people, the Jews and everybody else was known as Gentiles.

In the Israelite sanctuary, only the Israelites—and the Gentiles who had accepted the rituals of the law—were allowed to participate in the sanctuary service of the temple. The Gentiles, who numbered in the thousands, were not allowed into the inner court of the temple. The outer court was outside the sanctuary itself.

The inner court contained the altar of sacrifice. As the people brought their sacrifices to the sanctuary every day, a priest was present to escort the sinner and his or her offering into the inner court where the justification process began (see Leviticus).

The angel declared: "And the holy city shall they tread under foot forty and two months" (Revelation 11:2). The time period he mentions is the same as the one given to papal Rome to enforce their false Christianity on the world. In AD 70 the armies of Titus completely destroyed the Jewish temple, and the Jews were prohibited from coming near its ruins.

John continues: "And I will give power unto my two witnesses, and they shall prophesy a thousand two hundred and threescore days, clothed in sackcloth" (Revelation 11:3). The two witnesses referred to are the Old and New Testaments. "Search the scriptures; for in them ye think ye have eternal life: and they are they which testify of me" (John 5:39). During the time period of the 1260 years of papal supremacy, spanning from AD 538 to 1798, the Papacy changed the Scriptures and the laws of God to what they wanted. This period is symbolized by the two witnesses testifying "clothed in sackcloth," indicating a time of great sorrow. This was a time of great persecution for true Christians—this time period is also known as the Dark Ages.

Continuing with the next parallel, we read:

> And when the dragon saw that he was cast unto the earth, he persecuted the woman which brought forth the man child. And to the woman were given two wings of a great eagle, that she might fly into the wilderness, into her place, where she is nourished for a time, and times, and half a time [1260 years], from the face of the serpent. (Revelation 12:13, 14)

Revelation 8 covers how Lucifer deceived a third of the angels in heaven and our first parents in the Garden of Eden. We know who he is and what he stands for, and we know how he works to deceive all that he can. Besides deception, another tactic of the devil to gain followers is persecution. He puts pressure on believers to give up their belief in God's wonderful gift of salvation.

The woman in Revelation 12 represents God's true believers—all mankind from Creation to the second coming of Jesus. We call it His "church," which includes all who accept His gift of salvation given through Jesus' sacrifice. Jesus is the "man child" whom the devil tried to destroy in His infancy and all through His life.

A third parallel reads: "And there was given unto him a mouth speaking great things and blasphemies; and power was given unto him to continue forty and two months And he opened his mouth in blasphemy against God, to blaspheme his name, and his tabernacle, and them that dwell in heaven" (Revelation 13:5, 6). The power that is connected to the 1260 years is the papal power, which rules the Catholic Church. The papal power speaks "great things" and blasphemes God, His name, His tabernacle, and those who live in heaven. This is similar to Daniel's description of the little horn:

> I considered the horns, and, behold, there came up among them another little horn, before whom there were three of the first horns plucked up by the roots: and, behold, in this horn were eyes like the eyes of man, and a mouth speaking great things. (Daniel 7:8)

In order to find out what beast Revelation 13:5 is referring to, we need to go to the preceding verses in that chapter:

> And I stood upon the sand of the sea, and saw a beast rise up out of the sea, having seven heads and ten horns, and upon his horns ten crowns, and upon his heads the name of blasphemy. And the beast which I saw was like unto a leopard, and his feet were as the feet of a bear, and his mouth as the mouth of a lion: and the dragon gave him his power, and his seat, and great authority. And I saw one of his heads as it were wounded to death; and his deadly wound was healed: and all the world wondered after the beast. And they worshipped the dragon which gave power unto the beast: and they worshipped the beast, saying, Who is like unto the beast? who is able to make war with him? (Revelation 13:1–4)

A beast represents a king, kingdom, or earthly power. Here we have an earthly power with seven heads—seven different kingdoms—and ten horns. Horns represent power (see Daniel 8:7). Upon his horns were ten crowns. Kings wear a crown to show sovereignty over lands and peoples. That "his heads" carried "the name of blasphemy" (Revelation 13:1) signifies that the ten kingdoms were all pagan rulers—including the three that fell to the papal powers, leaving seven. This was completed in AD 538 with the downfall of the last of the three kingdoms who were the Goths, who were also Arians. (The siege of Rome took place in AD 537–538.) It was in AD 538 that Belisarius set up the pope as governor of Rome.

John describes the beast as bearing the qualities of three of the beasts of Daniel 7: "And the beast which I saw was like unto a leopard, and his feet were as the feet of a bear, and his mouth as the mouth of a lion …" This signifies that the beast had all of the pagan customs of the three nations that preceded Rome—Babylon, Medo-Persia, and Greece. The rituals and practices of this beast came from the rituals and practices of Babylon, Medo-Persia and Greece—all were pagans. These nations were essentially devil worshippers, which comes from the Bible text, "And the dragon gave him his power, and his seat, and great authority" (Revelation 13:2). In the Bible, "the dragon" is also known by other names: "And the great dragon was cast out, that old serpent, called the Devil, and Satan, which deceiveth the whole world: he was cast out into the earth, and his angels were cast out with him" (Revelation 12:9).

Then, John beholds something most startling: "And I saw one of his heads as it were wounded to death; and his deadly wound was healed" (Revelation 13:3). This symbolism reveals that the beast is an earthly power whose power was to be taken away and then restored. The loss of its power coincides with the time period of 1260 years of papal rule known as the Dark Ages. In AD 1798, at the end of the 1260 years, the pope was taken captive and the Catholic Church lost its dominance in the world, eventually even losing the territories of the papal states. Yet, later, the deadly wound is healed.

By 1929, the Vatican (the seat of the Catholic Church) had regained her status as an independent country. "On February 11, 1929, an historic treaty was signed between the Italian Government and the Vatican re-establishing the political power and diplomatic standing of the Catholic Church, which had been lost when Italy seized Rome, the last of the Papal States, on September 20th, 1870" ("Lateran Concordat of 1929—Papal Wound Healed!" Michael Scheifler's Bible Light, http://1ref.us/53). It was with the Lateran Concordat of 1929 that the papal wound was healed.

Now, according to Revelation 12:9 it is the devil who gives the papal system "his power, and his seat, and great authority." The leopard-like beast in Revelation 13 represents the papal power of Rome, while the dragon represents pagan Rome and the power behind it—the "old serpent, called the devil and Satan" (Revelation 12:9; 20:2)—who deceives the whole world through human agents doing his work. The devil uses deception, a little changing of God's Word. He also works openly as "a great red dragon, having seven heads and ten horns, and seven crowns upon his heads" (Revelation 12:3).

What else does Revelation say about the beast? "And they worshipped the dragon which gave power unto the beast: and they worshipped the beast, saying, Who is like unto the beast? who is able to make war with him?" (Revelation 13:4). It is interesting to note the words, "they worshipped the dragon." We have discovered that the dragon is the devil. Yet, the people also worshiped the beast, which is the Papacy. "And all that dwell upon the earth shall worship him, whose names are not written in the book of life of the Lamb slain from the foundation of the world" (Revelation 13:8).

Then the angel exhorts: "If any man have an ear, let him hear" (Revelation 13:9). Simply put, this means that, if people want eternal life and they know about the beast, they had better concern themselves with whether their name is written in the Lamb's book of life in heaven (Revelation 21:27). Salvation is through acceptance of the sacrifice that Jesus made and obedience to God's commandments by faith. That is how we get our names in the book of life.

Revelation 13 continues, depicting another beast in the prophecy that is connected to the beast that we just studied:

> And I beheld another beast coming up out of the earth; and he had two horns like a lamb, and he spake as a dragon. And he exerciseth all the power of the first beast before him, and causeth the earth and them which dwell therein to worship the first beast, whose deadly wound was healed. (Revelation 13:11, 12)

The first beast came out of the sea, a place of many people; the second beast came out of the earth, a place where only a few people live. It is interesting to notice that the ten kings of Daniel 7 also came up from "the earth" (Daniel 7:17). They came from a sparsely settled area now known as Europe. At first being nomadic tribes, each of the ten chose leaders and became kingdoms.

The world power represented by the second beast of Revelation 13 came into existence close to the same time as the deadly wound of the papacy was received. John described the second beast as having "two horns like a lamb." The horns still represent power, but these are separate, one on each side of its head, indicating a separation of powers. The representation of this beast aligns with the United States of America, which came into existence close to the same time as the deadly wound of the papacy was received. It also came up out of the earth, a sparsely populated region. The separation of powers aligns with the separation of church and state in the nation's formation. That separation was the very reason the Pilgrims came to the wilderness of the North American continent—to escape persecution by the dominate countries of Europe, countries that were ruled by the Papacy. The description goes on:

> And he doeth great wonders, so that he maketh fire come down from heaven on the earth in the sight of men, and deceiveth them that dwell on the earth by the means of those miracles which he had power to do in the sight of the beast; saying to them that dwell on the earth, that they should make an image to the beast, which had the wound by a sword, and did live. And he had power to give life unto the image of the beast, that the image of the beast should both speak, and cause that as many as would not worship the image of the beast should be killed. (Revelation 13:13–15)

The description tells of a future law regarding worship, in recognition of the Papacy's authority. What greater sign of authority is there than Catholicism's claim to having changed the fourth commandment to refer to Sunday rather than the Sabbath?

A Sunday law ordered by the United States government would exalt Catholic authority. In doing so, the second beast (the U.S.A.) would make an image to the first beast (the Papacy). The most striking conflicts down through the ages have been about the "day of worship"—the biblical seventh-day Sabbath versus the papal Sunday.

"And he causeth all, both small and great, rich and poor, free and bond, to receive a mark in their right hand, or in their foreheads" (Revelation 13:16). The "he" in this passage refers to the beast with the "horns like a lamb." Receiving a mark in the hand is a fitting symbol of active support of the Catholic Church's authority; a mark in the forehead is a fitting symbol of supporting Catholic authority as a true Catholic believer.

"And that no man might buy or sell, save he that had the mark, or the name of the beast, or the number of his name" (Revelation 13:17). This last verse includes possible means of going along with the beast: in order to support one's self, people will have to be able to buy necessities. They will have to be able to sell their goods and services if they work for themselves or are working for someone else. The name of the beast is the Papacy. The number of his name is given in Revelation 13:18—six hundred sixty-six. The text says that the number of the beast is also the number of a man. Many believe this man is the pope, the head or pontiff of the Catholic Church. In times past, he wore his name, *Vicarius Filii Dei*, as his title on the papal mitre or tiara, resembling a crown. This has been refuted by many Internet articles and people. What is that number?

"Here is wisdom. Let him that hath understanding count the number of the beast: for it is the number of a man; and his number is Six hundred threescore and six" (Revelation 13:18). The title of the Vatican pope is *Vicarius Filii Dei*. This has been known to be inscribed on his mitre and tiara, although this has also been refuted by many Internet articles and people. If you take the letters of his title, which represent Latin numerals (printed in upper case), and add them together, they equal 666—the "number of a man":

V	=	5	F	=	0	D	=	500
I	=	1	I	=	1	E	=	0
C	=	100	L	=	50	I	=	1
A	=	0	I	=	1			
R	=	0	I	=	1			
I	=	1						
U	=	5						
S	=	0						
		112	+		**53**	+	**501**	= **666**

Both the pope's tiara and mitre are shaped like three crowns on top of one another. It is of highest significance that the word "Vicarius" is on papal crowns, for the crowns symbolize the basis of his authority. The phrase *Vicarius Filii Dei* states it in full. The one who stands *in the place of the Son of God*. "Hence the Pope is crowned with a triple crown, as king of heaven and of earth and of the lower regions" (Ferraris, "Papa," *Prompta Bibliotheca Canonica, Juridica, Moralis, Theologica, Ascetica, Polemica, Rubristica, Historica*, column 1823).

Daniel 7:8, 20, 21, 24, 25 and Revelation 13:5–7 all identify the same power, which is depicted as the first beast of Revelation 13 and the little horn of Daniel 7 and 8. His special qualities are a different kind of kingdom, blasphemy against God, the purported changing of God's law, and the persecution of God's people. "And I saw as it were a sea of glass mingled with fire: and them that had gotten the victory over the beast, and over his image, and over his mark, and over the number of his name, stand on the sea of glass, having the harps of God" (Revelation 15:2). Paul described the people who gain the victory:

> But I would not have you to be ignorant, brethren, concerning them which are asleep, that ye sorrow not, even as others which have no hope. For if we believe that Jesus died and rose again, even so them also which sleep in Jesus will God bring with him.
>
> For this we say unto you by the word of the Lord, that we which are alive and remain unto the coming of the Lord shall not prevent them which are asleep.
>
> For the Lord himself shall descend from heaven with a shout, with the voice of the archangel, and with the trump of God: and the dead in Christ shall rise first: Then we which are alive and remain shall be caught up together with them in the clouds, to meet the Lord in the air: and so shall we ever be with the Lord. (1 Thessalonians 4:13–17)

This description is of the second coming of Jesus when the righteous dead are raised from their graves and the righteous living are caught up with them to be with Jesus forever.

The wicked who are alive at the second coming of Jesus will all be killed, as Paul wrote in his second Thessalonian letter: "And then shall that Wicked be revealed, whom the Lord shall consume with the spirit of his mouth, and shall destroy with the brightness of his coming" (2 Thessalonians 2:8). The first resurrection is the one you will want to be in: "Blessed and holy is he that hath part in the first resurrection: on such the second death hath no power, but they shall be priests of God and of Christ, and shall reign with him a thousand years" (Revelation 20:6). The first resurrection will take place at the second coming of Jesus. John describes those who are brought back to life: "And I saw thrones, and they sat upon them, and judgment was given unto them: and I saw the souls of them that were beheaded for the witness of Jesus, and for the word of God, and which had not worshipped the beast, neither his image, neither had received his mark upon their foreheads, or in their hands; and they lived and reigned with Christ a thousand years" (Revelation 20:4).

Jesus described two resurrections—the resurrection of life and the resurrection of damnation (John 5:29). Revelation declares: "But the rest of the dead lived not again until the thousand years were finished" (Revelation 20:5). That is, they do not come forth from the grave until the thousand-year period (Revelation 20:4), called the millennium, is complete.

Revelation echoes the cry that takes place as Jesus returns: "And the seventh angel sounded; and there were great voices in heaven, saying, The kingdoms of this world are become the kingdoms of our Lord, and of his Christ; and he shall reign for ever and ever" (Revelation 11:15).

When Jesus returns from earth to heaven at His second coming, He takes all of the saved with Him. These are the kingdoms of this world referred to in Revelation 11:15.

Chapter 21
The Saints and the Wicked

There is only one Saviour, as Peter declared: "Neither is there salvation in any other: for there is none other name under heaven given among men, whereby we must be saved" (Acts 4:12). Peter had just said: "Be it known unto you all, and to all the people of Israel, that by the name of Jesus Christ of Nazareth, whom ye crucified, whom God raised from the dead, even by him doth this man stand here before you whole" (Acts 4:10). Both Peter and John told the people, "For we cannot but speak the things which we have seen and heard" (Acts 4:20). What was the people's response to Peter and John? "And when they heard that, they lifted up their voice to God with one accord, and said, Lord, thou art God, which hast made heaven, and earth, and the sea, and all that in them is" (Acts 4:24). Their response was to praise the only Creator, the Maker of heaven and earth.

The final message before Jesus' return is a call to worship the Creator within the proclamation of "the everlasting gospel":

> And I saw another angel fly in the midst of heaven, having the everlasting gospel to preach unto them that dwell on the earth, and to every nation, and kindred, and tongue, and people, saying with a loud voice, Fear God, and give glory to him; for the hour of his judgment is come: and worship him that made heaven, and earth, and the sea, and the fountains of waters. (Revelation 14:6, 7)

In our last chapter, we discovered that the devil will be working through those who follow the beast and its image to get all mankind to worship the Papacy and the mark of its authority, which goes against the commandments of God. At the same time, God has sent an angel to remind all the earth that we owe our worship to the Creator God of the universe and to Him alone. As we saw from Acts 4, this is the natural response to accepting Jesus as our Savior and receiving the everlasting gospel—the same gospel that was preached by Peter and John.

The message the angel brings is to be preached "unto them that dwell on the earth." Someone must be willing to do what the angel called for and preach the everlasting gospel to the inhabitants of the earth. A single person cannot accomplish it by himself or herself. God needs a church of people who are willing to take on the task. We have looked at the fundamental beliefs of a long list of churches and we have compared them with what the Bible teaches.

There is only one denomination that most accurately meets all of their teachings based on the Bible. That denomination is the Seventh-day Adventist Church, a group of people who claim that they represent Christ by the way they live.

The Bible says that only a remnant of the people who are alive at the second coming of Jesus will be saved. There are many passages in the Old and New Testaments on the remnant. Here are several: "And the remnant of Jacob shall be among the Gentiles in the midst of many people" (Micah 5:8). "Esaias also crieth concerning Israel, Though the number of the children of Israel be as the sand of the sea, a remnant shall be saved" (Romans 9:27). "And the dragon was wroth with the woman, and went to make war with the remnant of her seed, which keep the commandments of God, and have the testimony of Jesus Christ" (Revelation 12:17).

There are many more texts describing the remnant of God, however the text in Revelation 12:17 is the best to show who the saints will be at the second coming of Jesus. Another parallel text on the remnant is Revelation 14:12: "Here is the patience of the saints: here are they that keep the commandments of God, and the faith of Jesus" (Revelation 14:12). The phrase, "the testimony of Jesus" in Revelation 12:17 is a bit puzzling. Is this talking about the testimony about Jesus in Scripture, or is it something else? Revelation 19:10 gives the answer, when John reported about his encounter with the angel: "And I fell at his feet to worship him. And he said unto me, See thou do it not: I am thy fellowservant, and of *thy brethren that have the testimony of Jesus:* worship God: for the testimony of Jesus is the spirit of prophecy" (Revelation 19:10, emphasis supplied). Of the forty-five English translations of Revelation 19:10, thirty-one of them record "the testimony of Jesus" as being "the spirit of prophecy."

If that verse is not clear enough that "the testimony of Jesus" means the Spirit-given gift of prophecy, when John went to fall down before the heavenly messenger again, the angel responded: "See thou do it not: for I am thy fellowservant, and of *thy brethren the prophets*, and of them which keep the sayings of this book: worship God" (Revelation 22:9, emphasis supplied). Thus, "the testimony of Jesus" is not the testimony of Jesus in Scripture, but the testimony borne through the gift of prophecy. This tells us that the remnant church was to be gifted with the gift of prophecy. The promise of a prophet to help guide the church (1 Corinthians 14:3).

In researching "the spirit of prophecy" on the Internet, I found 17,300,000 web pages. On one of these, I found the following information about the gift of prophecy in the Seventh-day Adventist Church.

> Arthur L. White, her grandson and biographer, writes that Ellen G. White is the most translated female non-fiction author in the history of literature, as well as the most translated American non-fiction author of either gender. Her writings covered creationism, agriculture, theology, evangelism, Christian lifestyle, education and health. She advocated vegetarianism. She promoted and was instrumental in the establishment

of schools and medical centers. During her lifetime she wrote more than 5,000 periodical articles and 40 books. Today, including compilations from her 100,000 pages of manuscript, more than 100 titles are available in English. Some of her most famous books include *The Desire of Ages*, *The Great Controversy* and *Steps to Christ*. Her work on successful Christian living, *Steps to Christ*, has been published in more than 140 languages. ("Ellen G. White," Wikipedia, http://1ref.us/54)

Seventh-day Adventists base this belief on the fact that one of the gifts of the Holy Spirit is prophecy (1 Corinthians 12:10). This gift is an identifying mark of the remnant church, and Seventh-day Adventists believe that it was manifested in the ministry of Ellen G. White.

Earlier we considered the biblical fact that the end-time church would only be a remnant (which literally means "that which is left over"). How then could a church of over seventeen million members be considered a "remnant"?

I personally believe in the Spirit of Prophecy and am convinced that all truly believing members should support it and that it should also apply to preachers within the Seventh-day Adventist Church who knowingly teach doctrines that are not in accordance with the Bible, and that, if they do not correct their teaching, they should be released from their duties.

How do we get the 17,000,000 members reduced to a "remnant"? The answer is in the statement "the remnant of her seed, which keep the commandments of God, and have the testimony of Jesus Christ" (Revelation 12:17).

Who are "her seed?" "Her seed" are all of God's faithful from the beginning of time until the last days, however many that might be. Some who profess to make the Word of God their claim are living in direct opposition to its plainest teachings. Their claim to be followers of the true end-time church is invalidated by the life that they live. Their lives make a mockery of the doctrines of the church and the teachings in the Bible. Ellen White herself wrote: "The Spirit was not given—nor can it ever be bestowed—to supersede the Bible; for the Scriptures explicitly state that *the word of God is the standard* by which all teaching and experience must be tested" (*The Great Controversy*, p. vii, emphasis supplied).

> … Sometimes that which men teach as 'special light' is in reality specious error, which, as tares sown among the wheat, will spring up and produce a baleful harvest. And errors of this sort will be entertained by some until the close of this earth's history. (White, *This Day With God*, p. 126)

There are only two powers that exist in the world—the power for good or the power for evil. All humans who live or have ever lived will have to make the choice of whom they will serve.

The greatest dangers of apostasy will come from within the church itself, and church members who do not have a firm commitment to God and the teachings of the Bible will be led away by the deceptions that come from church leaders—the very ones they are supposed to be able to trust. I will give you some examples later on.

There are many New Testament warnings against being deceived: "And he said, Take heed that ye be not deceived: for many shall come in my name, saying, I am Christ; and the time draweth near: go ye not therefore after them" (Luke 21:8). "But evil men and seducers shall wax worse and worse, deceiving, and being deceived" (2 Timothy 3:13). "For we ourselves also were sometimes foolish, disobedient, deceived, serving divers lusts and pleasures, living in malice and envy, hateful, and hating one another" (Titus 3:3). "And the devil that deceived them was cast into the lake of fire and brimstone, where the beast and the false prophet are, and shall be tormented day and night for ever and ever" (Revelation 20:10). "And the great dragon was cast out, that old serpent, called the Devil, and Satan, which deceiveth the whole world: he was cast out into the earth, and his angels were cast out with him" (Revelation 12:9). "And deceiveth them that dwell on the earth by the means of those miracles which he had power to do in the sight of the beast; saying to them that dwell on the earth, that they should make an image to the beast, which had the wound by a sword, and did live" (Revelation 13:14). In answer to the disciples' questions about the sign of His coming, Jesus responded:

> Take heed that no man deceive you. For many shall come in my name, saying, I am Christ; and shall deceive many. And ye shall hear of wars and rumours of wars: see that ye be not troubled: for all these things must come to pass, but the end is not yet. For nation shall rise against nation, and kingdom against kingdom: and there shall be famines, and pestilences, and earthquakes, in divers places. All these are the beginning of sorrows. (Matthew 24:3–8)

In the last half century (about 78 percent of which have been in the twenty-first century), there have been many who have come claiming to be Christ, and many of these have had large followings. According to an Internet search, following are the names of the people who have claimed to be Christ: Wayne Bent, Marshall Applewhite, Inri Cristo, Matayoshi Jesus, José Luis de Jesús Miranda, Jim Jones, David Koresh, Ariffin Mohamed, Laszlo Toth, Thomas Harrison Provenzano, Sergei Torop, Sun Myung Moon, Matthew Hale, Fred Phelps, Sr., Krishna Venta, Arnold Potter, Mitsuo Matayoshi, David Shayler, and Shoko Asahara. There have been many false christs, and there will be many more. Is Bible prophecy not being fulfilled?

Certainly these prophecies of Jesus are being fulfilled today as we look around us—terrible famines, numerous new diseases, an increase in tornados and earthquakes, nation warring against nation, people claiming to be Jesus. It seems that deception and wars have gone on forever from times past, yet Jesus said, "The end is not yet," and He added that there would be "kingdom against kingdom," "famines," "pestilences," and "earthquakes."

Then He said, "All these are the beginning of sorrows." It is like saying, *You have not seen anything yet; just wait till it happens!* "And many false prophets shall rise, and shall deceive many" (Matthew 24:11).

"For there shall arise false Christs, and false prophets, and shall shew great signs and wonders; insomuch that, if it were possible, they shall deceive the very elect" (Matthew 24:24). Who consider themselves to be "the elect"?

How do we reduce thousands of members to only a remnant? It is by deception within the very church that was given the three angels' message to preach to the world (Revelation 14:6–12).

Seventh-day Adventists take quite seriously the gospel commission of Jesus:

> Go ye therefore, and teach all nations, baptizing them in the name of the Father, and of the Son, and of the Holy Ghost. Teaching them to observe all things whatsoever I have commanded you: and, lo, I am with you alway, even unto the end of the world. Amen (Matthew 28:19, 20)

Seventh-day Adventists see themselves as responsible for proclaiming the gospel in the light of the three angels' messages of prophecy:

> The universal church is composed of all who truly believe in Christ, but in the last days, a time of widespread apostasy, a remnant has been called out to keep the commandments of God and the faith of Jesus. This remnant announces the arrival of the judgment hour, proclaims salvation through Christ, and heralds the approach of His second advent. This proclamation is symbolized by the three angels of Revelation 14; it coincides with the work of judgment in heaven and results in a work of repentance and reform on earth. Every believer is called to have a personal part in this worldwide witness (Revelation 12:17; 14:6–12; 18:1–4; 2 Corinthians 5:10; Jude 3, 14; 1 Peter 1:16–19; 2 Peter 3:10–14; Revelation 21:1–14). ("Remnant (Seventh-day Adventist belief)," Wikipedia, http://1ref.us/55)

The three angels' message is:

> And I saw another angel fly in the midst of heaven, having the everlasting gospel to preach unto them that dwell on the earth, and to every nation, and kindred, and tongue, and people, Saying with a loud voice, Fear God, and give glory to him; for the hour of his judgment is come: and worship him that made heaven, and earth, and the sea, and the fountains of waters.
>
> And there followed another angel, saying, Babylon is fallen, is fallen, that great city, because she made all nations drink of the wine of the wrath of her fornication. And the third angel followed them, saying with a loud voice, If any man worship the beast and his image, and receive his mark in his forehead, or in his hand.
>
> The same shall drink of the wine of the wrath of God, which is poured out without

mixture into the cup of his indignation; and he shall be tormented with fire and brimstone in the presence of the holy angels, and in the presence of the Lamb: And the smoke of their torment ascendeth up for ever and ever: and they have no rest day nor night, who worship the beast and his image, and whosoever receiveth the mark of his name. Here is the patience of the saints: here are they that keep the commandments of God, and the faith of Jesus. (Revelation 14:6–12)

The message of the angels is plain: God calls for true believers to worship the Creator God, leave the apostate churches because "Babylon is fallen," and refuse to worship the beast or his image and refuse the mark of the beast. People who have chosen church tradition above Bible truth and who choose not to follow the message of the second angel will receive the "mark of the beast."

It is a scary thought, but only through a vital and unbreakable relationship with God will anyone be able to stand untouched through the final events.

As the preaching of the third angel's message comes to a close, think about what the following events will be. These events are all described in Revelation 15 and 16. Just before the return of Jesus, the seven last plagues will fall on those who do not have the seal of God. Chapter 14 identifies the "remnant": "Here is the patience of the saints: here are they that keep the commandments of God and the faith of Jesus" (Revelation 14:12).

Following this identification comes these words of encouragement: "And I heard a voice from heaven saying unto me, Write, Blessed are the dead which die in the Lord from henceforth: Yea, saith the Spirit, that they may rest from their labours; and their works do follow them" (Revelation 14:13). Works demonstrate what kind of faith we have and, therefore, are the basis for reward: "For the Son of man shall come in the glory of his Father with his angels; and then he shall reward every man according to his works" (Matthew 16:27).

We already know about the resurrection of the dead, so what is the next event?

And I looked, and behold a white cloud, and upon the cloud one sat like unto the Son of man, having on his head a golden crown, and in his hand a sharp sickle. And another angel came out of the temple, crying with a loud voice to him that sat on the cloud, Thrust in thy sickle, and reap: for the time is come for thee to reap; for the harvest of the earth is ripe. And he that sat on the cloud thrust in his sickle on the earth; and the earth was reaped. (Revelation 14:14–16)

This is a description of Jesus' second coming when He gathers all His beloved saints and takes them to heaven. Jesus told His disciples, "That where I am, there ye may be also" (John 14:3). Does this mean that the saints are now up in heaven having begun their reign with Christ? No, John referred to this as taking place in the future after the second coming of Jesus:

"And after these things I heard a great voice of much people in heaven, saying, Alleluia; Salvation, and glory, and honour, and power, unto the Lord our God" (Revelation 19:1). "Blessed and holy is he that hath part in the *first resurrection:* on such the second death hath no power, but they *shall be* priests of God and of Christ, and *shall reign with him a thousand years*" (Revelation 20:6, emphasis supplied). The "thousand years," or millennium, begins at Jesus' return to heaven. When Jesus comes, He takes His people with Him to heaven (John 14:1–3). Thus, the millennium is spent in heaven. What happens in heaven during the millennium?

> And I saw thrones, and they sat upon them, and judgment was given unto them: and I saw the souls of them that were beheaded for the witness of Jesus, and for the word of God, and which had not worshipped the beast, neither his image, neither had received his mark upon their foreheads, or in their hands; and they lived and reigned with Christ a thousand years. (Revelation 20:4)

The reference to "they" and "them," means God's saints—both the remnant and the resurrected dead—who would not worship the beast or his image or receive his mark in their forehead or hand.

> And he laid hold on the dragon, that old serpent, which is the Devil, and Satan, and bound him a thousand years, And cast him into the bottomless pit, and shut him up, and set a seal upon him, that he should deceive the nations no more, till the thousand years should be fulfilled: and after that he must be loosed a little season. (Revelation 20:2, 3)

> And I saw a new heaven and a new earth: for the first heaven and the first earth were passed away; and there was no more sea. And I John saw the holy city, New Jerusalem, coming down from God out of heaven, prepared as a bride adorned for her husband. (Revelation 21:1, 2)

This will be an awesome time! Jesus has taken the saints up to heaven where they have thrones and dwell for 1000 years while "judgment was given unto them." With Jesus, they are given the judgment of all the wicked. They will be forever with Jesus, who received His kingdom just before His return to earth. There are no other redeemed. Then, Satan gets his last hurrah:

> And when the thousand years are expired, Satan shall be loosed out of his prison. And shall go out to deceive the nations which are in the four quarters of the earth, Gog and Magog, to gather them together to battle: the number of whom is as the sand of the sea. And they went up on the breadth of the earth, and compassed the camp of the saints about, and the beloved city: and fire came down from God out of heaven, and devoured them. (Revelation 20:7–9)

What a vivid picture the Bible portrays! The New Jerusalem has descended to the earth renewed, and Jesus and all the saints are in it. As the Holy City settles into place, Satan is loosed and all the wicked are raised in the second resurrection, and then Satan gathers all the wicked with all their instruments of war and deceives them into thinking that they are stronger than those in the city and that they can surround and capture it. Just then fire comes down from heaven upon the earth, destroys the rebels encircling the city, and cleansed all traces of sin, corruption, and evil.

The picture of the events described here is exactly as they will occur. The righteous will inhabit the new earth and the Eternal Father will make this earth His permanent throne. "And I saw a great white throne, and him that sat on it, from whose face the earth and the heaven fled away; and there was found no place for them" (Revelation 20:11).

Where are the rest of the people who have ever lived on this earth? "This is the second death. And whosoever was not found written in the book of life was cast into the lake of fire" (Revelation 20:14, 15). "And the devil that deceived them was cast into the lake of fire and brimstone, where the beast and the false prophet are, and shall be tormented day and night for ever and ever" (Revelation 20:10). They are completely destroyed, never to live again.

Who did it say was cast into the lake of fire? The devil, the beast, the false prophet, "and whosoever was not found written in the book of life" (Revelation 20:15). All the wicked are destroyed; the only thing that is left after fire completely burns anything is smoke. "And the smoke of their torment ascendeth up for ever and ever: and they have no rest day nor night, who worship the beast and his image, and whosoever receiveth the mark of his name" (Revelation 14:11). This is a picture of destruction that was well-known in Old Testament times. When an enemy set fire to a village and the people were unable to extinguish it, the smoke would rise on and on seemingly without end. Yet today there is no evidence of any smoke rising from old Israeli villages.

> Lift up your eyes to the heavens, and look upon the earth beneath: for the heavens shall vanish away like smoke, and the earth shall wax old like a garment, and they that dwell therein shall die in like manner: but my salvation shall be for ever, and my righteousness shall not be abolished. (Isaiah 51:6)

> It shall not be quenched night nor day; the smoke thereof shall go up for ever: from generation to generation it shall lie waste; none shall pass through it for ever and ever. (Isaiah 34:10)

> But the wicked shall perish, and the enemies of the Lord shall be as the fat of lambs: they shall consume; into smoke shall they consume away. (Psalms 37:20)

> For, behold, the day cometh, that shall burn as an oven; and all the proud, yea, and all that do wickedly, shall be stubble: and the day that cometh shall burn

them up, saith the LORD of hosts, that it shall leave them neither root nor branch. (Malachi 4:1)

Behold, they shall be as stubble; the fire shall burn them; they shall not deliver themselves from the power of the flame: there shall not be a coal to warm at, nor fire to sit before it. (Isaiah 47:14)

Therefore as the fire devoureth the stubble, and the flame consumeth the chaff, so their root shall be as rottenness, and their blossom shall go up as dust: because they have cast away the law of the LORD of hosts, and despised the word of the Holy One of Israel. (Isaiah 5:24)

But the heavens and the earth, which are now, by the same word are kept in store, reserved unto fire against the day of judgment and perdition of ungodly men.... But the day of the Lord will come as a thief in the night; in the which the heavens shall pass away with a great noise, and the elements shall melt with fervent heat, the earth also and the works that are therein shall be burned up.... Looking for and hasting unto the coming of the day of God, wherein the heavens being on fire shall be dissolved, and the elements shall melt with fervent heat. (2 Peter 3:7, 10, 12)

Therefore wait ye upon me, saith the Lord, until the day that I rise up to the prey: for my determination is to gather the nations, that I may assemble the kingdoms, to pour upon them mine indignation, even all my fierce anger: for all the earth shall be devoured with the fire of my jealousy. (Zephaniah 3:8)

Clearly, the Old and New Testaments teach eternal life for the righteous and eternal eradication for the wicked.

Chapter 22
The Final Reward

It is not enough for people to find and understand the truths of the Bible, they must be willing to obey them. God describes the kind of people He is looking for: "Here is the patience of the saints: here are they that keep the commandments of God, and the faith of Jesus" (Revelation 14:12).

The first part of the verse, "Here is the patience of the saints," points to the people who have endured—from Adam and Eve to the last living person on earth. Jesus declared: "And ye shall be hated of all men for my name's sake: but he that endureth to the end shall be saved" (Matthew 10:22).

The second part of the verse refers to those who "keep the commandments of God." The majority of Christians in this world do not qualify under this phrase, for they do not keep *all* of the commandments. They put tradition ahead of the Bible and claim to only keep some or most of the commandments.

Because it upholds keeping the commandments, some would like to make this verse about Jews. Yet, the third part of the verse, "and the faith of Jesus" identifies the "saints" as being Christian believers. John does not say that they keep certain parts of the commandments or that they keep the commandments of God and optionally have the faith of Jesus. It is both.

Revelation 14:12 links with Revelation 12:17. The latter says that the faithful remnant "keep the commandments of God, and have the testimony of Jesus." As we saw before, the "testimony of Jesus" is "the spirit of prophecy," or prophetic gift (Revelation 19:10; 22:9). These two characteristics—keeping the commandments and believing the spirit of prophecy—are placed on equal footing, even though many Seventh-day Adventists discount the writings of Ellen G. White.

Salvation is progressive. In judging people's progress, Jesus will judge their works by the amount of biblical truth they have been given, and compare that to their living up to what they know and understand. "For unto whomsoever much is given, of him shall be much required …" (Luke 12:48). All people will be judged by the Ten Commandment law. What is required is simple: "And now, Israel, what doth the LORD thy God require of thee, but to fear the LORD thy God, to walk in all his ways, and to love him, and to serve the LORD thy God with all thy heart and with all thy soul" (Deuteronomy 10:12).

The greatest threat for the Seventh-day Adventist Church is as it is for most all church organizations—the internal threat that is carried on in the name of brotherly love. It is in ignoring real dangers when they appear: "But if the watchman see the sword come, and blow not the trumpet, and the people be not warned; if the sword come, and take any person from among them, he is taken away in his iniquity; but his blood will I require at the watchman's hand" (Ezekiel 33:6).

When the leadership recognize ideas within their ranks that are not consistent with the Bible, what do they do about it? Some times it would seem that the teachers of these erroneous ideas are simply sent to another district where they can pursue their false doctrines and infect more people. The explanation of the leadership is: "We have to try to work with them and see if we can get them to see the wrong in what they are doing."

What is the end result of allowing people to preach their own doctrine mixed with the truths of the Bible? Precious souls will stumble and be lost, and woe be it to those who are responsible (Luke 17:1)!

Paul warned: "But evil men and seducers shall wax worse and worse, deceiving, and being deceived" (2 Timothy 3:13). Preachers—in whatever denomination—who mix the teachings of the Bible with their own ideas, will eventually believe their ideas to be the truth of God's Word as they place their own interpretations ahead of the Bible's true meaning. Paul wrote: "Now the Spirit speaketh expressly, that in the latter times some shall depart from the faith, giving heed to seducing spirits, and doctrines of devils" (1 Timothy 4:1). "For the time will come when they will not endure sound doctrine; but after their own lusts shall they heap to themselves teachers, having itching ears" (2 Timothy 4:3). "Now I beseech you, brethren, mark them which cause divisions and offences contrary to the doctrine which ye have learned; and avoid them" (Romans 16:17). Jesus said: "But in vain they do worship me, teaching for doctrines the commandments of men" (Matthew 15:9).

> **What is the end result of allowing people to preach their own doctrine mixed with the truths of the Bible? Precious souls will stumble and be lost, and woe be it to those who are responsible**

These inspired founders of the faith were so right in anticipating a departure from the truth in the latter times. There are hundreds of preachers today who preach only for their own glory, when Paul wrote: "whatsoever ye do, do all to the glory of God" (1 Corinthians 10:31).

When people "will not endure sound doctrine," they will be subject to preachers who teach what is pleasant and convenient and they latch onto a religious group that does not teach according to the truths found in the Bible but according to what the people want to hear. Churches then become social clubs that people attend to hear things they want to hear—even if it contradicts the Bible.

The apostle Paul warned, in Romans 16:17, not to have anything to do with preachers whose preaching is contrary to the teachings of the Bible. In the next verse he says: "For they that are such serve not our Lord Jesus Christ, but their own belly; and by good words and fair speeches deceive the hearts of the simple [the unlearned]" (Romans 16:18). Jesus said, "But in vain they do worship me, teaching for doctrines the commandments of men" (Matthew 15:9). His words are an indictment against preachers of any denomination who mix their own doctrine with Bible teaching.

"Then came to Jesus scribes and Pharisees, which were of Jerusalem, saying, Why do thy disciples transgress the tradition of the elders?" (Matthew 15:1, 2). Who was God's chosen people when Jesus was upon earth? It was the Jews. Who were the leaders of the Jews? The scribes and Pharisees. Of these Jesus sadly declared, "This people draweth nigh unto me with their mouth, and honoureth me with their lips; but their heart is far from me" (Matthew 15:8).

When Jesus and the apostles in the New Testament used the word "doctrine" they were referring to the teachings of the Scriptures. History has an uncanny way of repeating itself. God gave us not only sacred history but also His inspired word in the Bible. "Ye are my witnesses, saith the Lord, and my servant whom I have chosen: that ye may know and believe me, and understand that I am he: before me there was no God formed, neither shall there be after me. I, even I, am the Lord; and beside me there is no saviour" (Isaiah 43:10, 11).

Returning to the topic at hand, we ask again: How do we get from seventeen million people down to a "remnant"? To illustrate how this can be, I would like to use some history from the Bible, starting with Noah: "And the Lord said unto Noah, Come thou and all thy house into the ark; for thee have I seen righteous before me in this generation.... And Noah went in, and his sons, and his wife, and his sons' wives with him, into the ark, because of the waters of the flood" (Genesis 7:1, 7). Noah had three sons—Shem, Ham, and Japheth. The four men and their wives make eight. Thus, only eight people were saved out of the millions who lived upon the earth at that time.

Then there is the example of Elijah. "And he [Elijah] said, I have been very jealous for the Lord God of hosts: because the children of Israel have forsaken thy covenant, thrown down thine altars, and slain thy prophets with the sword; and I, even I only, am left; and they seek my life, to take it away" (1 Kings 19:14). How did the Lord God respond to Elijah? "Yet I have left me seven thousand in Israel, all the knees which have not bowed unto Baal, and every mouth which hath not kissed him" (1 Kings 9:18). In Elijah's day, there were several million Israelites. Yet, God told Elijah that there were only 7000 who were true to Him. The rest of the Israelites were to be slain. "... anoint Hazael to be king over Syria: and Jehu the son of Nimshi shalt thou anoint to be king over Israel and Elisha the son of Shaphat of Abelmeholah shalt thou anoint to be prophet in thy room. And it shall come to pass, that him that escapeth the sword of Hazael shall Jehu slay: and him that escapeth from the sword of Jehu shall Elisha slay" (1 Kings 19:15–17).

We can also turn to the example of Lot and his daughters. In Genesis 13 through 19, the Bible tells about the inhabitants of the Jordan River valley and about how Lot, Abram's nephew, chose to dwell in the city of Sodom. Sodom and Gomorrah and all the cities of the plains were exceedingly wicked, and the Lord came to visit the land and Abram. Abram saw three strangers walking up the road and invited them to rest and eat with him. When they did, Abram discovered that it was the Lord and two angels who were on their way down to Sodom and Gomorrah to see if all the cities were completely wicked.

Genesis also described how four kings who lived in the valley—Chedorlaomer king of Elam, Amraphel king of Shinar, Arioch king of Ellasar, and Tidal king of nations—attacked the five kings of Sodom and Gomorrah, Admah, Zeboiim, and Bela for rebelling against them. The four defeated the five and took all their people and possessions captive. Lot and his family were among them. When

Abram heard what had happened, he took all of his fighting men and went out against Chedorlaomer and his allies (Genesis 14:7) and recovered the people—including Lot and his family—and their possessions, returning them to their own cities. Lot and his family went back to Sodom, which is where they were when the angels came to visit.

The two angels sent by the Lord went to Sodom and saw firsthand just how wicked these cities were. The LORD had instructed the angels to find all who were righteous and take them out of the city because there were not even ten righteous people there, and the LORD would not destroy the righteous with the wicked. The angels instructed Lot and his family: "Escape for thy life; look not behind thee, neither stay thou in all the plain; escape to the mountain, lest thou be consumed" (Genesis 19:17). Lot was not eager to leave. The angels had to take them by the hand and lead them out of Sodom and send them to a little city called Zoar. The angels said to Lot:

> Haste thee, escape thither; for I cannot do any thing till thou become thither. Therefore the name of the city was called Zoar. The sun was risen upon the earth when Lot entered into Zoar. Then the Lord rained upon Sodom and upon Gomorrah brimstone and fire from the Lord out of heaven. And he overthrew those cities, and all the plain, and all the inhabitants of the cities, and that which grew upon the ground. (Genesis 19:22–25)

According to the Bible, the plains of the Jordan River were once lush and able to support large populations of people and animals. Today this region is a dried up desert where virtually nothing will grow. Lot and his daughters' rescue is another illustration of a small number of people being saved out of a larger population. These examples help explain how the righteous, who are saved, have always been a remnant from a much larger number of people.

There were eight saved from the flood, 7,000 from Israel, and only three from the Jordan valley and its cities. That amounts to 7,011 saved out of a billion people. Similarly, a remnant will stand firm in the midst of persecution and be ready when Christ returns.

> And I looked, and, lo, a Lamb stood on the mount Sion, and with him an hundred forty and four thousand, having his Father's name written in their foreheads.... no man could learn that song but the hundred and forty and four thousand, which were redeemed from the earth. These are they which were not defiled with women; for they are virgins. These are they which follow the Lamb whithersoever he goeth. These were redeemed from among men, being the firstfruits unto God and to the Lamb. And in their mouth was found no guile: for they are without fault before the throne of God. (Revelation 14:1, 3–5)

The 144,000 are the redeemed who are identified by three distinct features. The first feature is that they have the "Father's name written in their foreheads" (Revelation 14:1) This was previously mentioned in chapter 7: "And I saw another angel ascending from the east, having the seal of the living God: and he cried with a loud voice to the four angels, to whom it was given to hurt the earth and the sea" (Revelation 7:2). The angel tells what the seal is for: "Saying, Hurt not the earth, neither the sea, nor the trees, till we have sealed the servants of our God in their foreheads" (Revelation 7:3).

The second feature is that they have been "redeemed from the earth" (Revelation 14:3), yet redeemed from the earth at Jesus' coming but having gone through a period of great tribulation: "These are they which came out of great tribulation, and have washed their robes, and made them white in the blood of the Lamb" (Revelation 7:14).

The third feature is that they "are without fault." This characteristic identifies people who have gotten the victory over sin and have received the salvation given to them by grace through faith from God the Father and His Son, our Savior and Lord Jesus Christ.

Continuing in Revelation 7:4–8, God breaks down the total number into the number for each of the twelve tribes of Israel—12,000 each:

> And I heard the number of them which were sealed: and there were sealed an hundred and forty and four thousand of all the tribes of the children of Israel. Of the tribe of Judah were sealed twelve thousand. Of the tribe of Reuben were sealed twelve thousand. Of the tribe of Gad were sealed twelve thousand. Of the tribe of Asher were sealed twelve thousand. Of the tribe of Naphtali were sealed twelve thousand. Of the tribe of Manassas were sealed twelve thousand. Of the tribe of Simeon were sealed twelve thousand. Of the tribe of Levi were sealed twelve thousand. Of the tribe of Issachar were sealed twelve thousand. Of the tribe of Zebulon were sealed twelve thousand. Of the tribe of Joseph were sealed twelve thousand. Of the tribe of Benjamin were sealed twelve thousand. After this I beheld, and, lo, a great multitude, which no man could number, of all nations, and kindreds, and people, and tongues, stood before the throne, and before the Lamb, clothed with white robes, and palms in their hands. (Revelation 7:4–9)

Am I saying here that there will only be 144,000 saved? No. Revelation 7:9 says, "After this I beheld, and, lo, a great multitude, which no man could number, of all nations, and kindred's, and people, and tongues, stood before the throne, and before the Lamb, clothed with white robes, and palms in their hands." This great multitude is the same as the one described in Revelation 15:2. They represent the resurrected dead, now alive, who came from the earth at the second coming of Jesus (1 Thessalonians 4:13–17). Revelation identifies them as having white robes and palms in their hands. All the resurrected dead, together with the 144,000 who were redeemed from the earth, make up this great multitude. "And I saw as it were a sea of glass mingled with fire: and them that had gotten the victory over the beast, and over his image, and over his mark, and over the number of his name, stand on the sea of glass, having the harps of God" (Revelation 15:2). These are all of the saved—the 144,000 who are alive at Jesus' coming and the dead saints who will be resurrected.

Regarding "great tribulation," Jesus said: "For then shall be great tribulation, such as was not since the beginning of the world to this time, no, nor ever shall be" (Matthew 24:21). This tribulation is so fierce that even Jesus put limits on it: "And except those days should be shortened, there should no flesh be saved: but for the elect's sake those days shall be shortened" (Matthew 24:22). The second coming of Jesus is what will shorten those days and the tribulation.

Satan has asserted that angels did not need rules to govern them in their perfection. He later asserted that no human being could fully obey God's law. However, Job could, and so could the 144,000, which are God's prime examples: "These are they which were not defiled with women; for they are virgins. These are they which follow the Lamb whithersoever he goeth. These were redeemed from among men, being the firstfruits unto God and to the Lamb" (Revelation 14:4).

It was upon the Cross at Calvary, through "the shedding of His blood," that Jesus paid the penalty for sin. His blood paid the penalty for sin; His life was given to make us acceptable to the Father. And when we accept the gift of God, His blood covers our sins and gives us power to keep from sinning.

Paul and John both wrote about the remitting and cleansing of sin: "Whom God hath set forth to be a propitiation through faith in his blood, to declare his righteousness for the remission of sins that are past, through the forbearance of God" (Romans 3:25). "The blood of Jesus Christ his Son cleanseth us from all sin" (1 John 1:7). "If we confess our sins, he is faithful and just to forgive us our sins, and to cleanse us from all unrighteousness" (1 John 1:9).

Remission requires confessing our sins, believing that they are forgiven, and not committing them anymore. Unrighteousness is any act of sinning. "All unrighteousness is sin: and there is a sin not unto death" (1 John 5:17). The sin that is not unto death would be sin that is not premeditated or by our conscious choice. "He that committeth sin is of the devil; for the devil sinneth from the beginning. For this purpose the Son of God was manifested, that he might destroy the works of the devil" (1 John 3:8).

Our sins must be washed away in His blood: "And from Jesus Christ, who is the faithful witness, and the first begotten of the dead, and the prince of the kings of the earth. Unto him that loved us, and washed us from our sins in his own blood" (Revelation 1:5). We also are to overcome by Jesus' blood: "And they overcame him by the blood of the Lamb, and by the word of their testimony; and they loved not their lives unto the death" (Revelation 12:11).

Who was it that the living 144,000 are to overcome? It is the devil. How are they to overcome him? By "the blood of the Lamb and by the word of their testimony" (Revelation 12:11).

Hopefully, we understand how Jesus is our Savior, but what is "the word of their testimony"? In the topic about how a true Christian lives, the Christ-like life was covered. The Christ-like life is the word of their testimony.

Too many professed Christians have been deceived into thinking that a person can be a Christian and still live a life exactly like the people of the world. Did Jesus live just like the people of the world? He is our example. "And ye shall be hated of all men for my name's sake: but he that endureth to the end shall be saved" (Matthew 10:22). "I have given them thy word; and the world hath hated them, because they are not of the world, even as I am not of the world" (John 17:14).

True Christians make every effort to be Christ like, to live their life fulfilling the words of the Savior in Scripture and learning to do the will of the Father, as did Jesus, through Bible study and continual prayer. The promise is: "But as many as received him, to them gave he power to become the sons of God, even to them that believe on his name" (John 1:1).

The power of grace comes through adoption into Jesus' family. "For the law was given by Moses, but grace and truth came by Jesus Christ" (John 1:17). "And whosoever was not found written in the book of life was cast into the lake of fire" (Revelation 20:15). "He that overcometh shall inherit all things; and I will be his God, and he shall be my son" (Revelation 21:7).

Salvation is not just about what one thinks, but also about what one does. "But the fearful, and unbelieving, and the abominable, and murderers, and whoremongers, and sorcerers, and idolaters, and all liars, shall have their part in the lake which burneth with fire and brimstone: which is the second death" (Revelation 21:8). "Blessed are they that do his commandments, that they may have right to the tree of life, and may enter in through the gates into the city" (Revelation 22:14). "Not every one that saith unto me, Lord, Lord, shall enter into the kingdom of heaven; but he that doeth the will of my Father which is in heaven" (Matthew 7:21).

Does God want us to follow the traditions of a church or the instructions found in the Bible? "Beware of false prophets, which come to you in sheep's clothing, but inwardly they are ravening wolves" (Matthew 7:15). "Many will say to me in that day, Lord, Lord, have we not prophesied in thy name? and in thy name have cast out devils? and in thy name done many wonderful works" (Matthew 7:22)? Jesus answered them saying, "depart from Me, all ye workers of iniquity" (Luke 13:27). "Wherefore by their fruits ye shall know them" (Matthew 7:20).

When you listen to anyone who is supposedly working to better people's chances for the kingdom, do they relate it from the Bible or mostly from their church traditions? Jesus knew that preachers, elders, and priests who claim to glorify God would, in reality, be glorifying themselves. But such glorying is not the focus of those who follow the Lord: "Seeing that many glory after the flesh, I will glory also," "but he that glorieth, let him glory in the Lord" (2 Corinthians 11:18; 10:17).

God has great advantages for His children. "That the God of our Lord Jesus Christ, the Father of glory, may give unto you the spirit of wisdom and revelation in the knowledge of him" (Ephesians 1:17). "Make you perfect in every good work to do his will, working in you that which is wellpleasing in his sight, through Jesus Christ; to whom be glory for ever and ever. Amen" (Hebrews 13:21). "Now unto him that is able to keep you from falling, and to present you faultless before the presence of his glory with exceeding joy, to the only wise God our Saviour, be glory and majesty, dominion and power, both now and forever. Amen" (Jude 1:24, 25).

After researching the contents for this book, I do not understand how any person could not want to join the Seventh-day Adventist Church, even though the devil has his people within the

Seventh-day Adventist Church as in all other denominations. Churches cannot give you eternal life. Only through obedience to Jesus Christ and the Father's will can a person receive eternal life. "Here is the patience of the saints: here are they that keep the commandments of God, and the faith of Jesus" (Revelation 14:12).

Let us read the Bible and apply it to our lives so we may be among the saints that Jesus will take with Him into heaven. May God the Father, God the Son and God the Holy Spirit bestow upon you His loving kindness as you study the truths in His Word.

Bibliography

"28 Fundamental Beliefs." Seventh-day Adventist Church. http://1ref.us/4y (accessed February 17, 2014).

"A Comparison of Seventh Day Baptists with Seventh-day Adventists." Seattle Area Seventh Day Baptist Church. http://1ref.us/4x (accessed January 27, 2014).

"A Letter to the Pope." SDA Global. http://1ref.us/4k (accessed January 23, 2014).

"Astaroth." Wikipedia. http://1ref.us/47 (accessed January 21, 2014).

"Baptists." Wikipedia. http://1ref.us/56 (accessed February 5, 2014).

Bémont, Charles, and Gabriel Monod, with notes by George Burton Adams. *Medieval Europe from 395 to 1270*. New York: Henry Holt & Co., 1906.

Bailey, Francis Crawford Burkitt, Edwyn Robert Bevan, Jame Houston Baxter, and Cyril. *The History of Christianity in the Light of Modern Knowledge*. Blackie & Son Limited, 1929.

Blanc, D. A. "A Summary of the Gospel Message." Biblical Scholarship with a Global Perspective. http://1ref.us/4o (accessed February 5, 2014).

Brotherhood of St. Vincent of Paul. "Why Don't You Keep Holy the Sabbath-Day? A Question for All Bible Christians." *The Clifton Tracts*. New York: P. J. Kenedy, Excelsior Catholic Publishing House, 1856.

The Catholic Encyclopedia. Vol. 4. New York: Robert Appleton Company, 1908.

Catholic Mirror, September 23, 1894.

Catholic Press, August 25, 1900.

"Church of God." Wikipedia. http://1ref.us/4z (accessed January 27, 2014).

"Church of God, The Eternal." Church of God, The Eternal. http://1ref.us/50 (accessed January 27, 2014).

Conway, Bertrand L. *The Question-Box Answers*. New York: The Catholic Book Exchange, 1903.

Crews, Joe. "How the Sabbath Was Changed." SabbathTruth.com. http://1ref.us/4n (accessed February 5, 2014).

"Eastern Orthodox Church." Wikipedia. http://1ref.us/4v (accessed January 27, 2014).

"Ellen G. White." Wikipedia. http://1ref.us/54 (accessed March 26, 2014).

Emahiser, Clifton. "Daniel Prophesied the Roman Catholic Church." Israelite Watchmen. http://http://1ref.us/4b (accessed February 5, 2014).

"Evangelical Lutheran Church in America." Wikipedia. http://1ref.us/4q (accessed February 5, 2014).

"Exhort." The Free Dictionary by Farlex. http://1ref.us/52 (accessed January 21, 2014).

"Faith." The Free Dictionary by Farlex. http://1ref.us/44 (accessed January 21, 2014).

Ferraris, Lucius. "Papa," art. 2. In *Prompta Bibliotheca Canonica, Juridica, Moralis, Theologica, Ascetica, Polemica, Rubristica, Historica*. Vol. 5. Petit-Montrouge, Paris: J. P. Migne, 1858.

Frederick, William. *Three Prophetic Days*. Clyde, O., 1900.

Giermann, Peter. *The Convert's Catechism of Catholic Doctrine*. Reprint. Ringgold, GA: TEACH Services, Inc., 1995.

Goldstein, Clifford. "The Origin of Sunday Worship." From Sabbath to Sunday. http://1ref.us/4i (accessed January 21, 2014.

"History of the Catholic Church." Wikipedia. http://1ref.us/4e (accessed February 14, 2014).

"The History of the Change of God's Sabbath from Saturday to Sunday." http://1ref.us/4j (accessed January 21, 2014).

"History of Protestantism." Wikipedia. http://1ref.us/4g (accessed January 20, 2014).

"Hope." The Free Dictionary by Farlex. http://1ref.us/45 (accessed January 21, 2014).

Holtzmann, Heinrich Julius. *Kanon und Tradition*. Ludwigsburg: Druck and Verlag von Ferd Riehm, 1859.

Houdmann, S. Michael. "What is the origin of the Catholic Church?" http://1ref.us/4c (accessed February 14, 2014).

"Imputed Righteousness." Wikipedia. http://1ref.us/46 (accessed February 5, 2014).

Keenan, Stephen. *Doctrinal Catechism*. 1899.

Keohane, Steve. "Sabbath Changed to Sunday." Bible Probe. http://1ref.us/4m (accessed February 14, 2014).

Kreis, Steven. "Constantine the Great, c. 274–337." The History Guide. http://1ref.us/4d (accessed March 26, 2014).

"Lateran Concordat of 1929—Papal Wound Healed!" Michael Scheifler's Bible Light. http://1ref.us/53 (accessed January 27, 2014).

"List of Christian Denominations." Wikipedia. http://1ref.us/4p (accessed February 5, 2014).

"List of More Than 500 Sabbath Keeping Churches." Topix.com. http://1ref.us/4s (accessed January 27, 2014).

Maxwell, Mervyn. *God Cares*. Vol. 1. Nampa, ID: Pacific Press Publishing Association, 1998.

"Mithras & Sol Invictus ("the unconquered sun")." Tek Gnostics. http://1ref.us/49 (accessed January 16, 2014).

"Moloch." *Encyclopedia Mythica* from Encyclopedia Mythica Online. http://1ref.us/48 (accessed February 17, 2014).

"Nero Caesar." LUSENET. The Greenspun Family Server. http://1ref.us/4a (accessed September 23, 2014).

O'Brien, John Anthony. *The Faith of Millions: The Credentials of the Catholic Religion*. Our Sunday Visitor, 1974.

"Orthodox Church." Orthodox Wiki. http://1ref.us/4h (accessed January 20, 2014).

The Reluctant Messenger. http://1ref.us/4u (accessed January 27, 2014).

"Remnant (Seventh-day Adventist belief)." Wikipedia. http://1ref.us/55 (accessed January 27, 2014).

"The Roman Church's Admission of Changing The Sabbath." http://1ref.us/4l (accessed February 5, 2014).

"Sabbath Observing Denominations—Sabbath Churches." The Ten Commandments. http://1ref.us/4t (accessed January 27, 2014).

"Schism." Oxford Dictionaries. http://1ref.us/4f (accessed January 27, 2014).

Schroeder, John. *Heresies of Catholicism … The Apostate Church*. Lincoln, NE: iUniverse, Inc., 2003.

"Seventh Day Baptists." Wikipedia. http://1ref.us/4w (accessed January 27, 2014).

Tuberville, Henry. *An Abridgment of the Christian Doctrine*. 1828.

"United Church of God." Wikipedia. http://1ref.us/51 (accessed February 14, 2014).

Walch, Johann Georg, ed. *Auslegung des Alten Testaments* [Commentary on the Old Testament], in *Dr. Martin Luthers Sämmtliche Schriften* [Collected Writings]. Vol. 3. St. Louis, MO: Concordia Publishing House, 1880.

Wharey, James. *Sketches of Church History*. Philadelphia: Presbyterian Board of Publication, 1840.

White, Ellen G. *This Day with God*. Washington, DC: Review and Herald Publishing Association, 1979.

We invite you to view the complete
selection of titles we publish at:

www.TEACHServices.com

Scan with your mobile
device to go directly
to our website.

Please write or e-mail us your praises, reactions, or
thoughts about this or any other book we publish at:

P.O. Box 954
Ringgold, GA 30736

info@TEACHServices.com

TEACH Services, Inc., titles may be purchased in bulk for
educational, business, fund-raising, or sales promotional use.
For information, please e-mail:

BulkSales@TEACHServices.com

Finally, if you are interested in seeing
your own book in print, please contact us at

publishing@TEACHServices.com

We would be happy to review your manuscript for free.